'Chords of Freedom'

∕IVERSITY ∕

For Jack Pole: guide, mentor, friend

'Chords of Freedom'
Commemoration, ritual and British transatlantic slavery

J. R. Oldfield

Manchester University Press
Manchester and New York

distributed exclusively in the USA by Palgrave

The right of J. R. Oldfield to be identified as the author of this work has been asserted by him in accordance with the Copyright, Designs and Patents Act 1988.

Published by Manchester University Press
Oxford Road, Manchester M13 9NR, UK
and Room 400, 175 Fifth Avenue, New York, NY 10010, USA
www.manchesteruniversitypress.co.uk

Distributed exclusively in the USA by
Palgrave, 175 Fifth Avenue, New York,
NY 10010, USA

Distributed exclusively in Canada by
UBC Press, University of British Columbia, 2029 West Mall,
Vancouver, BC, Canada V6T 1Z2

British Library Cataloguing-in-Publication Data
A catalogue record for this book is available from the British Library

Library of Congress Cataloging-in-Publication Data applied for

ISBN   978 0 7190 6664 1 *hardback*

ISBN   978 0 7190 6665 8 *paperback*

First published 2007

16 15 14 13 12 11 10 09 08 07   10 9 8 7 6 5 4 3 2 1

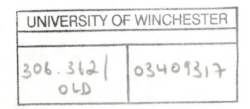
Typeset
by Frances Hackeson Freelance Publishing Serices, Brinscall, Lancs
Printed in Great Britain
by The Cromwell Press Ltd, Trowbridge

Contents

Illustrations

Acknowledgements

This book took shape over a long period of time (longer, certainly, than the normal RAE cycle) and along the way I have accumulated countless debts of gratitude. Pride of place must go to the many archivists and librarians who gave freely of their time and expertise. In particular, I would like to thank the staffs of the following libraries, galleries, and museums: the Bodleian Library, the British Library, the Corporation of London Record Office, the Hartley Library, University of Southampton, the Moorland-Spingarn Research Center, Howard University, Washington, DC, Ipswich Museum, Ipswich Record Office, London Guildhall Library, the National Maritime Museum, the National Portrait Gallery, Rhodes House Library, Oxford, the Library and Muniment Room, Westminster Abbey, Wilberforce House Museum (especially Vanessa Salter), and Wisbech and Fenland Museum.

While working on this project, I was also fortunate enough to spend three weeks at the New-York Historical Society. I am indebted to the Gilder Lehrman Institute of American History for giving me this opportunity, and to the staff at the New-York Historical Society for making my stay in New York so enjoyable. A grant from the British Academy also made possible a shorter trip to Washington, DC, while the University of Southampton very generously funded the cost of the illustrations. I am extremely grateful for their assistance.

No less important were those friends and colleagues who were prepared to share with me their thoughts about history, memory, and commemoration, among them Robert Blyth, Peter Gray, Neil Gregor, Douglas Hamilton, Tony Kushner, Kendrick Oliver, Gemma Romain, and Joan Tumblety. I also want to say a big 'thank you' to Alastair Duke. Alastair has been a colleague for over twenty years, and during that time he has been an unfailing friend and critic. From the first, he took a close interest in this project, read early drafts of most of the manuscript, and, as I have come to expect, was prompt in offering advice as to how it might be improved. I sometimes think that colleagues like Alastair are a dying breed, and I am only glad that I have been able to benefit from his knowledge and wisdom.

Once again, everyone at Manchester University Press worked hard to bring this project to fruition, even though the manuscript was delivered many months late. I am especially grateful to Alison Welsby, who commissioned the book, and to Jonathan Bevan and the press's excellent production staff. Finally, I would like to thank everyone at 7, Redhill (Veronica, Tom, and Matt) for their patience and good humour – and for their gentle (and sometimes not so gentle) reminders that I really ought to get the book finished. I could not have done it without you.

The dedication is, I hope, self-explanatory. Jack Pole shaped my life as a professional historian and I will always be grateful for his advice and encouragement and, most of all, for always being there. Thank you.

Introduction

In 1934, the Oxford historian, Reginald Coupland, told a meeting in Hull that Emancipation, by which he meant the abolition of British colonial slavery, was 'a striking example – perhaps the most striking example one can think of in modern history – of the power of pure idealism in the practical world'.[1] This was not an uncommon view. Throughout the celebrations that marked the bicentenary of Emancipation in 1933–34, Britain's decision to emancipate its slaves was variously described as a 'sublime' or 'disinterested' act, and, as such, a sign of the country's moral strength and superiority. Emancipation marked Britain out. One of the first countries to perfect the transatlantic slave trade, Britain had been the first to ban the trade (1807) and, subsequently, to free its slaves (1834). Such selfless actions, it was argued, legitimised Britain's role in the world, the country's stewardship over countless millions in Africa, India, and the Caribbean, and its particular claim to speak for those who were too weak to speak for themselves. Emancipation, in other words, helped to define Britain's national and imperial identity, her tradition of humanitarian interventionism, and, no less important, her status and authority in a rapidly changing and (during the 1930s, at least) depressed world.

Some three thousand miles away, Trinidadians also met to celebrate Britain's tradition of humanity. At a large 'demonstration' held in 1933 at the Prince's Building, Port of Spain, 2000 schoolchildren raised their voices in praise of Wilberforce, in a programme that included such favourites as 'Hurrah for England' and 'Flags of Empire', as well as a new piece, 'Chords of Freedom', that had been specially written for the occasion. 'Proudly swells a nation's breast,' the children sang,

> In honour of his worth,
> And joyous is the heart-throb
> Of Hull that gave him birth;
> But prouder, joyful more than these
> Our hearts pulsate across the seas.
> With the Empire's flag in view,

We sing the Empire's pride
In one whose love of country
Set justice as her guide.
Of purpose firm, and high in thought
He to that country honour brought.[2]

Large crowds gathered again in 1934 to celebrate Emancipation Day (1 August). The highlight was a masked pageant at the Queen's Park Oval. But before the festivities began, the mayor of Port of Spain, Arthur Andrew Cipriani, unveiled an oil painting of the 'great Liberator', William Wilberforce (a gift of Thomas Sheppard, Curator of Hull Museums), which was then carried around the stands so that everyone might have a chance to see it.[3] It was a deeply symbolic gesture, and one that, like 'Chords of Freedom', serves as a pointed reminder of how individual, national, and imperial narratives became intertwined, creating their own internal logic.

At the heart of this imperialistic discourse, however, was a glaring silence or omission. As these two examples suggest, Britons – and Britain's colonial subjects – were taught to view transatlantic slavery through the moral triumph of abolition, thereby substituting for the horrors of slavery and the slave trade a 'culture of abolitionism'. Whether seen through the lens of abolitionist relics or celebrations and commemorations, what is so often striking about this specific 'history' is its silencing of African perspectives, and, in particular, the suffering of the millions who were sold into slavery (that is, the victims in this story). Indeed, it was only after the Second World War that this dominant discourse was seriously contested, not least by independent black communities in the English-speaking Caribbean. One result, particularly evident since the 1980s, has been a greater insistence on the need to address African perspectives on transatlantic slavery, and to restore the lives of those who are forgotten, the 'people without history'.[4] This emphasis is perhaps most apparent in many of the country's slave museums, but it is also reflected in contemporary debates about reparations or the need in Britain for a Slavery Remembrance Day. Put a different way, since the 1980s the dominant discourse has been disrupted and, to some extent, replaced by overlapping narratives that, in turn, reflect broader cultural and political changes within British society.

This books attempts to plot these social and intellectual currents, and, in doing so, to understand how our collective memory of transatlantic slavery has been 'constructed'. Chronologically, it runs from the 1830s, when British colonial slavery was abolished, to the present day. Within this very broad time span, however, it is possible to identify a number of key dates or periods, each of which helped to frame our remembrance of British transatlantic slavery. The first of these came in the 1870s when, to all intents and purposes, the international struggle against slavery and the slave trade had come to an end. Memorial activity (at Wisbech and Wadesmill in Hertfordshire, for instance), as well as renewed interest in collecting and preserving abolitionist relics, all point to a pre-determined effort to commemorate an official (abolitionist) version of the past. The second key period was the early 1930s, which, if anything, reinforced this dominant nineteenth-century historiography. As we shall see, the anniversary celebrations held in 1933–34 were conceived, for the most part, as nationalistic rituals that re-affirmed Britain's position as a civilised, Christian nation – a discourse that inevitably placed huge emphasis on figures like William Wilberforce. And, finally, there have been the years since 1983, decades that have witnessed the setting of new agendas, chief among them being the recovery of African 'voices' and a wider recognition that what the British did was 'wrong'.[5]

Looking back across this chronological time span, it is also noticeable that while Britons have traditionally remembered some events and anniversaries (Emancipation, for instance), they have forgotten or neglected others, 1807 being an obvious case in point. Why? The answer undoubtedly has something to do with the fact that Emancipation was considered the greater moral victory, a grand imperial gesture that seemed to subsume all that had gone before it. Fortuitously, passage of the Emancipation Act (1833) also happened to coincide with the death of William Wilberforce, a conjunction of events that imbued Emancipation with a deeper personal significance that was inseparable from Wilberforce's own fifty years' struggle against transatlantic slavery. But it did not help either that abolitionists, in this case the Anti-Slavery and Aborigines' Protection Society, took little interest in the 1907 anniversary of the abolition of the slave trade, a decision that in retrospect proved a terrible miscalculation, if only because it allowed 1807 to slip out of the nation's historical consciousness. (It is significant, for instance, that there were no celebrations in 1957, either; instead, attention focused on 1933–34 and, later, 1983–84.) As the bicentenary of the abolition of the slave trade approaches, therefore, there is really no specific 'tradition' that Britons can fall back on, despite the fact that since the 1980s, at least, there has been growing interest in and emphasis on Britain's involvement in the transatlantic slave trade – a shift or transformation that is again particularly evident in the displays to be found in many of the country's slavery museums. Viewed in this light, 2007 takes on an added resonance and meaning, offering, as it does, an opportunity to fill what many see as a 'memory void'.[6]

More revealing still is the role of personality in this narrative. A key figure here is William Wilberforce, for many Britons the embodiment of Britain's tradition of humanitarian interventionism. But arguably this 'bias' would have been less apparent to his contemporaries than it was to later generations. Like so many British heroes, Wilberforce's image has been 're-arranged' (Halbwachs' term) to meet the demands of the present, so that at different times he has been viewed and adopted as a 'Christian philanthropist', an apostle of freedom, or, more recently, as a modern human rights campaigner. As we shall see, the 'making' of William Wilberforce began effectively with his burial in Westminster Abbey (1833) and Samuel and Robert Wilberforce's *Life* of their father, published in 1838, and continued through the 1930s and beyond. Perhaps just as important, as Wilberforce's stock rose so did that of his 'coadjutors' decline, to the point where Wilberforce's name became a by-word for

'Abolition', although, ironically, Wilberforce actually had very little to do with the Emancipation Act of 1833. This narrative within a narrative forms a central part of what follows, as does the recent rehabilitation of Thomas Clarkson, a controversial figure whose treatment by Wilberforce's sons raises important questions about the dynamics of publicly articulated views of the past.

How we as individuals and as a nation choose to remember events like transatlantic slavery is, of course, neither random nor unmediated. In recent years, what the sociologist Maurice Halbwachs described as 'collective memory' has become the subject of intense historical and philosophical inquiry.[7] As a result, we have become accustomed to thinking about the relationship between memory and the group (one of Halbwach's central concerns), as well as the role played in memory-work by official or 'state-sponsored' memory. For obvious reasons, official agencies are ideally placed to 'shape memory as they see fit, memory that best serves a national interest'.[8] But not all memory is state-sponsored. Sometimes, as in the case of transatlantic slavery, the impetus comes from semi-official agencies – church leaders, civic groups, and philanthropic societies and organizations – that fill the vacuum left by the state. Alternatively, the stimulus may come from strata that hitherto have been marginalised or 'forgotten'.[9] In other words, framing remembrance is neither an exclusive nor a privileged activity; on the contrary, in any given group there will often be a multiplicity of memories, as well as conflicts between memories.[10] Conversely, the strength of a group, particularly a group as large as the nation-state, will depend on there being some consonance or consistency between individual, official, and national memory – the last an elusive concept that is supposed to 'transcend the memory of particular groups that have a social, ethnic, or religious basis, and to include the collective memory of the entire nation'.[11]

Hence the importance of rituals, although the relationship between ritual and memory is itself complex. At one level, perhaps the most obvious, commemorative practices (festivals, anniversaries, memorial days) recollect important events or individuals in the past – that is to say, the content of these rituals (who or what is being remembered) is often more important than the form. But, as Paul Connerton reminds us, commemorative practices can also be read as bodily performances that involve the repetition or re-enactment of 'prior, prototypical actions'.[12] Put another way, it is the experience of *participating* in celebrations – the sights, sounds, and sensations – that as much as anything helps to shape a group's social memory. Monuments, another important site of memory, present similar interpretative problems. For some, chief among them Pierre Nora, monuments shut off or displace memory, 'supplanting a community's memory-work with its own material form'.[13] On the other hand, the circumstances surrounding the erection of public monuments, as well as their uses and adaptations, can reveal important clues about the construction of social memory. Like rituals and other memorial activities, monuments serve an integrative function. As James Young puts it, 'in the absence of common beliefs or common interests, art in public places may force an otherwise fragmented populace to frame diverse values and ideals in common spaces. By creating common spaces for memory monuments propagate the illusion of common memory'.[14]

As theorists remind us, however, every realm of memory is also a realm of contest.[15] If, in the case of transatlantic slavery, challenges to the dominant (white) discourse were slow to emerge, at least with any force, in recent years they have grown apace, stimulated in large part by societal changes, as well as broadly political and cultural forces, among them debates about diversity and multiculturalism. Another important impetus has come from 'below'. In the English-speaking Caribbean, for instance, the years following independence witnessed the emergence of alternative versions of the slave past, many of them shaped by the work of black intellectuals like Eric Williams and C. L. R. James. Similarly, in Britain and the United States black communities have reclaimed their history, aided in many cases by white scholars who have taken it upon themselves to revisit and revise traditional accounts of slavery and the slave trade.[16] Equally striking is the speed with which 'white' institutions have responded to these challenges, or, in other cases, have themselves initiated change. As we shall see, slave museums have been particularly active in involving the black community in the planning and organisation of their displays, and in devising programmes and activities (slave trails, for instance) that address black concerns. Indeed, in the past twenty years museums have emerged as key sites of memory in relation to transatlantic slavery, although, here again, it is important to stress that, like other representations of the past, slavery exhibitions can be approached as 'aesthetic, artistic creations'; that is to say, 'they juxtapose, narrate, and remember events according to the taste of their curators, the political needs and interests of their community, [and] the temper of the time'.[17]

It is these considerations, and the relationship between rituals, commemoration, and memory, that form the central theme of this study. For obvious reasons, I have not attempted to provide a representative survey of all memorial sites and all memorial activities connected with transatlantic slavery. Instead, I have concentrated on a number of key sites that enable us to probe the 'constructedness' of Britain's culture of abolitionism. Chapter 1 takes as its theme Benjamin Robert Haydon's painting, *The Anti-Slavery Convention, 1840*, an abolitionist relic whose troubled history provides not only an insight into how British abolitionists sought to preserve their version of the past, but also reveals their anxiety about 'race' and black self-determination, represented in this case by the imposing figure of Henry Beckford. Chapter 2 explores the controversy surrounding the publication of Robert and Samuel Wilberforce's life of their father, which is chiefly remarkable for its intemperate attack on Thomas Clarkson. As I argue, the *Life* played an important role in 'silencing' Clarkson, as well as in undermining the credibility of his famous *History*, published in 1808. But perhaps less well appreciated is the role that the book played in re-interpreting Wilberforce for a modern audience, not least by accentuating his patriotism, as well as the moderateness of his religious opinions. Chapters 3 to 5, which form the heart of the book, examine three other memory sites: abolitionist monuments, anniversary celebrations, and slavery museums. While each of these chapters can be read in isolation, taken together they plot the emergence of a culture of abolitionism in the nineteenth century, its apogee in the 1930s, and, ultimately, its demise. Chapter 5, which explores the role of museums in shaping contemporary views of transatlantic slavery, brings the narrative up to the present day, although for obvious reasons what is said here could just as easily be applied to other memorial activities.

The bulk of this book is concerned with British responses to transatlantic slavery. But in the final chapter I have extended my own frame of remembrance to include the United States and the English-speaking Caribbean. In the case of the United States, what I have been most interested to do is to trace the impact of 'West India Emancipation' on the development of American abolitionism and American abolitionist rituals. Here, at least, blacks and whites seem to have been able to celebrate Emancipation free from outside interference. In the Caribbean, on the other hand, blacks' attempts to mark 1 August (Emancipation Day), and to give it meaning, were constrained not only by the planter elite but also by white missionaries and British colonial officials who, in many cases, tried to impose their own (Eurocentric) views on Emancipation. It might be argued that the end result was the same, in the sense that in both regions blacks were obliged to work within white frames of remembrance. But, as we shall see, in the Caribbean at least, Emancipation continues to have relevance and purpose for black communities, many of which see in it a vehicle for articulating new, alternative versions of the black past. Perhaps just as important, these black frames of remembrance reverberate across the Atlantic, creating a collective consciousness (and a shared memory) that challenges us to rethink our own shared assumptions, as well as our own national identity.

Notes

1 Reginald Coupland, *The Empire in these Days: An Interpretation* (London, 1935), p. 264.
2 *Trinidad Guardian*, 29 July 1933; Wilberforce House Museum, Hull, Wilberforce and Anti-Slavery Collection: Wilberforce Centenary 1933, Box 14.
3 *Trinidad Guardian*, 3 August 1934. Cipriani was no stooge. In fact, he was fiercely critical of British colonial policy in the Caribbean. See Chapter 6.
4 Alex Van Stipriaan, 'July 1, Emancipation Day in Suriname: A Contested *Lieu de Memoire*, 1863–2003', *New West Indian Guide*, 78 (2004), pp. 269–70.
5 See, for example, the 2004 House of Commons debate on the (then) forthcoming bicentenary of the abolition of the slave trade, *Hansard*, sixth series, vol. 425, cols. 143WH–176WH. I pick up these debates in Chapter 4.
6 Iwona Irwin-Zarecka, *Frames of Remembrance: The Dynamics of Collective Memory* (New

Brunswick, 1994), p. 117.

7   Maurice Halbwachs, *On Collective Memory*, edited, translated and with an introduc-
    tion by Lewis A. Coser (Chicago, 1992). See also Pierre Nora, dir., *Realms of Memory:
    Rethinking the French Past*, edited and with a foreword by Lawrence D. Kritzman,
    translated by Arthur Goldhammer, 3 vols (New York, c. 1996–98); Alon Confino,
    'Collective Memory and Cultural History: Problems of Method', *American Historical
    Review*, 102 (1997), pp. 1386–1403; Noa Gedi and Yigal Elam, 'Collective Memory:
    What is it?', *History and Memory*, 8 (1996), pp. 30–50.

8   James Young, *The Texture of Memory: Holocaust Memorials and Meaning* (New Haven,
    CT, 1993), p. 3. For obvious reasons, a lot of the work on state-sponsored memory has
    focused on the Third Reich and other fascist regimes, but all states 'sponsor' memory,
    whether through state funerals, national memorial days (Remembrance Sunday, for
    example) or, in the British case, royal ceremonials. See Avner Ben-Amos, *Funerals,
    Politics, and Memory in Modern France, 1789–1996* (Oxford, 2000); David Cannadine,
    'Introduction: Divine Rites of Kings', in David Cannadine and Simon Price, eds,
    Rituals of Royalty: Power and Ceremonial in Traditional Societies (Cambridge, 1987), pp.
    1–19; Benedict Anderson, *Imagined Communities: Reflections on the Origin and Spread of
    Nationalism* (London, 1983); Eric Hobsbawn and Terence Ranger, eds., *The Invention
    of Tradition* (Cambridge, 1983).

9   Van Stipriaan, 'July 1, Emancipation Day in Suriname', p. 270.

10 Confino, 'Collective Memory and Cultural History', p. 1400; Irwin-Zarecka, *Frames of
    Remembrance*, pp. 67–85.

11 Ben-Amos, *Funerals, Politics, and Memory in Modern France*, p. 5.

12 Paul Connerton, *How Societies Remember* (Cambridge, 1989), p. 61.

13 Young, *The Texture of Memory*, p. 5.

14 Ibid., p. 6.

15 Van Stipriaan, 'July 1, Emancipation Day in Suriname', p. 270.

16 See Chapters 5 and 6.

17 Young, *The Texture of Memory*, p. viii.

❦ 1 ❦

Frames of remembrance:
Benjamin Robert Haydon and
The Anti-Slavery Convention, 1840

To a large extent, popular views of British transatlantic slavery, like most publicly articulated views of the past, were introduced from the top down; in this case, principally by those who had fought for many years to bring the institution to an end. Abolitionists (the 'Saints') were keenly aware of their place in history, as their voluminous memoirs and histories attest.[1] Occasionally, however, their insistence on celebrating their own achievements, and hence preserving their own version of the past, encountered resistance. A case in point is Benjamin Robert Haydon's painting, *The Anti-Slavery Convention, 1840*, which as its title suggests, was commissioned to commemorate the first World Anti-Slavery Convention, held in London in 1840. As we shall see, the engagement of abolitionists with the artistic world was hardly unproblematic. On the contrary, in Haydon they found a collaborator who not only had his own ideas about the meaning of the convention but who also seemed intent on turning their commission into a political act. The ensuing conflict between artist and patron resulted in a seriously flawed piece of work that ultimately satisfied no one. Yet, for all its faults, and despite the fact that for long periods it has been neglected or simply ignored, *The Anti-Slavery Convention, 1840* remains one of the nation's most enduring abolitionist relics. Moreover, its troubled history hints at silences and omissions ('realms of forgetting') that take us to the very heart of our sometimes difficult relationship with 'race' and transatlantic slavery.

The World Anti-Slavery Convention, held at Freemasons' Hall in London in June 1840, was a pivotal moment in the history of organised anti-slavery. Only a year before, British abolitionists had set up the British and Foreign Anti-Slavery Society (BFASS), whose aim was the abolition of slavery throughout the world. Keen to build on this initiative, the BFASS came up with the idea of a general anti-slavery conference, which was intended to take into account all aspects of the slavery question. Today, the convention is perhaps best remembered for the struggle between the BFASS and William Lloyd

Garrison and his supporters over the seating of American women delegates, among them Lucretia Mott and Maria Lydia Child. Important as this incident was, however, not least in exposing some of the differences that existed between British and American abolitionists, it hardly conveys a sense of the true significance of the gathering. As Howard Temperley has argued, the World Anti-Slavery Convention 'represented a drawing together of antislavery talent unique in the history of the movement'. Virtually all of the leading British abolitionists were present, as were many from the United States. There were also delegations from the British colonies, France, Spain, Switzerland and Haiti. Put simply, no one had ever seen anything quite like this before. Small wonder, then, that thousands of visitors crowded into the galleries at Freemason's Hall, or that the national press covered the two-week long convention in almost obsessive detail.[2]

With good reason, British abolitionists (or, at least, some of them) were keen to commemorate the convention and to exploit its propaganda value. The 1830s had witnessed a series of grand meetings and celebrations, most of them connected with Reform and most of them captured for posterity in prints and paintings, or sometimes both. One thinks, for instance, of William Salter's *The Waterloo Banquet of 1836* (1837) and Sir George Hayter's *The House of Commons, 1833* (1833–43). While it is true that none of the members of the BFASS was qualified or proficient in the visual arts, it seems likely that what they had in mind was something similar; a group portrait that would not only commemorate the Anti-Slavery Convention but also popularise it through cheap prints and, possibly, medals and ceramics.[3] What the BFASS was looking for, in other words, was a means of announcing itself to the world and of regaining some of the ground that had been lost by its predecessors, the Anti-Slavery Society (1823–39) and the Universal Abolition Society (1834–35).

To help them realise these ambitions, Joseph Cooper, John Beaumont, and James Tredgold, who were all members of the BFASS's guiding London Committee, approached Benjamin Robert Haydon.[4] A vain and self-opinionated man, Haydon had at an early stage in his career committed himself to the task of restoring the status and reputation of history painting, which within the academy, at least, was universally admitted to be the highest form of art because of its ability to 'raise nature' and 'heighten' emotion. Between 1810 and 1825 Haydon had produced a series of works, among them *The Judgement of Solomon* (1812–14), *Christ's Entry in Jerusalem* (1814–20), and *The Rising of Lazarus* (1823), which for a brief period were highly popular. In later years, increasing debts had forced him to turn to genre painting, where again he exhibited with some success. But his first love was history painting, and it was with understandable relief that he seized upon the opportunities offered by the political events of the 1830s. Having proposed and then lost a commission to paint the monster gathering of trades union at Newhall Hill, Birmingham, Haydon was invited by Lord Grey to paint *The Reform Banquet*, which was subsequently exhibited in London in 1834. Such works were considered 're-portage for posterity', and through them Haydon obviously hoped to 'promote

1   Benjamin Robert Haydon, self-portrait (c. 1845)

his claims for history painting of national significance that could attract public patronage'.[5]

Haydon's seriousness and his commitment to High Art may well have recommended him to Cooper and his friends. Whatever the reason, the choice was an unfortunate one. For one thing, *The Reform Banquet* had been a miserable failure: *Fraser's Magazine* went so far as to describe it as 'abominable'. For another, Haydon had little patience with portrait painting and regarded it with undisguised suspicion, believing that its popularity had done 'undue damage' to history painting.[6] To compound these difficulties, Haydon's not inconsiderable powers were obviously failing by the late 1830s. As a child, it seems that he had suffered from an eye condition, which left his sight so impaired that his assistants reported that Haydon worked with three pairs of large, round concave spectacles on his head 'all the time'. If anything, these problems got worse as time went on. C. R. Leslie, among others, has noted the 'almost regular decrease of excellence in [Haydon's] pictures, from the "Solomon" to the end of his life, parallel with his increasing troubles'.[7] What the members of the BFASS also failed to appreciate, until it was too late, was that Haydon was highly opinionated, impetuous, and fiercely independent.

Haydon later recalled that at first he had been unwilling to accept the BFASS's commission. Nevertheless, he did agree to attend the opening session of the World Anti-Slavery Convention on 12 June.[8] What he witnessed clearly affected him deeply. By prior arrangement, the veteran abolitionist, Thomas Clarkson, then in his eighty-first year, had agreed to act as chairman of the convention, although it was not anticipated that he would take an active part in the proceedings. At the appointed hour he was led into the hall, supported by Joseph Sturge and William Crewdson, and greeted by the delegates, who received him in respectful silence. The formalities over, Clarkson's grandson, also Thomas, was introduced to the convention in what was, in effect, a ritual laying-on of hands. It was his mother's dearest wish, Sturge told the delegates, that 'her darling child should devote his life to the cause in which [his grandfather] had worked for nearly half a century'. The effect was electric. Amelia Opie, who was sitting at the back of the hall, opposite the platform, noted that Sturge's address was listened to with the 'deepest emotion'. 'The young subject of it was himself deeply affected,' she went on, 'and I saw tears stealing down many a manly cheek, while many a manly brow was hidden awhile from observation.'[9]

Clarkson himself then came forward. In what was to be his last public address, he began by taking the delegates back to his early labours against the slave trade. He spoke warmly of Wilberforce and William Smith, MP for Norwich, as he did of Samuel Hoare and Richard Phillips, who had both been members of the London Committee of the Society for Effecting the Abolition of the Slave Trade. But then he seemed to falter. 'There were other dear friends,' he added, drawing the back of his hand across his eyes, 'whose names I am sorry to say I cannot recollect at the moment'. Rousing himself, Clarkson went on to remind the delegates of the enormity of the task before them. He even offered them a word of advice, pressing the case for an economic boycott of American slave-grown produce. Then lifting his arm as if pointing to heaven, 'his face quivering with emotion', Clarkson ended by exhorting the delegates: 'May the Supreme ruler of all human events at whose disposal are not only the hearts, but intellects of men, may He in his abundant mercy guide your councils and give his blessing on your labours'.[10]

Sitting in the gallery, Haydon realised at once that he had found 'the moment of interest' he had been looking for.[11] But there was more drama to follow. Before Clarkson left the hall and the real work of the convention began, Joseph Sturge brought forward Henry Beckford, an ex-slave from Jamaica and one of only four black delegates attending the convention. After shaking hands with Clarkson, Beckford proposed a vote of thanks to 'British ladies', and to the assembled delegates. 'I have seen the blood run down the negro's back', he told them. 'I have seen the poor creatures confined to chains; but how shall I rejoice when I return to my native land to tell my friends that I have seen those gentlemen who delivered us from the accursed system which was the ruin of men's souls as well as their bodies'. Significantly, Beckford presented himself as both living proof of the benefits of Emancipation and as a source of hope and inspiration to others. 'I came here as a free man, and shall return the same,' he reminded the delegates, rousing them to further exertions. 'I was a slave for twenty-eight years, but look at me, and work on.'[12]

The significance of this moment was not lost on Haydon, and almost at once he resolved to work Beckford into his painting. Indeed, in the finished composition Beckford sits in the centre foreground, 'the hand of a friend resting with affection on his arm, in fellowship and protection', listening to Clarkson as he concludes his speech. As Haydon explained in his description of the painting, 'this is the point of interest in the picture … the African sitting by the intellectual European, in equality and intelligence, whilst the patriarch of the cause points to heaven as to whom he must be grateful'.[13] Even today, this central image, which dominates the completed canvas, is arresting; it is what surrounds it that lacks conviction. Be that as it may, Haydon's decision to place Beckford on terms of rough equality with white abolitionists was a bold move calculated to create unease, not least in the minds of the very people who had commissioned the painting. For not only was Haydon challenging abolitionist sensibilities by placing his own construction on the meaning of the World Anti-Slavery Convention, he was also challenging white aesthetic notions that more often than not relegated blacks to the realm of crude, comic caricatures. As it turns out, in the 1810s Haydon

2   Benjamin Robert Haydon, *The Anti-Slavery Convention, 1840* (1841)

had himself subscribed to many of these same notions of alleged black 'inferiority', and in this sense *The Anti-Slavery Convention, 1840* also can be viewed as a work of catharsis.

The vast majority of eighteenth- and early nineteenth-century images of blacks portrayed anonymous and largely passive men and women in domestic service. There were exceptions, of course. John Singleton Copley, for one, gave blacks more active roles in two of his most famous paintings, *Watson and the Shark* (1778) and *The Death of Major Pearson* (1782–84). Perhaps just as significant, Géricault included three black figures in his *Raft of the Medusa* (1819).[14] But far more often blacks were depicted as servants or slaves. Typical of the genre is Francis Wheatley's painting of *A Family Group with a Negro Servant* (1774–75), in which a black attendant, probably a boy, kneels respectfully at the far left of the picture, that is, at the margins. Other blacks are portrayed serving tea, holding their masters' horses, or occasionally, playing with or looking after white children. In other words, they fill supporting or subsidiary roles. More often than not, the blacks portrayed in these pictures are objects of display, intended to tell the viewer something about the owner's wealth, status, and respectability. They are props, fashionable possessions that in their way are every bit as important as a piece of china or the cut of a dress.[15]

Alternatively, blacks were portrayed as supplicants of one kind or another, a trope that went back to the sixteenth century and beyond.[16] The figure of the kneeling slave pleading for his or her freedom became a popular abolitionist motif during the late eighteenth century, and many of the images surrounding Emancipation in 1833–34 reinforced hierarchical notions of (white) power and authority, not least by representing Emancipation as a 'gift' bestowed upon slaves in the British Caribbean by beneficent whites.[17] The language of empire gave such images added relevance and meaning. In Thomas Jones Barker's *The Secret of England's Greatness* (c. 1863), Queen Victoria presents an ornately decorated bible to a native African prince (sometimes referred to incorrectly as the 'Sultan of Zanzibar') who kneels before her with his arms outstretched to receive this symbol of civilisation. While Barker included other figures in *The Secret of England's Greatness*, including Prince Albert, Lord John Russell, and Viscount Palmerston, the picture is dominated by the transaction taking place in front of them. Victoria, as one might expect, is resplendent in court dress (the scene is set in the audience chamber at Windsor Castle). Her visitor, however, is dressed more unconventionally in flowing robes, sashes, a leopardskin cape, earrings, bracelets, and a magnificent turban, complete with what looks like an ostrich feather. His dress, like his pose, marks him out as an exoticised 'other', thereby accentuating and legitimising Britain's civilising mission and, with it, the victory of the Christian Saxon world over the whole 'dark' continent.[18]

Satirical prints also tended to reinforce notions of black inferiority. From Hogarth to Rowlandson, British satirists helped to popularise an image of

3 Thomas Jones Baker, *The Secret of England's Greatness* (c. 1863)

blacks as servants, sailors, rioters, prostitutes, and beggars; in short, as part of plebeian culture. Worse, they were often the butt of jokes or introduced only to make a wider political point. During the Westminster election of 1784, for instance, Rowlandson portrayed the Duchess of Devonshire in the act of buying the vote of a disreputable-looking black publican. Another engraving from this period, again by Rowlandson, depicts Mrs Hobart rounding up more potential voters, in this case 'an old and decrepit Chelsea pensioner and a negro supported on stumps and crutches'. Many of these prints also had obvious sexual overtones, revealing a prurient interest in 'overt and frequently socially compromised sexual unions'.[19] If anything, the black iconography of the early nineteenth century was cruder and certainly more vicious in its comic intent. Prints like Edward Clay's *Life in Philadelphia* (1829) and *Tregear's Black Jokes* (1834) mercilessly lampooned blacks' speech and manners, as well as their over-fondness for extravagance and display. The popularity of black minstrels and characters like 'Jim Crow' were part of the same broad phenomenon. As Hugh Honour puts it, 'paintings of blacks by white artists often seem to have been based on the assumptions crudely embodied in the black face act'.[20]

Negative images of blacks were legitimised by contemporary attitudes towards 'race' and human diversity. Whether framed in terms of climate, the environment or cultural relativism, this discourse invariably identified Africans as the antitype of civilised Europeans. Some went further. Immanuel Kant, for instance, thought that the differences between blacks and whites were so 'fundamental' that they were 'as great in regard to mental capacities as in colour'. Analyses of skull types tended to reinforce these prejudices. Diagrammatic charts of comparative skulls, like those accompanying the works of the Dutch physiologist Peter Camper (1722–89), usually placed the European with a facial angle of 80 degrees next to the Greek god Apollo (the ideal vertical profile), and the African with an angle of 70 degrees next to the ape. While Camper himself did not regard these distinctions as fixed or immutable, they went on to assume a rigid status during the nineteenth century. According to David Bindman, by about 1850 'a racial science based on a scale of relative intelligence and measurable skull type, with the European at the upper end and the African at the lower, had become well established in a number of European universities'.[21]

One obvious result of this obsession with racial hierarchies and 'ideal form' was that artists and writers came to attach overwhelming importance to the Greek sculptural canon. Recently, Kirk Savage has shown how in the United States during the nineteenth century 'classical sculpture served as the benchmark of whiteness'. The classical or canonical body, in this formulation, was erect and contained. As Savage points out, the head of Apollo, in particular, 'was a widely recognised standard of male beauty and, by implication, a lesson in the relationship of physical beauty to intellect and culture'. The black body, by contrast, was characterised by 'swaying contours, wildly scattered limbs, protruding buttocks, [and] spread-eagle legs'. Popular images of blacks served only to reinforce these stereotypes. Black minstrels, for instance, exploited the comic potential of the black body, as did satirists and illustrators. Savage also notes that the principle of 'opposition' embedded in these popular images of blacks was very similar to the principle operating in so-called 'scientific' works, 'where the vertical profile of the canonical face [was] contrasted with the supposedly jutting jaw of the more animal-like Negro'. In the United States, of course, this polarity was accentuated by the experience of slavery (the enslaved body could hardly be considered noble or dignified), but it was by no means unique to America or, indeed, to the English-speaking world.[22]

Haydon's own reflections on the heroic or classical standard of form are well documented. In 1810, while working on his *Macbeth*, he had encountered a black American from Boston by the name of Wilson. Haydon immediately engaged him for a month and began drawing and casting him, 'without a moment's loss of time in all the attitudes wanted for my picture'. He had all his joints moulded in every stage, from their greatest possible flexion to their greatest possible extension. Haydon even attempted a plaster cast of Wilson's entire torso, a difficult and dangerous procedure that very nearly cost Wilson his life.[23] It is obvious that Haydon greatly admired the beauty of Wilson's body. As he put it: 'What was excellent was the great flexibility and vigour of his movements ... The great principle that the form of a part depends on its actions was here confirmed.' Nevertheless, he also observed a number of glaring defects, which he recorded in meticulous detail; for instance, that Wilson's 'calf was high and feeble, his feet flat, and heel projecting, his forearm as long as his arm bone, his deltoid short, his jaw protrusive, and his forehead receding'. In other words, he found in Wilson 'all the positive marks characteristic of brutality'.[24]

Significantly, Haydon concluded that these defects were inherent 'racial' characteristics. All blacks, he argued, whether Africans or American 'Negroes', shared the same tragic flaws: 'their lobes of ear small, their teeth frequent, lower jaw retreats, the skull is diminished – they have longer bodies, longer fore arms, greater projection of elbows, deficient Deltoids'. Haydon went further. Because blacks were deficient in the great muscles that kept the human form erect, he argued, they walked 'feebly, with a shuffling want of firmness'. Monkeys, he added, had 'more of these characteristics and can neither walk or run, but only hop irregularly'. Crucially, Haydon attributed differences in human and animal form to what he called 'distinct characteristics of intellect'. What he was putting forward, in other words, was a crude racist theory that explained black 'brutality' in terms of ignorance and 'deficiency of intellect'. These speculations, moreover, shaped Haydon's heroic standard of form. As he frankly admitted in his autobiography, 'I made the basis of it to be the *reverse* of all the … approaches to deficiency in the Negro.' In short, Haydon's experiments with Wilson served only to confirm what he already believed, namely that the black body was the antithesis of classical whiteness.[25]

The Anti-Slavery Convention, 1840 struck a very different note, however. Haydon's decision to give Beckford such a prominent role in his painting undoubtedly had less to do with aesthetic considerations than with his own professed radicalism. Characteristically, he wanted to make a statement, not least about his own abolitionist credentials. He also wanted his painting to have moral influence.[26] Whatever the reason, Haydon succeeded in portraying Beckford with 'conspicuous directness'. Immaculately attired in 'English' morning dress, itself an important badge of power and identity, Beckford is unmistakably a free man and the equal of any European in the picture (Haydon said as much himself).[27] Moreover, his posture, and the casual way he rests his left arm on a neighbour's chair, suggests someone who is perfectly at ease with his surroundings. He is neither cowed nor submissive. On the contrary, Beckford maintains a quiet dignity, accentuated by his upturned gaze (his eyes remain fixed on Clarkson) and his unruffled appearance. Here, in other words, is a figure to admire and respect – and, just as important, to be taken seriously.

The irony of this situation was not lost on Haydon. As he wrote to Thomas Clarkson in March 1841: 'Is it not singular that I who carried on a controversy 31 years ago, against the intellectual powers of the Negro, however deep his sympathies, should be the man to paint a Picture in his honour?'[28] What Haydon did not anticipate is how others would respond to his decision to place Beckford at the dramatic centre of his painting. When he told John

Scoble, who was later to become Secretary of the BFASS, that he proposed to place him in a group together with Beckford and George Thompson, Haydon noted that Scoble 'sophisticated immediately on the greater propriety of placing the Negro in the distance, as it would have much greater effect'. Haydon was clearly taken aback; abolitionists, he thought, should take pride in being placed close to 'the Negro'. Over the next few days he tested out other sitters on the same subject. William Lloyd Garrison, who sat for Haydon on 30 June, 'met [him] at once directly'. George Thompson, on the other hand, merely said that saw 'no objection' to the idea. For Haydon, however, this was not enough. He remained convinced that 'a Man who wishes to place the Negro on a level must no longer regard him as *having been* a Slave! & not feel annoyed at sitting by his side'.[29]

Haydon had put his finger on a sensitive issue. In the United States many white abolitionists were divided over the question of social intercourse with blacks, fearing that it would strengthen white prejudice and fasten the chains of bondage even tighter. There were similar debates over the expediency of admitting blacks as members of anti-slavery societies. In 1835, for instance, William Lloyd Garrison had found it necessary to reprimand a fellow abolitionist for expressing his belief that 'we ought never to have permitted our colored brethren to unite with us in our associations'.[30] Clearly, Scoble and Thompson shared some of these same concerns. Mixing blacks and whites in public was always a delicate issue, as was anything that encouraged social intercourse between the races. Seen in this context, the reassuring hand that George Stacey, another BFASS committee member, places on Beckford's left arm takes on an added significance. However laudable or well intended, such gestures hinted at a degree of intimacy that threatened to collapse the boundaries between black and white, Christian and heathen, liberator and liberated.[31]

Nevertheless, Haydon stood firm. As if to make his point, he put in Scoble's head (his first portrait) on 1 July and started work on Beckford two days later.[32] The rest of the composition proved more problematic, however. In all, some 350 delegates attended the World Anti-Slavery Convention, and from the start it must have been obvious that not all of them could be included in Haydon's picture. In fact, Haydon painted considerably less than half of the delegates, or 137 portrait heads.[33] Some, like the BFASS committee, selected themselves. Space also had to be made for many of the foreign delegates, although here again there were some notable omissions, among them William Lloyd Garrison. Finally, the BFASS committee selected a number of delegates from local anti-slavery societies, various benevolent organizations, and church groups, although on what basis is not entirely clear. The committee was also largely responsible for the arrangement of the delegates. Haydon noted in his diary on 16 July that 'John Beaumont called, & we ticketed all the heads *according to desert*, as the Duke of Sussex and I did with the Reform Banquet'.[34]

In some cases, the arrangement of delegates was obviously seen as an opportunity to settle old scores. According to Haydon, Sir Thomas Fowell Buxton 'had behaved so bad to the society that they resolved not to give him but a second rate place'. Buxton, it appears, was not at all pleased at being squeezed into the group sitting behind Clarkson, and neither was James Birney, one of the American delegates.[35] It had been the same thing with Haydon's picture of *The Reform Banquet*. 'No body would be put in Shadow,' he recalled, 'and some people, old Reformers, came 50 miles to insist on their right of being put in.'[36] In other cases, political or organizational rivalries were the decisive factor. The Philadelphian Abby Kimber, herself a loyal Garrisonian, claimed that someone (she did not know who) had got Samuel Prescod placed in front of George Thompson, leader of the British Garrisonians, 'so that he is not seen in that position so common to him with his arm thrown over his chair'. Garrison, meanwhile, was excluded entirely from the finished picture, even though Haydon had clearly intended to do him *'life* size' and to place him among the women delegates. Either Haydon subsequently changed his mind, or, as seems more likely, the BFASS committee quashed the idea.[37]

Eventually, the committee whittled the number of 'heads' down to about 100. The challenge for Haydon was to arrange these portraits into a plausible composition. He had struggled with this problem in *The Reform Banquet*, where at least the long rows of tables, with Lord Grey at their head, had provided a satisfactory point of focus. However, in *The Anti-Slavery Convention, 1840* his

4   Benjamin Robert Haydon, *The Reform Banquet* (1834)

arrangement of the space and the figures was much less assured. Working at speed and hampered by poor eyesight, Haydon failed miserably to control the transition from the group of the figures in the foreground to the dim and distant background of the hall. Some of the heads in the half-distance appear as large as those in the foreground. Many of them are suspended in mid air, as if dismembered from their bodies, while others face each other awkwardly in poses that are frankly implausible, given that the delegates are meant to be seated on a level plane facing the podium. Clarkson, for his part, seems dwarfed by the figures around him. The outsized portraits of Joseph Sturge and William Crewdson, immediately under Clarkson's upraised left arm, are particularly clumsy, as are many of the portraits crowded into the seats immediately behind him.[38]

Clearly, as a composition *The Anti-Slavery Convention, 1840* was seriously flawed. A lot of this must be put down to Haydon's failing powers, but the BFASS committee was at fault, too. Haydon later complained that even 'after the Composition was settled, I used to get notes from Joseph Sturge, "Friend Haydon, I would thank thee to put in the bearer (an old abolitionist)"'. A diary entry for November 1840 notes wearily: 'Their bringing me 31 heads more, after arranging 103, is rather a joke, but if they like, they shall have heads all over, like a peacock's tail.' Haydon estimated that as a result 'there were at least 50 heads where no bodies could be squeezed, according to perspective'.[39] None of this is to deny that Haydon had limitations as an artist. Yet there is no doubt that the BFASS committee's incessant demands seriously compromised his ambitions for the painting, or that their interventions left an indelible mark on *The Anti-Slavery Convention, 1840* and how it was received. Haydon noted in March 1841 that 'some swear the Quakers are too prominent'. 'This is the way,' he went on. '[The] Men who have paid for work, ordered a work, & spent hundreds in the Cause, are considered *too* predominant in their *own* picture.' But for some abolitionists this was precisely the point: *The Anti-Slavery Convention, 1840* was a 'Quaker picture'.[40]

As his diary makes clear, Haydon worked non-stop on *The Anti-Slavery Convention, 1840* for almost ten months, from June 1840 until April 1841. It was an astonishing effort: Sir George Hayter took nearly ten years over *The House of Commons, 1833*. Haydon put in his last head on 24 April. Then, as a final flourish, he inscribed the names of Wilberforce, Sharp, and Toussaint L'Ouverture on the curtains above the convention hall. Haydon obviously meant this as a mark of respect. However, the BFASS committee would have none of it. The following day Haydon received a curt note from Beaumont telling him that the names 'must come out'. Haydon obliged but not for the first time he was left smarting at what he regarded as a lack of imagination on the part of his Quaker friends. 'The gratitude of posterity!' he snapped. 'Without Wilberforce, Toussaint, or Sharpe [sic], no Convention would have been held on the subject. And here is my friend Beaumont insisting on their names (introduced merely in allusion to their services) being struck out.' By this stage Haydon clearly had had enough of both Beaumont and the painting.

'The delight I had in turning to one of my historical Compositions after I had got rid of that infernal collection of faces, is not to be described', he wrote in his diary on 30 April.[41]

Haydon's frustration is hardly surprising. *The Anti-Slavery Convention, 1840* had been conceived in a state of impassioned idealism. A diary entry for 27 June 1840 reads: 'My sketches & the great Picture is sublime.' At other times during these early months he refers to his painting as 'a glorious practice in heads'. As time went on, however, his references to the commission became shorter and less effusive. His assessment of the finished painting, for instance, was that it was 'original, natural & effective'. Clearly, he was disappointed. Nevertheless, *The Anti-Slavery Convention, 1840* still had value as a piece of commemorative art, or so he thought. Haydon wrote to Thomas Clarkson on 19 March 1841: 'I trust in God, it will have a moral influence on the sacred cause, and by exciting attention ... keep up the desire the ultimate extinction of the greatest curse ever afflicted on creatures gifted with life & sensibility'. Significantly, he picked up the same theme in his description of the painting, published in 1841.[42] It was as if he wanted people to appreciate the picture for what it represented, rather than for its artistic merit. The question was whether others would be quite so understanding or forgiving.

Having completed his painting, Haydon decided to exhibit it at the Egyptian Hall in Piccadilly. Originally built in 1811–12 to house William Bullock's private museum, the Egyptian Hall had later been converted into a vast exhibition space. Rooms were available to anyone who could pay a deposit on the rent, and the hall often housed three or four different exhibitions at the same time. Over the years, the Egyptian Hall hosted a variety of attractions: freak shows, performers, clairvoyants, and what Richard Altick describes as 'unclassifiables,' ranging from Monsieur Guadin's model of Switzerland (1825) to the Royal Clarence Vase (1832).[43] From a relatively early date the Egyptian Hall also served as a gallery for the exhibition of large dramatic paintings. Géricault's *Raft of the Medusa*, for instance, was first exhibited at the Egyptian Hall in 1820, and in 1843 Sir George Hayter exhibited four of his paintings there, including *The House of Commons, 1833*. For Haydon, who was increasingly at odds with both the Royal Academy and the British Institution, the venue provided a popular alternative to the annual mixed exhibitions, although it undoubtedly exposed him to financial risk. Haydon first exhibited at the Egyptian Hall in 1820 when he hired Bullock's great room to exhibit *Christ's Entry into Jerusalem*, and he repeated the experiment again in 1823, 1828 and 1832. But none of these exhibitions was anything like as successful as *Christ's Entry into Jerusalem*, which makes his decision to exhibit again at the Egyptian Hall all the more surprising.[44]

We can only surmise that Haydon felt that this time he had a subject that by its very nature would attract widespread interest. (It is also possible that exhibiting *The Anti-Slavery Convention, 1840* in this way was part of the agreement that Haydon had reached with Cooper, Beaumont, and Tredgold.) Sadly, he was to be disappointed. None of the art journals covered the exhibition, which opened on 11 May 1841, and neither did *The Times*.[45] Those papers that did were either non-committal or downright hostile. The London *Morning Post*, for instance, described the painting as 'a great abortion in historical art', pointing out that the drawing was 'defective' and the perspective 'null and void'. But it was the 'vulgar' composition that appears to have caused greatest offence. Claiming that there were 137 'professed heads' but only six or eight bodies, the *Post* likened the serried ranks of faces to 'a pattern card of Birmingham buttons, or a batch of baker's rolls stuck up on edge' (significantly, the *Post*'s critic made no mention of Henry Beckford). 'It is altogether a most grievous affair,' the paper went on. 'Several of the faces behind are twice as large as those in the foreground, and there is no keeping, even of the commonest kind, in any part of the composition.' Worse still, the *Post* succeeded in turning Haydon's painting into an Egyptian Hall freak show, predicting that its very awfulness would indulge the public's curiosity in 'what is monstrous and absurd'.[46]

The *Athenaeum* was equally critical. 'It cannot satisfy an artistic eye,' the journal observed contemptuously, 'unless a pavement of heads laid over one third of the canvas, almost as formally as the skulls in Cruikshank's Monument to Napoleon, could be permitted to stand for composition.' Neither did it satisfy the viewer as 'a merely prosaic transcript of things as they are'; indeed, the *Athenaeum* claimed that but for the 'skeleton catalogue' they would not have known that many of their 'friends' were in the painting.[47] Even those sympathetic to the cause were critical. William Lucas, for example, dismissed the painting as 'a wagon load of heads, poor as a work of art but interesting from the number of portraits,' adding that 'though most may be recognised, are none of them faithful.' Catherine Clarkson's friend, Patty Smith, agreed. 'His [Haydon's] sketches are fine,' she confessed, 'and he has given immense variety of character to the delegates but I doubt whether he is an adept in the peculiarity of likeness. Grandeur is his forte. Mr C looks like a Homer or a Belisarius – an affecting noble head, but not quite his Mr C's Eye.' (Lucas, for his part, thought that Haydon's portrait of Clarkson did not reveal 'enough of the feeble old man'.) Only Catherine Clarkson seemed to be pleased with the painting, describing it as 'the most wonderful thing I ever saw'.[48]

Understandably, Haydon was disappointed and angered by the press's response to *The Anti-Slavery Convention, 1840*. 'The Criticism of this Picture has been absurd,' he wrote on 13 May. 'Because it looks like mere Nature, the Cricks [sic] think the *Art* has been overlooked; whereas, there is as much, or more Art, in this artless look than in many Compositions of more profundity.' Yet in the same breath he admitted that the 'the Picture as an Exhibition has failed entirely'.[49] What made the criticism all the more difficult to bear, certainly for the British and Foreign Anti-Slavery Society, was that abolitionists were already under mounting pressure as a result of the high cost of Emancipation in the British Caribbean. Rising sugar prices, together with popular images of an idle and well-fed Caribbean peasantry, inevitably caused resentment among many Britons, particularly as Emancipation coincided almost exactly with a long depression in the British Isles. Not surprisingly, some of this frustration was vented on abolitionists. In 1840 Chartists broke up an anti-slavery meeting in Norwich, and, perhaps more disconcerting still, the following year the annual meeting of the BFASS was disrupted by Chartist hecklers.[50]

Seen in this context, the failure of Haydon's painting took on a much wider significance. What ought to have been a cause for celebration and an opportunity to regain lost ground, turned instead into a retreat and another exercise in damage limitation. It is clear that the exhibition in the Egyptian Hall had been conceived as a publicity exercise. The official catalogue, for instance, included an appendix setting out the aims of the BFASS, as well as a long list of BFASS publications. Strenuous efforts had also been made to ensure that abolitionists were present to greet visitors, certainly during the first week of the exhibition. There were even hopes in some quarters that Queen Victoria would visit the exhibition, thereby guaranteeing the popularity of the painting.[51] The critical response to the picture, however, seems to have convinced the BFASS committee that it was probably best to draw a veil over the whole episode. Significantly, the society's official organ, *Anti-Slavery Reporter*, limited its coverage of the exhibition at the Egyptian Hall to a brief notice in a leader on 5 May 1841, and a poem dedicated to 'Haydon's Picture of the Anti-Slavery Convention' printed two weeks later. Needless to say, any thoughts of producing an engraving of the picture were quickly abandoned.[52]

Once the exhibition had closed, Haydon's picture was put into store, presumably at the BFASS's offices in London. Haydon later estimated that he had lost nearly £250 by exhibiting *The Anti-Slavery Convention, 1840*, a huge sum of money when one takes into account the fact that he had received only

5   Sir George Hayter, *The House of Commons, 1833* (1833–43)

£525 for the painting in the first place. In desperation, in 1842 he tried to sell his sketches of the convention to John Beaumont for £50, 'though 100 is less than their value', but without success. Reflecting on his experience in 1843, after visiting Sir George Hayter's crowded exhibition at the Egyptian Hall, he conceded that he had mismanaged the whole affair. 'Hayter has acted like a sensible Man who knows the World', he noted in his diary. 'He has made every body pay £10 10s. and gave them their sketch. I sketched every body and made them pay nothing.' Haydon also blamed himself for not having the strength of his own convictions. If he ever tackled such a subject again he vowed that he would 'compose it as if I was composing an ancient subject and fit on modern heads on principles of Art, not bend principles of art to modern Vanity'.[53]

Haydon never fully recovered from the failure of *The Anti-Slavery Convention, 1840*, but he did live long enough to see it enjoy a brief revival. In 1843 the Second World Anti-Slavery Convention took place at Freemason's Hall in London. To coincide with this event, Haydon's painting was hung at one end of the hall, opposite Auguste Briard's *Scene on the African Coast* (1835), which had been bought and presented to Thomas Fowell Buxton by the Anti-Slavery Society in 1841. Subsequently, it was moved to the Hall of Commerce in Threadneedle Street, where it remained on public display until October 1843.[54] Interest in the painting also led George Baxter, perhaps at the instigation of the BFASS, to propose publishing it as an ornamental print. Trained as a lithographer and engraver, Baxter had pioneered a process to produce colour prints from blocks and plates using oil-based inks. His output was prolific. Perhaps best known for his popular series of missionary prints, Baxter also produced large numbers of portraits, genre paintings, and historical works. Two of his most successful prints, for instance, were *The Coronation of Queen Victoria*, after Sir George Hayter, and *The Opening by Queen Victoria of Her First Parliament* (both 1841). Although constantly in debt, Baxter was also well connected, having been presented twice to Queen Victoria and Prince Albert at Buckingham Palace.[55]

Baxter's prospectus was first published in *Anti-Slavery Reporter* in September 1843. The following month it was announced that Prince Albert had consented to become a patron, and early in 1844 Baxter reportedly began work on the print, although it seems to have immediately run into difficulties.[56] The problem undoubtedly was money. To judge from the prospectus, Baxter was looking for a minimum of 150 subscribers, but the indications are that subscriptions fell some way short of this target. What scuppered the project, in others words, was public indifference, not least among abolitionists themselves. This latest setback signalled the complete failure of *The Anti-Slavery Convention, 1840* as a piece of abolitionist propaganda. Despite the intrinsic interest of the subject matter, Haydon had been unable to produce an image that gripped the public imagination. If anything, his clumsy and poorly executed painting seems to have alienated many abolitionists, Garrisonians and non-Garrisonians alike. (It is striking, for instance, that *The Anti-Slavery Convention, 1840* attracted little interest or excitement in the United States, although this undoubtedly had as much to do with the politics of the 1840 Convention as it did with the intrinsic merits of the painting.) Perhaps Haydon was right when he said that the 'Time [was] fast coming when we shall get sick of these bastard "High Art Works"', but his own painting belonged to the same genre, and reflected the same uneasy blend of group portraiture and history painting.[57]

After 1843 Haydon's painting was once again put into store. It might have remained there indefinitely but for the intervention of the trustees of Ipswich Museum. There had been a museum of sorts in Ipswich since the 1790s but over the years its premises in the Town Hall had become cramped and over-crowded. During the 1840s a subscription was raised for a new museum building, which was eventually opened to the public in December 1847.[58] To mark this event the trustees arranged to borrow *The Anti-Slavery Convention, 1840*. The painting had obvious local associations, chief among them being Thomas Clarkson, who for many years had been resident outside Ipswich at Playford Hall. George William Alexander, who was the Treasurer of the BFASS, also had local connections, as did Josiah Conder, another committee member. The idea of bringing Haydon's painting to Ipswich probably originated with George Ransome, honorary secretary of the Ipswich Museum. It must have helped, too, that several members of the Alexander family were actively involved in the museum. Less easy to assess is the influence of the Marquis of Bristol, who besides being patron of Ipswich Museum also owned Playford Hall.[59]

To judge from local newspapers, the appearance of Haydon's painting at the opening of the museum proved a popular attraction, and it is no surprise that the trustees sought to retain the picture on a permanent basis. (For its part, the BFASS appears to have been only too willing to accept the trustees' offer.) In its new surroundings, however, *The Anti-Slavery Convention, 1840* took on a very different resonance and meaning. The shift is evident in the way in which the painting was usually described. The *Bury Post*, for instance, referred to it grandly as 'Haydon's large and interesting picture of our Suffolk worthy Thomas Clarkson delivering his last address to the Anti-Slavery Convention in 1840.' Even the museum's official guide was wont to describe the painting as 'Clarkson's last Address to the Anti-Slavery Convention'.[60] In other words, the museum's trustees claimed *The Anti-Slavery Convention, 1840* as a site of local memory. Central to this process was the particular claim placed on Clarkson as a 'Suffolk worthy'. Clearly, in the eyes of Ransome and his fellow trustees, Clarkson – and not Beckford, or Haydon's self-conscious attempt to place blacks on an equal footing with whites – was the real subject of the picture. It is striking, for instance, that at one stage Haydon's painting was to have been suspended prominently against the museum's staircase wall, while a bust of Clarkson, 'resting on an Indian cabinet', was to have occupied a niche above it on the highest landing.[61] None of this is to deny that *The Anti-Slavery Convention, 1840* could be read in different ways. But the Ipswich authorities obviously placed a construction on it that, by valorising white civic identity, subtly altered its original meaning.

In all, *The Anti-Slavery Convention, 1840* remained on display in Ipswich Museum for nearly thirty years. But then during the early 1870s it was suddenly rediscovered by British abolitionists. The timing was significant. The ending of the American Civil War (1861–65) and, with it, the emancipation of some four million slaves had marked the close of another chapter of anti-slavery effort in Britain. Some activists subsequently moved on to the question of the Islamic slave trade, but for many of them slavery became a thing of the past.[62] Seen in this light, the importance of Haydon's painting, not least as an abolitionist relic, was obvious; the only question was how to exploit it. As a first step, in 1873 John Alfred Vinter, 'Lithographic Artist to Her Majesty Queen Victoria', was commissioned to produce an engraving of *The Anti-Slavery Convention, 1840*, which was subsequently published by Samuel Harris & Co., London. Although the precise details are unclear, there is little doubt that this was an official image. Not only was it approved by the London Committee of the British and Foreign Anti-Slavery Society at a meeting held in April 1873, but according to local advertisements it was published 'by direction of Samuel Gurney, Esq., President of the Anti-Slavery Society'.[63]

Interestingly, it was also Gurney who in 1877 proposed moving Haydon's painting from Ipswich to London with a view to placing it in the National Portrait Gallery. Again, the timing was significant. In 1873 Joseph Cooper (the only surviving member of the three original trustees) had transferred legal ownership of the picture to the Anti-Slavery Committee in London. It made sense, therefore, for Gurney and his colleagues to reclaim the painting; after all, it was part of their past. The trustees of Ipswich Museum obviously had other ideas, however. The sticking point, it seems, was the question of ownership. In the absence of any proof to the contrary (for some reason no one thought to produce Joseph Cooper's indenture until January 1879), the Ipswich authorities claimed that Haydon's painting 'belonged' to them. Not only had they housed the picture for nearly thirty years, but they had also spent money on its care and restoration. It had become a part of the town's common history. Finally, after nearly eighteen months of protracted legal negotiations, the museum's trustees were forced to give way. But it is a measure of the importance that they attached to *The Anti-Slavery Convention, 1840* as a local relic that in December 1879 they offered to take it back, 'on condition of it being legally assigned to them in perpetuity'.[64]

Having at last acquired Haydon's painting, the Anti-Slavery Committee could now think about donating it to the National Portrait Gallery. Overtures were made early in July 1879 but it was not until the following January that George Scharf, secretary and curator of the gallery, viewed it for the first time at the BFASS offices in New Broad Street.[65] Scharf, in turn, arranged for the painting to be transferred to South Kensington, where the gallery's trustees inspected it on 6 February. The trustees, who included the Marquess of Bath and Lord Ronald Gower, were clearly caught in two minds. In their view, the picture had 'evidently suffered severely from neglect and bad treatment'. Scharf, in fact, calculated that at least £40 would need to be spent on the painting – 'for relining and cleaning and restoring' – before it could be shown to the public. Nevertheless, after careful consideration the trustees agreed to accept the donation. They also authorised the necessary repairs. The conservation work, which appears to have been carried out under the general supervision of George Wallis, FSA, took about six weeks. Scharf noted in his diary on 10 April that 'Mr Stafford Allen [Secretary of the BFASS] came by appointment to see the large Haydon picture & expressed himself greatly pleased with its much improved appearance'. A few days later Gurney himself came to view the painting, bringing with him 'impressions of the engraved key to the picture'.[66]

Early in May 1880 *The Anti-Slavery Convention, 1840* was mounted in the western recess of the National Portrait Gallery, together with Sir George Hayter's *The House of Commons, 1833*, and soon afterwards it was opened to the public.[67] The dance was over. As David Lowenthal has argued, 'Transplantation may infuse a work with new life, lending it decorative or iconographic value.'[68] Haydon's painting was no exception. It was not just that the picture was now hanging in a national art gallery, although that was undoubtedly important. Transplantation also invested it with a new meaning. As we have seen, in Ipswich *The Anti-Slavery Convention, 1840* had been valued and preserved primarily as a local relic. In its new surroundings, however, it formed part of a broader historical narrative (a specific national 'history') that celebrated the 'great cause of human freedom'. By mounting Haydon's painting beside *The House of Commons, 1833* the gallery staff made this association abundantly clear, linking Reform and Emancipation together into a coherent 'island story' that spoke to and reinforced Britain's civilising mission.[69]

Interestingly, the celebrations held in London in August 1884 to mark the 50th anniversary of Emancipation picked up the same theme. Emancipation was 'a historical landmark', Lord Derby told a special jubilee meeting at London's Guildhall, 'interesting, not merely to philanthropists, but to all thoughtful students of the evolution of society'.[70] For obvious reasons, the publicity surrounding the 50th anniversary of Emancipation created renewed interest in Haydon's painting, so much so that George Scharf arranged for the National Portrait Gallery to be open on Friday 1 August (the gallery was normally closed on Fridays) so that the general public could view *The Anti-Slavery Convention, 1840* on the actual anniversary date.[71] Nevertheless, it is surely significant how quickly and easily this interest, and the excitement surrounding the reappearance of Haydon's painting, was dispelled. In fact, what we might describe as the 'modern' history of *The Anti-Slavery Convention, 1840* proved to be every bit as turbulent as its 'past'. In 1911, following its move to its present site in St Martin's Place, the National Portrait Gallery loaned Haydon's painting to the Royal Courts of Justice, where it remained on display in the Great Hall until 1931.[72] The painting was returned to the NPG in time for the 100th anniversary of the passage of the Emancipation Bill in 1933, when at the suggestion of the Anti-Slavery Society it was moved temporarily to 'a more public part' of the gallery, but from the mid-1970s onwards it spent long periods in store. Indeed, with the exception of a very brief period in 1994, when the picture was put on display as part of a Charles Darwin exhibition in Dresden, the *Anti-Slavery Convention, 1840* remained out of the public gaze for almost thirty years.[73]

Happily, there is a postscript to this story. In the autumn of 2003 the National Portrait Gallery opened its new 'Regency Gallery'. Here, for the first time in nearly 100 years, *The Anti-Slavery Convention, 1840* and Hayter's *The House of Commons, 1833* have been reunited in a section called, appropriately enough, 'The Road to Reform'. Reassuring though it is, the gallery's narrative strategy belies the fact that Haydon's painting, like British anti-slavery itself, has for long periods been forgotten, ignored or simply confined to the margins. While it has been customary to turn to *The Anti-Slavery Convention, 1840* from time to time, as in the case of the anniversary celebrations in 1884, 1933, and now 2007, the painting has just as often appeared expendable. Of course, a lot of this can be put down to the picture's lack of artistic merit. As Hugh Honour has argued in a different context, the 'distinction [of] a work of art distinguishes the subject'.[74] But it did not help, either, that Haydon's painting defied easy categorisation, or that it challenged many white racist assumptions. Haydon had wanted *The Anti-Slavery Convention, 1840* to speak to a great moral principle, namely that blacks were capable of standing on equal terms with white Europeans. Yet, as we have seen, the tendency of museums and curators was to try (not always successfully) to fold the painting into an imperialistic discourse that highlighted Britain's tradition of humanitarian interventionism, thereby interposing a safe distance between Beckford and his liberators. Fashions change, of course, as do values and priorities: modern audiences are much more likely to respond to Beckford, or, indeed, to seek him out, not least because they have a very different notion of who and what constitutes the British nation. In this sense, *The Anti-Slavery Convention, 1840* has proved a remarkably durable and pliable relic. Transplanted and re-transplanted, its history is emblematic of our complex relationship with British transatlantic slavery and, just as important, its place in our collective memory.

Notes

1   See, for example, Thomas Clarkson, *The History of the Rise, Progress and Accomplishment of the Abolition of the Slave Trade by the British Parliament*, 2 vols (London, 1808); Prince Hoare, *Memoirs of Granville Sharp* (London, 1820); *The Life of William Wilberforce. By his Sons, Robert Isaac Wilberforce [and] Samuel Wilberforce*, 5 vols (London, 1838); Joseph Sturge, *A Visit to the United States in 1841* (London, 1842); Charles Buxton, *Memoirs of Sir Thomas Fowell Buxton, Bart., with Selections from His Correspondence* (London, 1848); George Stephen, *Anti-Slavery Recollections: In a Series of Letters addressed to Mrs. Harriet Beecher Stowe* (London, 1854).

2   Howard Temperley, *British Anti-Slavery, 1833–1870* (London, 1972), pp. 86–92.

3   Rhodes House Library, Oxford, British and Foreign Anti-Slavery Society (BFASS)
    Papers, MSS Brit. Emp. S18, C9/147, Robert Russell to John Tredgold, 9 July 1840,
    and C11/13; John Backhouse to John Beaumont, 1 July 1841. While it is true that
    medals and ceramics were produced to commemorative the World Anti-Slavery Con-
    vention, including a number of pieces commemorating Clarkson, there is nothing to
    suggest that these artefacts were commissioned by the British and Foreign Anti-Sla-
    very Society. Examples can be found in the British Museum, Wisbech and Fenland
    Museum in Wisbech, and the British Empire and Commonwealth Museum in Bristol.
4   Willard Bisell Pope, ed., *The Diary of Benjamin Robert Haydon*, 5 vols (Cambridge,
    MA, 1960–63), IV, p. 640. For Haydon, see Penelope Hughes-Hallet, *The Immortal
    Dinner: A Famous Evening of Genius and Laughter in Literary London, 1817* (London,
    2001); Alethea Hayter, *A Sultry Month: Scenes of London Literary Life in 1846* (London,
    1965); Clarke Olney, *Benjamin Robert Haydon: Historical Painter* (Atlanta, GA, 1952);
    Eric George, *The Life and Death of Benjamin Robert Haydon, 1786–1846* (Oxford, 1948);
    George Paston, *B. R. Haydon and His Friends* (London, 1905).
5   David Blayney Brown, '"Fire and Clay": Benjamin Robert Haydon – Historical
    Painter', in David Blayney Brown, Robert Woof, and Stephen Hebron, *Benjamin Rob-
    ert Haydon, 1786–1846: Painter and Writer, Friend of Wordsworth and Keats* (Grasmere,
    1996), pp. 2–22; Paston, *B. R. Haydon and His Friends*, pp. 193–4.
6   George, *The Life and Death of Benjamin Robert Haydon*, pp. 167–70; Paston, *B. R. Haydon
    and His Friends*, pp. 213–14.
7   George, *The Life and Death of Benjamin Robert Haydon*, pp. 13–14; Brown, '"Fire and
    Clay"', p. 14; Robert Woof, 'Haydon, Writer, and the Friend of Writers', in Brown,
    Woof, and Hebron, *Benjamin Robert Haydon, 1786–1846*, p. 26; Hayter, *A Sultry Month*,
    pp. 58–9.
8   Benjamin Robert Haydon, *Description of Haydon's Picture of the Great Meeting of Del-
    egates at the Freemason's Tavern, June 1840, for the Abolition of Slavery and the Slave Trade*
    (London, 1844), p. 7.
9   Chapin Library, Williams College, Massachusetts, MS, Amelia Opie, 'Description of
    the Opening Session of the World Anti-Slavery Convention'.
10 Haydon, *Description of Haydon's Picture*, pp. 8–9; *Proceedings of the General Anti-Slavery
    Convention called by the Committee of the British and Foreign Anti-Slavery Society, and held
    in London, from Friday, June 12 to Tuesday, June 23, 1840* (London, 1841), pp. 2–3.
11 Haydon, *Description of Haydon's Picture*, p. 9.
12 *Proceedings of the General Anti-Slavery Convention*, p. 22. Beckford came to Britain with
    the Baptist missionary, William Knibb, and another freedman, Edward Barrett. The
    two men subsequently 'travelled up and down the country with Knibb, appearing on
    platforms and speaking of their gratitude to the British public for the gift of freedom'.
    See Catherine Hall, *Civilising Subjects: Metropole and Colony in the English Imagination,
    1830–1867* (London, 2002), pp. 141, 159–60.
13 Haydon, *Description of Haydon's Picture*, p. 10.
14 Hugh Honour, *The Image of the Black in Western Art, vol. 4, From the American Revolu-
    tion to World War I*, 2 parts (Cambridge, MA, 1989), I, pp. 37–50. Even when blacks are
    given more prominent roles, they sometimes seem detached or cowed and submis-
    sive. To take one obvious example, the black figure in William Powell's *The Battle of
    Lake Erie* (1817) shields his face from the impact of a cannonball, while his white
    companions remain impassive and seemingly oblivious to the danger. See Albert
    Boime, *The Art of Exclusion: Representing Blacks in the Nineteenth Century* (London and
    Washington, DC, 1980), pp. 185–6.
15 Mary Webster, *Francis Wheatley* (London, 1970), pp. 24, 118–19. See also Honour,
    The Image of the Black in Western Art, I, pp. 28–30; Marcus Wood, *Blind Memory:*

Visual Representations of Slavery in England and America, 1780–1865 (Manchester, 2000), pp. 152–4; David Dabydeen, *Hogarth's Blacks: Images of Blacks in Eighteenth-Century English Art* (Manchester, 1987). On both sides of the Atlantic there was also a tradition of sorts of black portraiture. Recent research has unearthed an increasing number of these individual studies, although relatively few of them in the British case date from the pre-1840 period. See Jan Marsh, ed., *Black Victorians: Black People in British Art, 1800–1900* (Aldershot, 2005); Richard J. Powell, 'Cinque: Antislavery Portraiture and Patronage in Jacksonian America', *American Art*, 11 (1997), pp. 48–73; Wood, *Blind Memory*, pp. 131, 152–4.

16   Honour, *The Image of the Black in Western Art*, I, pp. 63–4, 79 (plate), 97 (plate), 98 (plate), 128 (plates), 131 (plate), 168 (plate), 192 (plate).

17   See, for instance, 'Slaves Receiving News of Emancipation, British West Indies, ca. 1834', http://hitchcock.itc.virginia.edu/Slavery/details.php?filename=cass2 accessed 6 March 2005 (taken from *Cassells' Illustrated History of England*, London, 1863).

18   Jan Marsh, 'Quest for the Queen's Secrets', *Guardian*, 27 January 2001; Wood, *Blind Memory*, pp. 189–95.

19   J. R. Oldfield, *Popular Politics and British Anti-Slavery: The Mobilisation of Public Opinion against the Slave Trade, 1787–1807* (Manchester, 1995), pp. 172–3; Wood, *Blind Memory*, pp. 152–72.

20   Honour, *The Image of the Black in Western Art*, II, pp. 58–64.

21   David Bindman, *From Ape to Apollo: Aesthetics and the Idea of Race in the Eighteenth Century* (London, 2002), pp. 201–9, 223; Honour, *The Image of the Black in Western Art*, II, pp. 12–21.

22   Kirk Savage, *Standing Soldiers, Kneeling Slaves: Race, War, and Monument in Nineteenth-Century America* (Princeton, 1999), pp. 8–15.

23   Malcolm Elwin, ed., *The Autobiography and Memoirs of Benjamin Robert Haydon* (London, 1950), pp. 123–4; Pope, *The Diary of Benjamin Robert Haydon*, I, pp. 182–89.

24   Elwin, *The Autobiography and Memoirs of Benjamin Robert Haydon*, p. 123.

25   Pope, *The Diary of Benjamin Robert Haydon*, I, pp. 188–9; Elwin, *The Autobiography and Memoirs of Benjamin Robert Haydon*, p. 125.

26   Haydon, *Description of Haydon's Picture*, pp. 10–12; British Library, Add MS 41,267A, ff. 205 and 232, Haydon to Mary Clarkson, 26 June 1840 and Haydon to Thomas Clarkson, 19 March 1841.

27   Honour, *The Image of the Black in Western Art*, II, p. 168. As if anticipating his critics, Haydon insisted that Beckford's head was 'as fine in physical construction of brain as any European in the picture'. See Haydon, *Description of Haydon's Picture*, p. 10.

28   British Library, Add MS 41,267A, f. 284, Haydon to Thomas Clarkson, 30 March 1841.

29   Pope, *The Diary of Benjamin Robert Haydon*, IV, p. 644.

30   Leon F. Litwack, *North of Slavery: The Negro in the Free States, 1790–1860* (Chicago, 1961), pp. 216–26. See also Henry Mayer, *All on Fire: William Lloyd Garrison and the Abolition of Slavery* (New York, 1998), pp. 351–2; Richard S. Newman, *The Transformation of American Abolitionism: Fighting Slavery in the Early Republic* (Chapel Hill, 2002), pp. 121–3. According to Mayer, there was 'a continuum of integrationist and separatist tendencies' within the American abolitionist movement.

31   There is a growing literature on blacks in Victorian Britain. See, in particular, Audrey Fisch, *American Slaves in Victorian England: Abolitionist Politics in Popular Literature and Culture* (Cambridge, 2000), esp. pp. 52–68; Wood, *Blind Memory*, esp. pp. 103–17, 152–205. Both authors imply that at some level (white) notions of national well-being were inextricably linked to notions of racial superiority. See also J. R. Oldfield, 'Transatlanticism, Slavery and Race', *American Literary History*, 14 (2002), pp. 131–40.

32   Pope, *The Diary of Benjamin Robert Haydon*, IV, pp. 644–5. There is no way of knowing how Scoble and others responded to Haydon's intransigence, or whether the matter was ever discussed, but it seems reasonable to suppose that this was not quite what the members of the BFASS had in mind when they commissioned the painting.

33   The roll of the Convention contained the names of over 500 delegates, although the number actually present was about 350, of whom 40 were from the United States. See *Proceedings of the Anti-Slavery Convention*, pp. 573–84; *Liberator*, 24 July 1840.

34   Pope, *The Diary of Benjamin Robert Haydon*, IV, p. 648. My emphasis.

35   Ibid., p. 661; British Library, Add MS 41,267A, f. 252, Catherine Clarkson to Mary Clarkson, May 1841. Haydon appears to have taken an instant dislike to Buxton. 'Buxton sat and I never saw such childish vanity & weakness', he noted in his diary on 15 August. 'That Man so bedimmed my brain, a bad head was the consequence, and what with his (Buxton's) dictating letters, signing, correcting, & talking, I passed literally a most distracting morning, & told him so.' See Pope, *The Diary of Benjamin Robert Haydon*, IV, p. 661.

36   Pope, *The Diary of Benjamin Robert Haydon*, V, pp. 259–60.

37   Boston Public Library, Boston, Garrison Papers, Abby Kimber to an unknown correspondent, 25 August 1840 and Haydon to William Lloyd Garrison, 30 June 1840; Mayer, *All on Fire*, pp. 292–3. Garrison sat for Haydon on 30 June and again on 9 July.

38   Hayter notes that Haydon's 'defective eyesight', as well as his cramped studio, 'produced the errors of proportion – particularly the shortness of leg – which give a fatally ludicrous look to so many of his heroic figures'. See Hayter, *A Sultry Month*, p. 59.

39   Pope, *The Diary of Benjamin Robert Haydon*, V, pp. 15, 259.

40   Ibid., pp. 39–40. Haydon often referred to *The Anti-Slavery Convention* as 'the Quaker picture'.

41   *Ibid.*, V, pp. 49–50.

42   *Ibid.*, IV, pp. 643, 649; British Library, Add MS 41,267A, f. 232, Haydon to Thomas Clarkson, 19 March 1841; Haydon, *Description of Haydon's Picture*, pp. 10–12.

43   Richard Altick, *The Shows of London* (Cambridge, MA, 1978), pp. 249–53; London Guildhall Library, Scrapbook, Granger 2. 5. 7; *Notes & Queries*, 5th series, 10 April 1875, p. 284 and 10th series, 4 March 1905, pp. 163–4.

44   Altick, *The Shows of London*, pp. 243, 413; Brown, '"Fire and Clay"', pp. 12–19. Haydon exhibited at the Egyptian Hall for the last time in May 1846, when he hired one of the rooms on the upper floor to show *The Banishment of Aristides* and *The Burning of Rome*. Again, the exhibition was a failure. While thousands flocked to see Tom Thumb in an adjacent room, Haydon received only 133 visitors, producing £5 13s 6d. The experience broke Haydon. On 22 May he shot himself in the head and then cut his throat.

45   This undoubtedly had something to do with Haydon's alienation from the art establishment. The editor of the *Art-Union*, for instance, described Haydon as 'a quack of the worst order' – this in response to his (Haydon's) repeated attacks on the Royal Academy. 'The pen of Mr Haydon has obtained for him a notoriety his pencil has failed to achieve', he went on, 'for thirty years he has been writing himself up and painting himself down'. See the *Art-Union. A Monthly Journal of the Fine Arts*, 3 (1841), pp. 92–3. Not surprisingly, the *Art-Union* ignored *The Anti-Slavery Convention, 1840*, as did the *Polytechnic Journal*.

46   *Morning Post*, 10 May 1841.

47   *Athenaeum*, 15 May 1841.

48   G. E. Bryant and G. P. Baker, eds., *A Quaker Journal: Being the Diary and Reminiscences of William Lucas of Hitchin (1804–1861)*, 2 vols.(London, 1934), I, p. 214 (entry for 18 May 1841); British Library, Add MS 41,267A, ff. 207 and 252, Patty Smith to Catherine Clarkson, 26 June 1840 and Catherine Clarkson to Mary Clarkson, May 1841.

49 Pope, *The Diary of Benjamin Robert Haydon*, V, pp. 50, 53.

50 Seymour Drescher, *The Mighty Experiment: Free Labor versus Slavery in British Emancipation* (New York, 2002), p. 161.

51 Haydon, *Description of Haydon's Picture*, pp. 14–20; BFASS Papers, MSS Brit. Emp. S18, C11/83, John Morgan to John Beaumont, 3 May 1841.

52 *Anti-Slavery Reporter*, 5, 19 May 1841.

53 Pope, *The Diary of Benjamin Robert Haydon*, V, pp. 135, 259–60. In the same breath, however, Haydon avowed that he 'would rather be confined under the Bridge of Sighs for Life, than have painted such a hideous bit of wretchedness as his [Hayter's] little Portrait of the Queen'. *Ibid.*, V, p. 260.

54 Ibid., p. 284; personal communication from Jan Marsh, November 2002.

55 C. T. Courtenay Lewis, *George Baxter (Colour Printer): His Life and Work* (London, 1908), esp. pp. 16, 25, 93.

56 *Anti-Slavery Reporter*, 6, 20 September, 4, 18 October, 15 November 1843, 10, 24 January and 7 February 1884. Baxter attended the BFASS annual meeting in May 1844, presumably to solicit more subscriptions, but there are no further references to the print after that date. Experts conclude that it was never produced. See Lewis, *George Baxter*, p. 113.

57 Pope, *The Diary of Benjamin Robert Haydon*, V, p. 259.

58 For the history of Ipswich Museum, see Frank Woolnough, *A History of Ipswich Museum* (Ipswich, 1908); Ipswich Record Office, S Ips 069, George Ransome, scrapbook, 1846–48.

59 Woolnough, *A History of Ipswich Museum*. In 1846, W. H. Alexander was treasurer of Ipswich Museum, while another member of the family was on the board of trustees.

60 *Bury Post*, 17 November 1847; Anon, *A Guide to Ipswich Museum* (Ipswich, 1871), p. ii. See also *Suffolk Chronicle*, 20 November 1847.

61 *Suffolk Chronicle*, 4 December 1847.

62 Temperley, *British Anti-Slavery*, pp. 261–2.

63 MSS Brit. Emp. S18, C46/47, John Vinter to Benjamin Millard, 4 March 1873, and BFASS Papers, MSS Brit. Emp. S20, E2/10, BFASS Committee Minutes, entry for 4 April 1873; *Sketch of the Life of Thomas Clarkson* (London, 1876), outside back cover.

64 BFASS Committee Minutes, entries for 2 January 1874, 16 January, 2 March, 4 May, 6 July, 5 October, 7 December 1877, 4 January, 31 October, 5 December 1878, 2 January, 6 March, 3 April, 3 July, 31 July 1879; MSS Brit. Emp. S18, C157/264, J. Castle Gant to Rev. Aaron Buozacott, 2 March 1877, and John Lee to E. Sturge, 18 December 1878; MSS Brit. Emp. S18, C157/265, Lee to C. H. Allan, 16 September 1879 and Joseph Cooper to unknown correspondent, 25 September 1879; Ipswich Record Office, DB/1/1, Town Council of Ipswich, Reports of Committees, February 1871 to November 1879, Reports of the Museum Committee for 14 August 1878 and 12 August 1879; Ipswich Museum, Museum Committee Minutes, entries for 3 December 1879, 7 January, and 4 February 1880.

65 BFASS Committee Minutes, entries for 2 October, 4 December 1879 and 5 February 1880; National Portrait Gallery, Secretary's Journals, Private MSS, 1876–80, entries for 10 July, 4 September 1879 and 23 January 1880; National Portrait Gallery, Archives Correspondence, 599, Stafford Allen to George Scharf, 7 November 1879 and 9 January 1880, Charles Allen to Scharf, 14 January 1880 and NPG to Stafford Allen, 13 November 1879.

66 National Portrait Gallery, Minutes of Trustee Meetings, vol. 3, entries for 6 February and 24 March 1880; Secretary's Journals, entries for 6 March and 5, 10, 14, 16 April 1880. The BFASS raised a subscription to help cover the cost of the repairs and other incidental expenses. See BFASS Committee Minutes, 4 March 1880; *Anti-Slavery*

Reporter, 1 March and 1 May 1880.

67   National Portrait Gallery, Secretary's Journals, entries for 16 April and 1, 3 May 1880; Minutes of Trustee Meetings, vol. 3, 11 May 1880.

68   David Lowenthal, *The Past is A Foreign Country* (Cambridge, 1985), p. 287.

69   For the notion of 'island stories', see Raphael Samuel, *Islands Stories: Unravelling Britain, Theatres of Memory, Volume II*, edited by Alison Light (London, 1998). The terms itself comes from Alfred, Lord Tennyson's ode on the death of Wellington and was also taken as the title of H. E. Marshall's classic history for children, *Our Island Story*, first published in 1905.

70   *The Times*, 2 August 1884.

71   *The Times*, 1 August 1884.

72   National Portrait Gallery, 599, Keys, Lists, Photos, Studies, correspondence between Office of Works, Westminster, and NPG, 7 May 1912 to 5 June 1931.

73   *The Friend*, 27 July 1934; *Harrogate Advertiser*, 28 July 1934; National Portrait Gallery, 599, hanging history, 1971–97.

74   Honour, *The Image of the Black in Western Art*, I, p. 17.

2

Literary memorials: Clarkson's *History* and *The Life of William Wilberforce*

The early abolitionist movement (1787–1807) was dominated by two key figures, Thomas Clarkson and William Wilberforce. The two men could not have been more different. Where Wilberforce was slight and angular, Clarkson was tall and well-built; where Wilberforce was confident, articulate, and at ease in the best of company, Clarkson was brusque and inclined to be awkward; where Wilberforce moved effortlessly in the world of the club and the Commons chamber, Clarkson preferred the company of his Dissenting friends. For these and other reasons, Clarkson and Wilberforce were never particularly close. Yet theirs was a special relationship borne out of a common interest and a common sense of purpose. As *The Times* put it succinctly in 1881, '[Clarkson] might not have done without Wilberforce, but neither could Wilberforce have done without him.'[1] While Wilberforce provided leadership in the House of Commons, Clarkson to all intents and purposes led the agitation 'out of doors'. Like the American abolitionist, William Lloyd Garrison, Clarkson was one of the earliest full-time, professional reformers. And through his researches and his tours, his books and his pamphlets, he helped to push Britain into the abolitionist era.

For all that, Clarkson and Wilberforce are perceived and remembered in quite different ways. Today, Wilberforce is generally regarded as the personification of British anti-slavery, a 'statesman-saint' who almost single-handedly was responsible for ending the British transatlantic slave trade and, with it, British colonial slavery.[2] Clarkson, on the other hand, is much more difficult to place. In part, Clarkson's relative obscurity can be explained in terms of his peculiar role within the early abolitionist movement. But it did not help, either, that his reputation was contested, not least by Wilberforce's two sons, Robert and Samuel, and his nephew, James Stephen. The result was an undignified scramble for status and authority that in essence revolved around two important books: Clarkson's *The History of the Rise, Progress and Accomplishment of the Abolition of the Slave Trade by the British Parliament* (1808); and *The*

Life of William Wilberforce. By His Sons, Robert Isaac Wilberforce and Samuel Wilberforce (1838).

Clarkson seems to have conceived of the idea of writing a history of the early abolitionist movement soon after the Abolition Bill passed both houses of Parliament in 1807. The pitfalls were obvious. As Clarkson himself put it: 'I always foresaw that I could not avoid making myself too prominent an object in such a history, and that I should be liable, on that account, to the suspicion of writing it for the purpose of sounding my own praise.' Anticipating these criticisms, he disclaimed all merit on his own account, pointing instead to the 'influence of a superior Power'. Somewhat more disingenuously, he also insisted that his relationship with Wilberforce and the other members of the London Committee of the Society for Effecting the Abolition of the Slave Trade (SEAST) had been one of mutuality and interdependence, likening the Committee to a human body 'made up of a head and of various members, which had different functions to perform'. Clarkson hoped that 'this would be so obvious to the good sense of the reader, that if he should think me vainglorious in the early part of [his history] he would afterwards, when he advanced in the perusal of it, acquit me of such a charge'.[3] Sadly, his confidence was to prove misplaced. In truth, Clarkson never successfully resolved the problem of integrating his own activities into a broader history of the early abolitionist movement, with the result that his book inevitably invited comment and, from some quarters, outright hostility.

As its title suggests, Clarkson's *History* purported to be a work of historical record but in fact it is much more than that. Part history, part autobiography, part personal testimony, it is a sprawling work that runs to over 1,100 pages. The book opens with a panoramic view of abolitionism, which traces the activities of four 'classes' of 'forerunners and coadjutors' who had been active in the cause between the sixteenth and eighteenth centuries. Clarkson even appended a detailed map to help the reader, which presented abolition as a series of tributary streams and rivers, each with the name of a supposed abolitionist attached.[4] All of this was by way of introducing the reader to the subject of abolition and providing historical depth, but, just as important, the map also helped to establish the London Committee of the SEAST (organised in May 1787) as the 'junction' where these different classes of coadjutors 'met together and were united'. Clarkson went further. It was the London Committee, he maintained, 'labouring afterwards with Mr. Wilberforce as a parliamentary head', that, 'in the space of twenty years', contributed 'to put an end to a trade, which, measuring its magnitude by its crimes and sufferings, was the greatest practical evil that ever afflicted the human race'.[5]

It is at this point that the work becomes autobiographical. Indeed, some of the most arresting passages in the first volume of the *History* concern Clarkson's introduction to the slave trade as a student at Cambridge (coincidentally, Clarkson and Wilberforce were both undergraduates at St John's, although their paths do not seem to have crossed), his near religious experience at Wadesmill in Hertfordshire in 1785, where he began to conceive the idea of trying to do something to bring the traffic to an end, and his role in the founding of the SEAST.[6] This autobiographical thread continues throughout the rest of the *History*. While it is true that Clarkson is often at pains to adopt a historical perspective, not least when he is describing the slave trade debates in the Commons and the House of Lords, time and time again the narrative returns to Clarkson and his own special 'office'. This might not have mattered so much if Clarkson had been writing his memoirs or a series of anti-slavery recollections, but in what purported to be an historical work it inevitably sounded a discordant note.[7] Viewed critically, Clarkson's *History* suffers because it lacks a reliable or consistent narrative voice. It is rather a hybrid text that moves uneasily between established genres, even at the risk of subverting them altogether.

Perhaps just as important, the *History* is incomplete or, at least, selective. What one might describe as the 'first phase' of the early abolitionist movement came to an end in 1793 when the House of Commons refused to revive the subject of the slave trade, having only the year before passed resolutions providing for its gradual abolition.[8] As it turned out, this was the signal for Clarkson to withdraw from the struggle, his health broken by a punishing round of tours and meetings. The campaign went on, of course, but for the next ten years Clarkson was in the Lake District. During this period he married, had a son, also Thomas, and befriended the Wordsworths, the Southeys, and the Coleridges. All of this was bound to have an effect. By the time Clarkson resumed his labours in 1804 at the start of a fresh parliamentary campaign, abolitionism had changed appreciably. Moreover, with the passage of time new leaders had emerged, among them Zachary Macaulay and Wilberforce's brother-in-law, James Stephen. Not surprisingly, it took time for Clarkson to adjust to these changes. Whereas he had once been a driving force, Clarkson now found himself on the periphery and in all likelihood shut out of the deliberations that finally led to the Commons victory of 1807.[9]

Clarkson's growing isolation in the final years of the campaign is reflected in the shape and structure of the *History*. Less than one tenth of the completed book, or roughly 90 pages, deals with the period 1804 to 1807. The inevitable result is that it provides only a partial view of the history of the abolition of the slave trade. Macaulay and Stephen, for instance, are mentioned only once by name.[10] In fairness to Clarkson, it seems unlikely that this oversight was intentional; given the autobiographical nature of the *History* there were bound to be silences and omissions. Yet it is easy to see why some critics should have viewed the book as a monument to Clarkson's vanity. To many of those who knew and admired Wilberforce, Clarkson's blurring of the distinction between personal and public history also had a more invidious purpose, namely to denigrate Wilberforce and to set himself up as the true leader of the early abolitionist movement.

For this reason the book met with a mixed reception. Years later, Clarkson's wife, Catherine, recalled that Francis Jeffray, editor of the *Edinburgh Review*, had seen fit to make 'some alterations and additions' to Coleridge's review of the *History*, because he thought that Coleridge's object was to exalt Clarkson at Wilberforce's expense; 'and so put in a Paragraph which does not harmonize with the rest and worse insinuates something of the same kind with respect to the Author of the "History" itself because Mr Wilberforce's name does not appear in the dedication'.[11] Zachary Macaulay, for his part, observed in 1816 that the book was 'remarkable chiefly for the earnest warmth of heart which it manifests, and for the strange redundancies, and still stranger omissions, and, above all, the extravagant egotism with which it abounds'.[12] Even Wilberforce was moved to say that, though substantially 'true', the *History* 'by no means [conveyed] a just conception of all that deserves commemoration', a view evidently shared by many of his family and friends.[13]

Needless to say, Wilberforce's critics took a very different view of the matter. Among radicals and Dissenters, Clarkson was already acknowledged as the progenitor of the slave trade agitation, if not its leader. This was certainly Wordsworth's view of the matter. Wordsworth's sonnet *To Thomas Clarkson, on the final passing of the Bill for the Abolition of the Slave Trade* (1807) hailed Clarkson as 'Duty's intrepid liegeman' who 'Didst first lead forth that enterprise sublime'.[14] The *History* did little to challenge or alter these perceptions; if anything, it gave them greater credence and reliability. To William Hazlitt's mind, for instance, 'the man that effected [the abolition of the slave trade] by Herculean labours of body and equally gigantic labours of mind was Clarkson, the true Apostle of human Redemption on that occasion'. Wilberforce, he went on, 'was but the frontispiece to that great chapter in the history of the world – the mask, the varnishing and painting'.[15] It was difficult to know which was more striking (or, indeed, more provoking), Hazlitt's celebration of Clarkson as 'the true Apostle of human Redemption', or his calm dismissal of Wilberforce as a 'mask' or 'frontispiece'.[16]

Statements like these convinced many in Wilberforce's intimate circle of friends that the whole tale would need to be rewritten. That opportunity came with Wilberforce's death in July 1833. Almost immediately, Robert and Samuel Wilberforce started work on a five-volume life of their father, which finally appeared in 1838. As Tories and High Churchmen, the Wilberforces had every reason to distrust Clarkson. For one thing, he was a radical who was known to have sympathised with the French Revolution. For another, while Clarkson was nominally an Anglican and at one stage had even contemplated a career in the Church of England, having taken deacon's orders in 1783, he moved in Dissenting circles and counted Dissenters – especially Quakers – among his closest friends.[17] But the Wilberforces' real quarrel with Clarkson concerned their father. The *History*, they argued, created the erroneous impression that Clarkson had 'originally engaged' Wilberforce in the cause and that he (Wilberforce) had subsequently become 'a sort of Parliamentary agent, of whom you availed yourself'.[18] In effect, there were two points at issue here. The first touched upon the origins of Wilberforce's abolitionism. The other was about leadership, both inside and outside Parliament. On both counts, the Wilberforces believed that Clarkson was misinformed or, worse, simply wrong.

In their view, Wilberforce was not a 'tributary flood', as Clarkson's controversial map had seemed to indicate, but the 'main channel' of British anti-slavery.[19]

An important impetus also came from James Stephen (later Sir James Stephen and from 1836 to 1847 Colonial Under-Secretary), who appears to have disliked Clarkson with an almost pathological intensity. Stephen confided to Robert Wilberforce in September 1833 that 'there is no question on earth on which I am more clear than the necessity of your reclaiming for your Father the hardly earned Laurels of which Clarkson has but too successfully laboured to deprive him'. To Stephen's mind, Clarkson was an impostor. For many years before the final victory, he reminded Robert Wilberforce, Clarkson had actually given up the whole affair. Those years, moreover, or some of them, had been 'passed in a sort of English Jacobinism', and by 'alarming George III, Mr Pitt and the whole race of anti-Jacobins' Clarkson had done 'as much to frustrate and delay the abolition, as he ever did to promote it'. As if that were not enough, 'in the day of triumph this modest man [had been] found in his place ... and soon after did all that in him lay to exclude every one else from any share in the honour'. For these reasons, Stephen believed that it was the Wilberforces' 'urgent private duty' to 'put down this Charletanerie'. He also advised them to take the fight to Clarkson by giving him 'direct notice' of their intention to challenge his version of events, 'and to preserve, with a view to Publication, any correspondence which may pass between you on the subject'.[20]

The Wilberforces obviously took this advice to heart, but in truth they needed very little encouragement. To judge from their personal correspondence, they found everything about Clarkson unappealing. Take the question of his politics. 'How despicably mean, vain and pottering are all Clak's letters [from France]: his admiration of Lafayette, the bustle of the French', Samuel wrote to Robert Wilberforce in January 1836. 'Twaddle's vanity is exquisite'.[21] Both brothers, moreover, were inclined to think the worst of him. In March 1837, for instance, Robert Wilberforce conjectured that 'the notion of his [Wilberforce's] suspending his operations [in 1801] except as individual considerations', had been introduced by Clarkson 'in order to show that nothing was done during those years when he [Clarkson] was withdrawn'. In fact, nothing was further from the truth, and Robert thought that he could prove as much.[22] At other times, they were reduced to treating Clarkson as a figure of fun. 'Why is Thomas Clarkson like Solomon's Seal?' Samuel joked in the summer of 1836. 'Because he compressed a genius'. In a more extended metaphor, Robert Wilberforce likened Clarkson to one of 'your buoys with its solemn head spinning round on the Portsmouth coast'.[23]

Even at this distance there is something chilling about the calm and deliberate way in which the Wilberforces set about undermining Clarkson's reputation, in effect 'silencing' him.[24] Nothing was left to chance. Seizing upon Clarkson's intemperate response when Wilberforce refused to use his influence to secure a naval promotion for Clarkson's brother, John, Samuel Wilberforce proposed publishing most of the relevant correspondence, 'without the name', as an illustration of 'the collateral trials of the Aboln. Leader'.

If Clarkson hit back, Samuel explained, they could then publish 'three or four of his meanest letters which he knows not that we have, published with the name, for the world's benefit'.[25] To the last, they tried to anticipate any line of attack. Late in December 1837 Samuel confessed to Robert that the only point on which he thought they might be caught out was their claim that their father had refused to read Clarkson's *History*, 'lest he should be compelled to remark upon it'. What if Wilberforce had 'expressed himself pleased etc. in such a way as to seem to imply that he had read it'? Samuel was sure that Clarkson ('the vain old goose') would have kept any such letters, 'and so may seem to contradict our statement'.[26] After further consideration, they decided to take the risk and leave the passage as it stood, but the exchange is revealing, not least because it suggests how determined the Wilberforces were to dismiss Clarkson and to undermine his credibility.

The full extent of the Wilberforces' case against Clarkson became apparent when *The Life of William Wilberforce* was finally published in 1838. With remarkable ingenuity the brothers traced their father's interest in the abolition of the slave trade back to a letter written to a York newspaper when he was only fourteen years of age. They also claimed that between 1783 and 1786 Wilberforce had discussed the subject with James Ramsay, as well as African merchants, and 'that it was by this general acquaintance with West Indian matters, and not from any accidental summons [meaning Clarkson], that he was led to turn his attention to the slave trade'.[27] With equal vigour, the Wilberforces invested the London Committee of the SEAST with a very different significance, insisting that 'from the first' their father had directed its endeavours.[28] Clarkson, accordingly, was pushed into the background. Strangely, there was no mention of his role in the founding of the London Committee, or the part he had played in its opinion-building activities. Not to be outdone, the Wilberforces appended a fold-out 'Tabular View of the Abolition of Slavery and the Slave Trade', which traced the history of British anti-slavery from the Somerset case of 1772 through to the Emancipation Act of 1833. Clarkson's name appears only twice, the first time in 1785, the year he was awarded the senior Latin prize at Cambridge University for his 'Essay' on the slave trade; and the second time in 1787, when he was 'employed to collect evidence'.[29] The Wilberforces, in short, had produced a counter-narrative to Clarkson's *History*, which recast Clarkson in the role of their father's 'agent'. Understandably, Clarkson bridled at the use of the term (it was later removed from the abridged version of the *Life*, following representations from Clarkson's supporters), yet somehow it proved difficult to shake off.[30]

It was the tone of the *Life*, however, that was calculated to cause most offence. Clarkson and his *History* were dismissed at the first opportunity:

> Of this book it is necessary to declare at once, and with a very painful distinctness, that it conveys an entirely erroneous idea of the Abolition struggle. Without imputing to Mr Clarkson any intentional unfairness, it may safely be affirmed that his exaggerated estimate of his own service has led him unawares into numberless misstatements. Particular instances might be easily enumerated,

but the writers are most anxious to avoid any thing resembling controversy on this subject. Contenting themselves, therefore, with this declaration, they will henceforth simply tell their own story, without pointing out its contradictions to Mr Clarkson's 'History'.[31]

Clarkson was not only unreliable, the Wilberforces implied, but also vain and petty. There was the business over his brother's naval promotion, of course, where Clarkson's irritation with Wilberforce had clearly got the better of him. Equally unwarranted, or so the Wilberforces thought, was his ill-advised meddling in a scheme to provide him (Clarkson) with an annuity.[32] By concentrating on these episodes, as opposed to Clarkson's voluminous writings or his work organising committees and petitions, the *Life* came close to dismissing Clarkson's significance altogether. Perhaps just as important, the Wilberforces left readers in no doubt as to the nature of Clarkson's political loyalties, or, indeed, the dangers they posed to the success of the cause their father had 'taken in hand'.[33]

How much this unflattering portrait owed to James Stephen it is impossible to say. But Stephen clearly discussed the project with the Wilberforces and read large sections of the *Life* in manuscript, including the sections on slavery.[34] By a curious coincidence he also reviewed the book in the *Edinburgh Review*. Not surprisingly, Stephen warmly endorsed the position that the Wilberforces had taken with regard to Clarkson. In fact, he went further by casting doubts on Clarkson's stamina, as well as on his achievements. Clarkson, he could not help pointing out, had withdrawn from the slave trade agitation at a critical stage. Wilberforce, on the other hand, had 'returned to the conflict [this was in 1794] with unabated resolution', even though 'sustaining labours not less severe, and a public responsibility incomparably more anxious than that under which the health of his colleague [Clarkson] had given way'. Stephen also drew a further damaging comparison. 'It was within the reach of ordinary talents to collect, to examine, and to digest evidence, and to prepare and distribute popular publications', he maintained. 'But it required a mind as versatile and active, and powers as varied as those of Mr Wilberforce, to harmonize all minds … to negotiate with statesmen of all political parties, and, above all, to maintain for twenty successive years the lofty principles of the contest unsullied even by the seeming admixture of any lower aims'.[35] Put simply, Clarkson was the lesser man – emotionally, physically, and mentally.

Understandably, the vehemence of the Wilberforces' attack on Clarkson caused dismay in some quarters. The Tory diarist, J. W. Croker, dismissed the two brothers as 'little children'. 'Even if they were incontestably right', he confessed to Henry Brougham, 'their father's fame would not be a jot elevated; but 'tis extraordinary, or rather not extraordinary, how little scratches will fester in little minds.'[36] Baron Denman, the Lord Chief Justice, was equally dumbfounded. Struggling to account for the Wilberforces' behaviour, he could only conclude that they were 'clearly repeating' what their father must have told them, a circumstance that to his mind 'lowered [Wilberforce] as a rational and sensible man, fit to pass judgement on his fellow mortals'. Whatever the truth of the matter, both men agreed that the Wilberforces' conduct was 'abominable'. Perhaps just as important, Denman thought the whole proceeding betrayed a want of 'gentlemanly feeling', a stinging rebuke that spoke volumes about Victorian preoccupations.[37]

Vital support also came from the barrister and man of letters, Henry Crabb Robinson. Like many others, Robinson was not blind to the failings of Clarkson's two-volume *History*. 'Had they been called *Memoirs*,' he freely admitted, 'no man could have taken exception to anything contained or omitted.' At the same time, however, he distrusted the Wilberforces' motives, as well as their methodology. In his review of the *Life* in the *Eclectic Review* and elsewhere, Robinson accused the Wilberforces of deliberately 'garbling' extracts from letters and of publishing correspondence 'written in the confidence of friendship'. He also believed that the *Life* had been written under the 'manifest influence of ill will', not just towards Clarkson personally but towards abolitionists in general. Pointing out that Robert and Samuel Wilberforce were 'High Conservatives' and 'High Churchmen', Robinson argued that the two brothers were naturally 'strenuously opposed' to the great body of Wilberforce's former associates, most of whom had been Protestant Dissenters.[38] The Wilberforces, he added, 'barely tolerate the survivors and representatives of the original Abolitionists, and betray even an antipathy towards the religious and political bodies with whom their father was connected'.[39]

Clarkson, for his part, was clearly taken aback by the tone and contents of the *Life*, although, in truth, Robert Wilberforce had already given him fair warning of what to expect. His first instinct had been to fight back, enlisting the help of 'impartial witnesses', among them the MP, William Smith, and his old friend, Joseph Plymley, later Archdeacon Corbett.[40] When that did not work, Clarkson had resorted to less subtle pressures. 'Be assured,' he wrote to Samuel Wilberforce in May 1835, 'that after the Statements which I have it in my Power to make your Memoirs would, after the Publication of them, soon fall into Discredit, if your Brother should pursue the Course which he once intended to take'. In saying this, Clarkson was careful to appeal to the memory of his erstwhile 'coadjutor'. As he put it, it was immaterial to him whether Robert Wilberforce persisted in his original design; but it was not immaterial whether 'you bring your intended Memoirs into Discredit; for I wish your Father's life to be universally known and duly appreciated'. Such thinly veiled threats only strengthened the Wilberforces' resolve, however, forcing Clarkson 'to take an apparently hostile Part against the Sons of Mr Wilberforce'.[41]

Two things in particular seem to have bothered him. One was the question of order, or precedence. To Clarkson's mind, the real issue was not 'in whose heart benevolent feelings were first excited', but rather 'who first put the shoulder to the wheel, who first conceived the project and acted upon it of rousing a whole nation to a sense of national iniquity'.[42] Not surprisingly, Clarkson claimed this distinction for himself, pointing to his labours in 1785 and 1786. He also took offence at the suggestion that Wilberforce had been the presiding genius of the London Committee of the SEAST.[43] (Wilberforce, in fact, did not join the Committee until April 1791, although he clearly had an input into its deliberations before that date, even if this was not quite the same thing as leadership; Wilberforce, for instance, did not initiate policies, at least not where the Committee's opinion-building activities were concerned.)[44] Clarkson had covered most of this territory in his *History*, but the Wilberforces' attack made it vitally important to reassert the independence of the London SEAST Committee, as well as the enterprise of its members. For, in divorcing Clarkson from the Committee, by skipping over the fact that he had been a member of the Committee at all, the Wilberforces had been able to make good their claim that Wilberforce, and not Clarkson, had been the driving force outside Parliament.[45]

Clarkson set out all of this in his *Strictures on a Life of William Wilberforce* (1838), edited by Henry Crabb Robinson, obviously hoping for some kind of retraction. In the meantime, he worked tirelessly to rally his friends and supporters. Henry Brougham, for instance, was urged to procure 'a fair and honest Reviewer of [the *Strictures*] in the Edinburgh Review, or to *prevent*, if you can, one of the *Family* [meaning James Stephen] from reviewing it'.[46] With the same insistence, Clarkson's wife, Catherine lobbied William Wordsworth, hoping to enlist his support in the controversy; and, indeed, in a new edition of his sonnets, published in 1838, Wordsworth added a note standing by his earlier statement that Clarkson had been the 'first [to] lead that enterprise sublime'.[47] No less important was the support that Clarkson received from the Corporation of London, which in November 1838 granted him the freedom of the City of London, in recognition of his role in 'originating the great struggle for the deliverance of the enslaved African'.[48] Again, the choice of language was significant and, like the honour itself, clearly intended to reaffirm Clarkson's pre-eminent position among British abolitionists.

In a related move, Clarkson's friends also arranged for the publication of a new, one-volume edition of the *History*, complete with a lengthy preface (probably written by Brougham) that not only brought the story up to date but also carried the fight to the Wilberforces. Hailing the *Strictures* as a 'model of excellence in controversial writing', Brougham boldly announced that 'the vindication of Thomas Clarkson has been triumphant; the punishment of his traducers has been exemplary. His character stands higher than ever; his name is lofty and it is unsullied'.[49] Yet, despite these efforts – and despite Clarkson's dramatic appearance before the World Anti-Slavery Convention – the controversy refused to go away. In 1840 the Wilberforces published their long-awaited response to the *Strictures*, which, in turn, was answered by Robinson in his *Exposure of Misrepresentations contained in the Preface to the Correspondence of William Wilberforce* (1840). Eventually, the two sides reached an uneasy truce: the Wilberforces removed all of the offending passages from an abridged version of the *Life*, published in 1843, and later apologised for the 'tone' of the original work, which they acknowledged had been 'practically unjust'.[50] Nevertheless, the effect of the controversy on Clarkson's status and reputation is incalculable. Henry Crabb Robinson put things into perspective when he wrote in 1838 that the *Life* invited a comparison that

> not one reader in a hundred will have the inclination to make. Their book, they are aware, will be in every house, the owner of which makes pretension to both religion and gentility, while Mr. Clarkson's *History* is to be met with chiefly in the houses of a few quakers. His style being characterized only by quaint simplicity renders it unattractive to worldlings and Messrs. Wilberforce may be quite certain the field will be their own.[51]

Robinson's words were to prove prophetic. Not only did the *Life* become the standard source for all subsequent biographies of Wilberforce, but it also helped to shape perceptions of Clarkson, just as it shaped perceptions of his relationship with Wilberforce and the other members of the London Committee.

The results were predictable. While many of Wilberforce's early, nineteenth-century biographers were willing to concede that Clarkson was a pioneer (sometimes even 'the pioneer') of British anti-slavery, they nevertheless tended to assign him a subordinate or menial role within the movement.[52] Henry Wheeler, for instance, whose *The Slaves' Champion* was published privately in 1859, describes Clarkson as 'the *agent* and compeer by whom the weapons for the coming struggle were to be collected, set in order, and placed in the hands of the "Champion" [Wilberforce]'. In much the same way, John Campbell Colquhoun in his *William Wilberforce: His Friends and His Times* (1866), likens Clarkson to a 'quartermaster-general', drawing a sharp distinction between his services and those of the 'commander-in-chief'. Furthermore, Colquhoun maintains that Clarkson and the London Committee were 'independent of each other', the implication being that he was some sort of agent. A very similar impression is created by Travers Buxton in his *Wilberforce: The Story of a Great Crusade*, published in 1907, where Clarkson is portrayed as 'a journeyman labourer' (the phrase was originally coined by Jeremy Bentham), who was 'always ready to undertake the drudgery connected with the cause'.[53]

By and large, modern biographers have tended to take the same line. Reginald Coupland, in his *Wilberforce* (1923), describes Clarkson as the London Committee's 'almost indispensable agent'. Coupland's portrait of Clarkson, moreover, owes a great deal to the *Life*. While Coupland justifiably applauds Clarkson's achievements 'out of doors', he nevertheless characterizes him as indiscreet, petulant (as witness his behaviour over his brother's naval promotion), and impulsive. Coupland also goes a stage further by charging that Clarkson had spoken 'slightingly' of Wilberforce after his death, an extravagant claim based on his (Coupland's) misreading of Coleridge's brutal assertion that Wilberforce 'cared nothing about the slaves, nor if they were all damned, provided he saved his own soul'.[54] John Pollock is equally caustic. Clarkson, he argues

> tended to regard himself as the prime mover in any undertaking. Thus, though recording that Wilberforce, when thanking him for the gift of the Essay, said he had thought about the subject often and it was near to his heart, Clarkson convinced himself that it was he who first supplied details; and he who made

Wilberforce aware of Newton. Even more absurd, Clarkson believed he introduced Pitt to the question in 1788, and stuck to that story in old age though confronted with evidence that Pitt and Wilberforce had been negotiating with France on Abolition for several months before Pitt interviewed him.[55]

As this language suggests, Clarkson is invariably seen as vain and conceited. Most of Wilberforce's biographers also refer to Clarkson's advanced political views, his impetuosity, and his lack of judgement. Wilberforce, by contrast, is generally regarded as astute, patriotic, and politically moderate.[56]

Yet, as we shall see, the Wilberforces did not have everything their own way. If anything, their attack on Clarkson and his *History* fuelled a lingering sense of injustice that, ironically, helped to keep Clarkson's public memory alive (this, after all, is the wider significance of the Clarkson memorial tablet recently unveiled in Westminster Abbey). Though hardly a popular biographical subject – at least, when compared with Wilberforce – Clarkson has continued to attract scholarly interest, much of it determined, in one way or another, to set the record straight. James Elmes, for instance, in his *Thomas Clarkson: A Monograph* (1854), reinterprets Clarkson's alleged 'vanity' and 'egotism' as 'self-sufficiency', a quality he apparently shared with Horace, Ovid, Milton, Hogarth, and Johann Kepler. Other biographers focus, instead, on Clarkson's 'calm intrepidity' or his 'Christian heroism'; or else, like Earl Griggs, tackle the 'Wilberforce controversy' head on by trying to effect some sort of reconciliation between the two protagonists.[57]

As Ellen Wilson Gibson's excellent 1990 biography attests, Clarkson has proved a remarkably durable figure. Equally pertinent, his stock has risen as historical fashions have changed, and as perspectives on the early abolitionist movement have shifted away from the narrow confines of Parliament to the wider world outside Westminster. Adam Hochschild's *Bury the Chains* (2005) is but one example of how interest in what Hochschild describes as the 'first grassroots human rights campaign' has brought with it a reappraisal of Clarkson's achievements; Clarkson, in fact, is the book's 'central character'.[58] For all that, the *Life* continues to cast a long shadow. Even today there is a tendency to take sides in this debate, as if Wilberforce and Clarkson should be viewed as rivals rather than as allies or coadjutors: 'Clarkson did all the work, Wilberforce took all the credit' is one typical comment.[59] The tragedy, of course, is that Clarkson has never been allowed to find his own level. As David Lowenthal reminds us, all reputations are to some extent manufactured. In Clarkson's case, however, the 'alterations' have been particularly exaggerated, creating a discourse that is every bit as meaningful as the man himself.[60]

As it turns out, the Wilberforces' attack on Clarkson and his *History* was part of a more far-reaching attempt to (re)position their father. At first glance, this might seem surprising. Even during his own lifetime Wilberforce was freely acknowledged as a 'Christian philanthropist', 'the conscience of his country', 'the foremost moral subject of the crown'.[61] Following his death, many eulogists struck the same note. Earl Fitzwilliam, for instance, speaking at a large county meeting in York in October 1833, declared that it was 'impossible to do otherwise than to love and venerate a man whose whole study, thought and purpose appeared to be to help and assist others'. Echoing these sentiments, the Archbishop of Canterbury told the same meeting that Wilberforce had been 'a burning and shining light in his generation, and that in all his actions he had glorified God'. Let Britons look fully into that character, he went on, 'and they would find that, in every point, there was something worthy of imitation'. Others went further, likening Wilberforce's considerable achievements to those of Nelson and Wellington, a comparison that seems to have come easily to men and women who thought of abolition as 'warfare' and, more often than not, described Emancipation as a 'victory' or 'triumph'.[62]

Yet, for many, Wilberforce was a controversial figure. As a prominent and vocal member of the Evangelical 'party' within the Church of England, he was bitterly distrusted by reactionary Tories, many of whom regarded him as a subversive radical bent on 'the overthrow of church, crown and constitution'.[63] He was equally distrusted by radicals and 'liberals'. Nominally an independent MP, Wilberforce's motto was 'measures, not men'. Over the years, however, this stance (and Wilberforce's determination, wherever possible, to support the government of the day) laid him open to the charge of inconsistency or, worse, hypocrisy. During the French Revolutionary Wars (1793–1802), for instance, Wilberforce pressed repeatedly for 'peace with France', thereby offending the 'partisans of administration', while at the same time supporting the supply of 'due resources' to 'carry on the war vigorously'.[64] More controversially, he also defended the suspension of habeas corpus, as he was to do again in 1800 and 1817. In fact, as Wilberforce's record shows, he was a reluctant and unenthusiastic reformer, favouring 'moderate, gradual, and almost insensibly operating Parliamentary Reform', and distancing himself from 'demagogues' like William Cobbett, who, to his mind, were intent on nothing less than 'privy conspiracy and rebellion'. It was these same considerations, and his fear of social unrest, that led Wilberforce to support the repressive Six Acts (1819), which, among other things, banned meetings of more than fifty people and made the publication of blasphemous and seditious libels a transportable offence.[65]

Part of the problem here, of course, was that Wilberforce's identification with Abolition naturally raised expectations. It was assumed, wrongly as it turned out, that Wilberforce's politics were fundamentally 'liberal', and that once the African slave trade had been abolished he would turn his attention to social and economic conditions 'at home'. Much to the dismay of radicals, however, Wilberforce refused to be drawn on issues like industrial 'slavery' or the Irish peasantry, except insofar as those issues could be addressed by means of bibles and missions.[66] 'Is it to be presumed,' Cobbett asked, barely disguising his frustration, 'that [George] Washington, for instance, was not as good and just and humane a man as *Massa Wilby who voted and spoke even for the continuation of the Dungeon-bill, in 1818?*'[67] Hazlitt, who suspected Wilberforce of serving two masters, God and Mammon, was more scathing still. In an excoriating essay, later included in *The Spirit of the Age* (1825), Hazlitt accused Wilberforce of preaching 'vital Christianity to untutored savages; and [tolerating] its worst abuses in civilized states'. 'Mr Wilberforce is far from being a hypocrite,' he went on, 'but he is, we think, as fine a specimen of *moral equivocation* as can well be conceived'. Rounding on Wilberforce and his friends, who included figures like Hannah More, Hazlitt demanded angrily: 'What have the SAINTS to do with freedom or reform of any kind?'[68]

For some, Wilberforce's conservatism and his seeming disrespect for liberty at home remains the most troubling part of his legacy.[69] His sons, however, appear to have felt no need to defend his record. Instead, they adopted a rather different strategy, highlighting, first, their father's independence and, then, his patriotism. It is clear from the *Life* that Wilberforce conceived of his role as an independent MP as both a duty and a calling; it was his particular 'part', as he saw it, to 'give the example of an independent member of parliament, and a man of religion, discharging with activity and fidelity the duties of his trust'.[70] Indeed, it was a matter of pride to Wilberforce (and to his sons) that throughout his career he had remained firm in his 'resolution to take neither place, pension, nor peerage'. As the Wilberforces put it, in the very first volume of the *Life*: 'He too would no doubt have been entangled in the toils of party, and have failed of those great triumphs he afterwards achieved, but for the entrance into his soul of higher principles.' 'His later journals,' they go on, 'abound in expressions of thankfulness that he did not at this time [1782–83] enter on official life, and waste his days in the trappings of greatness.'[71]

Seen in this light, Wilberforce's independence was not simply admirable but, in its way, heroic. If anything, this effect was heightened by the inclusion in the *Life* of lengthy extracts from Wilberforce's private diaries and journals, which offered the reader a rare insight into the mind of a 'Christian politician'. What emerged from these sometimes anguished reflections was not only a clearer sense of Wilberforce's astuteness, particularly in public affairs, but also a better understanding of his values and priorities, as he struggled to adhere to what he 'saw to be his line of duty, neither deterred by opposition, nor piqued by unmerited reproach into irritation or excess'.[72] Viewed up close in this way, Wilberforce's motives and his seemingly erratic political behaviour assumed a very different shape and character. His guiding principle, it was made clear, was a deep religious faith that 'could know no remission and yield to no delay'. The *Life*, in other words, presented Wilberforce as a 'statesman-saint', for whom 'true Christianity [lay] not in frames and feelings, but in diligently doing the work of God'.[73] Picking up this theme in its review of the book, published in June 1838, the *British Magazine* aptly observed that 'no one can read the work without increased respect for the man, for his popular talents, his sincerity, his courage, his boundless charity, [or] his zeal for all that he believed to be good'.[74]

With equal vigour, Robert and Samuel Wilberforce repeatedly stressed their father's patriotism. Predictably, the *Life* made no secret of Wilberforce's hostility to 'French principles' or his 'abhorrence of the Revolution party'.[75] Even

the ticklish issue of Wilberforce's support for peace with France was con-
strued as a patriotic act, designed, it was said, to protect the national interest,
'cultivate our own internal resources', 'gain the hearts of our people', and to
'economize in our expenditure'.[76] As the *Life* made clear, Wilberforce feared
the consequences of a costly war with France, not least because he thought it
would demoralise the British people and set back his own plans for the 'refor-
mation of manners'. But he was not a pacifist. Faced with the threat of inva-
sion, he took an active part in raising local militia, and even offered advice on
home defence to Henry Dundas at the War Office. No matter that some of
Wilberforce's fiercest Tory critics thought this stance weak and vacillating.
Keen to set the record straight, the Wilberforces noted with approval their
father's statement in 1812 that he had 'strongly opposed' war with France, 'but
once it had begun, I did not persist in declaiming against its impolicy and mis-
chiefs, because I knew that by doing so I should only injure my country'.[77]

Significantly, the Wilberforces were less forthcoming about their father's
religious activism; that is, his attempts to reform the nation's morals (his other
'great object'). Ford Brown has estimated that during his lifetime Wilberforce
was connected with some thirty or forty philanthropic societies, among them
the London Missionary Society and the Church Missionary Society, the British and Foreign Bible Society, the Proclamation Society, the Lock Hospital
and the Lock Asylum, the Small Debts Society, the Sunday School Society,
the Naval and Military Bible Society, and the Bettering and Philanthropic
Societies.[78] The *Life*, however, makes little or no reference to these different
organizations. An obvious exception is the British and Foreign Bible Society,
but even here the *Christian Observer*, a leading Evangelical journal, believed
that the Wilberforces were guilty of misrepresentation, 'their allusions to it
being chiefly an apology for their father's being a member of it'.[79] These silences are revealing, not least because they suggest that the Wilberforces were
uneasy about the religious complexion of groups like the Bible Society and, in
particular, their connections with organised Dissent. Just as important, they
also had the effect of pushing their father's other activities into the background,
giving greater weight and authority to his role as 'the Great Emancipator'.

Brown, of course, suspected that the Wilberforces meant to go further by
remaking their father in their own image. This argument has some merit.
But, even if we accept that the Wilberforces were inclined to play down their
father's role within the Evangelical 'party', there is little to suggest that they
deliberately set out to 'conceal' Wilberforce's Evangelicalism (as David
Newsome argues, the 'very lengthy quotations from Wilberforce's religious
journals, throughout the work, could leave no doubt whatever in any reader's
mind that Wilberforce was an ardent Evangelical'); even less to suppose that
Wilberforce himself eventually went over to the High Church 'party'.[80] Be
that as it may, the Wilberforces were careful to avoid any hint of controversy,
particularly when it came to the question of Dissent. Sensitive to the charge
that their father, like other early Evangelicals, had been willing (perhaps too
willing) to cooperate with Dissenters, Robert and Samuel glossed over

Wilberforce's links with organised Dissent, while at the same time emphasising that those Dissenters he did cooperate with 'professed an affectionate regard for the national establishment'.[81] To this extent, the *Life* is selective. The figure that emerges from these five volumes is not only a Christian patriot, but also a religious moderate whose overriding concern was to bring 'light' to benighted Africa.

Clearly, one of the principal aims of the *Life* was to re-affirm Wilberforce's position as the leader and orchestrator of the early abolitionist movement. This still left the question of colonial slavery, however. While there is no doubt that Wilberforce endorsed Emancipation, or, at least, gradual emancipation, his retirement in 1825–26 left the campaign in the hands of a group of younger men, among them Henry Brougham and Thomas Fowell Buxton. It was these figures who negotiated the difficult path from 'gradual' to 'immediate' emancipation, and who eventually won over Lord Grey and his Cabinet. The anti-slavery campaign of 1832–34 was also helped by groups like the Agency Committee, which not only took the lead in popularising 'immediatism' but also brought 'pressure from without by appealing directly to the public conscience'. Abolition, in other words, was multi-faceted and, perhaps more to the point, drew on the talents of a wide array of individuals, including George Stephen, Daniel O'Connell, and Joseph Pease.[82]

A lot of this was reflected in popular images of Emancipation. If anything, the iconography associated with the campaign to end colonial slavery tended to concentrate not on the 'Saints' but on the slaves themselves. Typical of the genre was a series of medals produced by John Davis of Birmingham, each of which depicts a (kneeling) slave now transformed into a (standing) freedman, arms raised, clasping broken chains. Other medals produced in 1834 and again in 1838 (when apprenticeship came to an end) depict small family groups of freed slaves, sometimes accompanied by their white 'liberators'. When the 'Saints' are referred to at all it is usually in the form of a roll call: 'Penn, Granville Sharp, Wilberforce, Benezet, Clarkson, Buxton, Brougham, Sturge, Sligo'. Occasionally, Toussaint L'Ouverture is included in the list of 'coadjutors', as are James Stephen and David Barclay. But significantly there is no single reference point, as there had been in 1807 when Wilberforce's name and profile dominated popular images of Abolition.[83]

The Wilberforces obviously thought long and hard about how best to integrate Emancipation into their narrative. Part of their strategy was to create a sense of continuity between the first and second acts of 'the great Slavery Drama'. As Robert Wilberforce put it, writing to his brother in January 1835: 'The more I see the more am I convinced that by care and study you may make an interesting corpus historia of the two connected. I shall hope you will establish it [the campaign against the slave trade] as the approved "précis" of that interesting part of our public history.' And, indeed, the final volume of the *Life* is careful to stress that in committing himself to Emancipation Wilberforce was 'but following up his former steps'.[84] At the same time, the brothers were eager to establish that Emancipation was their father's 'cause'. It was Wilberforce, they argued, who proposed to Thomas Fowell Buxton a 'secret cabinet council' to decide what course to pursue (this was in 1822); Wilberforce who was chosen to introduce the subject of colonial slavery in the House of Commons; and Wilberforce who subsequently decided to entrust the cause to Buxton, as 'the depository of his principles on West Indian matters'.[85]

What is revealing about this narrative is what it leaves out; indeed, in many ways the *Life* is every bit as selective and incomplete as Clarkson's *History*. For instance, the Wilberforces make no mention of the Society for the Mitigation and Gradual Abolition of Slavery, which was organised in 1823, or the efforts of its members, among them Thomas Clarkson, to take Emancipation out into the country. It was the same thing with the post-1826 period. Here again, the *Life* is largely silent on the progress and development of the anti-slavery campaign, both inside and outside parliament. Buxton, for instance, slips out of the narrative after 1826, while little notice is taken of either Brougham or activists like George Stephen. Instead, the Wilberforces content themselves with a few scattered references to Emancipation, usually involving their father's appearances at anti-slavery meetings (in 1828 and 1830).[86] Of course, given the nature of the project, these silences could easily be justified – after all, the *Life* was intended to be a biography and not a history – but they also had the effect of making Wilberforce and Emancipation appear synonymous with one another, which was clearly the intention.

The Wilberforces returned to this theme in the closing pages of the *Life*. By a curious twist of fate, Wilberforce died at just the moment that the Government's Emancipation Bill was passing through the House of Commons; indeed, it is said that 'the last public information he received was, that his country was willing to redeem itself from the national disgrace at any sacrifice'. For obvious reasons, the congruence of these two events added 'signal interest' to Wilberforce's death, creating a 'corpus historia' of a rather different kind. As Robert and Samuel Wilberforce put it: 'His state of health had latterly induced many of his friends to express their hope that he might be allowed to witness the consummation of the fifty years' struggle, and might then retire in peace; and so strong was this presentiment, that one of them speaks of writing to take leave of him so soon as the Bill for the Abolition of Slavery was known to be in progress.'[87] Here again, Emancipation is linked to the earlier campaign against the slave trade. But, just as important, it is also linked to Wilberforce; the 'fifty years' struggle' is clearly his struggle. In other words, the circumstances surrounding Wilberforce's death in 1833 are used here to sustain a narrative strategy that places him at the very centre of British anti-slavery.

As we have seen, the *Life* was a carefully constructed text, designed to reinterpret William Wilberforce for future generations, and, in doing so, to secure his place in the nation's pantheon of heroes. Put simply, Robert and Samuel Wilberforce cleared a path for their father. If the first two volumes of the book were designed to meet the challenge posed by Clarkson and his *History*, the final volume did much the same thing for Buxton and Brougham, albeit in a less obvious and confrontational way. The project was an ambitious one. Wilberforce emerges from these volumes not only as the dominant force in British anti-slavery, but also as a 'statesman-saint'. Here again, the *Life* has proved highly influential. Today, our collective memory of Wilberforce is shaped and influenced by two complementary images, both of which can be traced back to the 1830s; that of Wilberforce as a 'liberator', and that of Wilberforce as a 'Christian statesman'. As the Conservative MP, Patrick Cormack, puts it in his *Wilberforce: The Nation's Conscience* (1983): 'Of all the great figures of the last two centuries whose names come most readily to mind, few are politicians. Those who are do so not only because of their abilities but because they held high office in difficult times. Wilberforce alone is remembered because he did great good.'[88]

Cormack's characterisation of Wilberforce as a 'Christian politician' – Garth Lean, another of Wilberforce's recent biographers, refers to him as 'God's Politician' – is a vindication of the Wilberforces' biographical strategy. For Christians, in particular, Wilberforce remains 'one of the giants of British politics'. To quote Tim Montgomerie, former Director of Conservative Christian Fellowship: 'Not only did he [Wilberforce] show that a Christian can succeed at the highest level in politics in service of great causes, and against the greatest odds, he demonstrated a biblical model for political involvement'.[89] But arguably that is not how most Britons view Wilberforce; for them, he is simply the 'man who freed the slaves' – a 'great name' who ranks alongside Nelson, Wellington, Florence Nightingale, and Churchill. Ironically, the Wilberforces would have recognised and applauded this impulse. By moving their father closer to the national establishment, and away from heterodoxy and Dissent, Robert and Samuel Wilberforce succeeded in creating a heroic figure whose sincerity and perseverance came to embody a certain type of British philanthropy and, just as important, a certain type of Britishness.[90]

Notes

1 *The Times*, 12 November 1881.
2 See, for instance, the tribute in the *Sheffield Daily Telegraph*, 26 July 1933. Lord Hemingford coined the phrase 'statesman-saint' to describe Wilberforce in his address at the celebrations in Westminster Abbey in 1969 to commemorate the bicentenary of Wilberforce's birth. Rhodes House Library, Oxford, Anti-Slavery and Aborigines' Protection Society Papers, MSS Brit. Emp. S19 D/11/11/1.
3 Clarkson, *The History of the Rise, Progress and Accomplishment of the Abolition of the Slave Trade*, I, pp. 269–75.
4 For the significance of this map see Wood, *Blind Memory*, pp. 16–21.
5 Clarkson, *The History of the Rise, Progress and Accomplishment of the Abolition of the Slave Trade*, I, p. 257.
6 Ibid., p. 210.

7   Clarkson appears to have been aware of some of these issues, although he still insisted on calling his book a 'history'. See Clarkson, *The History of the Rise, Progress and Accomplishment of the Abolition of the Slave Trade*, I, p. 269.

8   Oldfield, *Popular Politics and British Anti-Slavery*, pp. 45–62.

9   Ibid., pp. 84–5. For Clarkson's years in the Lake District, see Ellen Wilson Gibson, *Thomas Clarkson: A Biography* (London, 1990), pp. 88–90, 96–104; Robert Gittings and Jo Manton, *Dorothy Wordsworth* (Oxford, 1985), pp. 108–11, 164, 182–4, 211–12; Pamela Woof, ed., *Dorothy Wordsworth: The Grasmere Journals* (Oxford, 1991), pp. 30, 47–8, 50, 53, 54–7, 76–7, 83–4.

10 Clarkson, *The History of the Rise, Progress and Accomplishment of the Abolition of the Slave Trade*, II, pp. 502–3.

11 Wisbech and Fenland Museum, Wisbech, Clarkson Papers, TCC/34, Catherine Clarkson to Elizabeth Shewell, 31 March 1836; *Edinburgh Review*, 24 (July 1808), pp. 355–79; Earl Leslie Griggs, *Thomas Clarkson: The Friend of Slaves* (London, 1936), p. 97.

12 *Christian Observer*, 15 (January 1816), p. 29. Macaulay was reviewing *Reasons for establishing a Registry of Slaves in the British Colonies: being a Report of a Committee of the African Institution* (1815).

13 Quoted in Gibson, *Thomas Clarkson*, p. 119. There is some debate as to whether Wilberforce actually read Clarkson's *History*. See below.

14 The sonnet was composed in March 1807 and originally published in *Poems, in Two Volumes by William Wordsworth* (London, 1807).

15 William Hazlitt, *The Spirit of the Age* [1825] (Plymouth, 1991), p. 243; Tom Paulin, *The Day-Star of Liberty: William Hazlitt's Radical Style* (London, 1998), p. 266. Hazlitt first met Clarkson in Bury St Edmunds some time in 1799 and was later commissioned to paint his portrait. See A. C. Grayling, *The Quarrel of the Age: The Life and Times of William Hazlitt* (London, 2000), pp. 67–8, 140, 143; Herschel Moreland Sikes, ed., *The Letters of William Hazlitt* (London, 1979), p. 132.

16 In a similar vein, Thomas Noon Talfourd described Clarkson as 'the true annihilator of the slave trade'. Wilberforce, he maintained, was merely an 'oratorical' philanthropist. See Thomas Noon Talfourd, *The Letters of Charles Lamb, with a Sketch of his Life*, 2 vols (London, 1837), I, pp. 218–19.

17 *Alumni Cantabrigiensis*, Part II, vol. ii, p. 58. By 1785 Clarkson was domestic chaplain to the Earl of Portmore. For Dissent and the Church of England, see Owen Chadwick, *The Victorian Church*, 2 vols (London, 1966), I, pp. 60–100; Ford K. Brown, *Fathers of the Victorians: The Age of Wilberforce* (Cambridge, 1961), pp. 487–533. Chadwick notes that relations between Church and Dissent reached 'a low point' during the 1830s.

18 Thomas Clarkson, *Strictures on a Life of W. Wilberforce by the Rev. R. I. Wilberforce and the Rev. S. Wilberforce. With a Correspondence between Lord Brougham and Mr Clarkson; also a Supplement containing Remarks on the Edinburgh Review of Mr Wilberforce's Life* (London, 1838), p. 7. This charge was originally made in a letter from Robert Wilberforce dated 18 July 1834. See also Bodleian Library, Oxford, Wilberforce MS, c. 57, f. 76, Robert Wilberforce to Samuel Wilberforce, 14 November 1833. Erroneous or not, Clarkson's version of events had obviously gained some currency in literary and intellectual circles. The *Gentleman's Magazine*, for instance, in its obituary of Wilberforce, noted in passing that 'it was at the particular solicitation of the celebrated Mr. Clarkson that Mr. Wilberforce was first induced to interest himself on the subject of Slavery'. See *The Gentleman's Magazine*, September 1833, p. 273.

19 This is James Stephen's gloss on the Wilberforces's position. See *Edinburgh Review*, 67 (1838), p. 158.

20 Wilberforce MS, c. 65, f. 25, James Stephen to Robert Wilberforce, 25 September

1833. See also Wilberforce MS, c. 65, f. 61, Stephen to Wilberforce, 30 October 1833. Stephen uses 'modest' here in the sense of 'mediocre' or 'small'.

21 Wilberforce MS, c. 58, f. 3, Samuel Wilberforce to Robert Wilberforce, 13 January 1826. Clarkson's radicalism clearly offended the Wilberforces. One detail that preoccupied and irritated Samuel Wilberforce, for instance, was Clarkson's membership of 'the Friends of the People'. See Wilberforce MS, c. 58, ff. 3, 7, 17, Samuel Wilberforce to Robert Wilberforce, 13, 22 January and 14 March 1836.

22 Wilberforce MS, c. 58, f. 89, Robert Wilberforce to Samuel Wilberforce, 13 March 1837.

23 Ibid., c. 58, ff. 27, 35, Robert Wilberforce to Samuel Wilberforce, May 1836 and Samuel Wilberforce to Robert Wilberforce, August 1836. Samuel at this time was living on the Isle of Wight. The use of nicknames was also highly significant. Samuel appears to have coined 'Clak', a play on 'clack', meaning 'senseless chatter' or 'to chatter', in 1836. See Wilberforce MS, c. 58, f. 3, Samuel Wilberforce to Robert Wilberforce, 13 January 1836. 'Twaddle' was a variation on the same theme.

24 I use 'silence' here in the sense of an 'active and transitive process'. See Michel-Rolph Trouillot, *Silencing the Past: Power and the Production of History* (Boston, 1995), p. 48.

25 Wilberforce MS, c. 58, f. 17, Samuel Wilberforce to Robert Wilberforce, 14 March 1836. See also Wilberforce MS, c. 58, f. 19, Robert Wilberforce to Samuel Wilberforce, March 1836.

26 Wilberforce MS, c. 59, f. 35, Samuel Wilberforce to Robert Wilberforce, 28 December 1837.

27 Robert Isaac Wilberforce and Samuel Wilberforce, *The Life of William Wilberforce. By his Sons, Robert Isaac Wilberforce [and] Samuel Wilberforce* (hereafter referred to as *Life*), 5 vols (London, 1838,) I, pp. 9, 140–9. With equal vigour the Wilberforces rejected any suggestion that Lady Middleton had enlisted their father in the cause. Wilberforce's interest in abolition, they maintained, was 'the fruit of his religious change [in 1785]'.

28 *Life*, I, pp. 151–2.

29 This table appears as the frontispiece to the second volume of the *Life*. Also significant is the importance that the Wilberforces attached to James Ramsay. 'In 1786 was published Mr. Clarkson's first pamphlet on the trade,' they note, 'but through the years 1784 and 1785 Mr. Ramsay fought alone, nor did he ever quit the strife until he sunk under its virulence in the summer of 1789.' See *Life*, I, p. 148. Here again, the language was very carefully chosen, and was clearly meant as an implied criticism of Clarkson.

30 *The Life of William Wilberforce. By his sons, Robert Isaac Wilberforce and Samuel Wilberforce* (new edition, abridged, London, 1843).

31 *Life*, I, p. 141n.

32 Ibid., II, pp. 38–44, 51–5.

33 Ibid., I, pp. 342–3.

34 See Wilberforce MS, c. 58, f. 94 and c. 59, f. 38, Robert Wilberforce to Samuel Wilberforce, 23 March and 29 December 1837. Also see Wilberforce MS, Diaries of Samuel Wilberforce, e. 5 (entry for 2 September 1833), e. 6 (entries for 26 and 27 February 1836), and e. 7 (entries for 28 January, 14 February, 27 and 28 March 1837).

35 *Edinburgh Review*, 67 (1838), pp. 153–4, 159.

36 University College, London, Brougham Papers, HB/14,319, J. W. Croker to Henry Brougham, 14 September 1838.

37 Brougham Papers, HB/39,339, Thomas Denman to Henry Brougham, 20 October 1838. See also Brougham Papers, HB/39,338, Denman to Brougham, 15 October 1838. Others, like Thomas Babington Macaulay, were inclined to attribute the Wilberforces' meanness of spirit to their mother, or, at least, to their mother's family. See Edith J.

Morley, *Henry Crabb Robinson on Books and their Writers*, 2 vols (London, 1938), II, p. 590. In a similar vein, Marianne Thornton observed that it was 'pitiable to hear the measured calculating un-Wilberforced like tone of [Robert Wilberforce]'. 'He is not to be blamed though', she went on, 'nature has made him a thorough Spooner from Birmingham and this is where his blameless useful existence should have passed. I wish there was a law obliging men to take their mother's names when so utterly unlike their fathers.' See E. M. Forster, *Marianne Thornton, 1797–1887: A Domestic Biography* (London, 1956), p. 139.

38   *Eclectic Review*, 67 (1838), pp. 681–7.

39   Henry Crabb Robinson, *Exposure of Misrepresentations contained in the Preface to the Correspondence of William Wilberforce* (London, 1840), p. 4.

40   Wilberforce MS, c. 7, ff. 94 and 104, Clarkson to Samuel Wilberforce, 12 August 1834 and 22 May 1835; c. 65, f. 88, Clarkson to Robert Wilberforce, n.d.; c. 7, f. 100, William Smith to Catherine Clarkson, n.d. The Wilberforces later claimed that 'Clarkson's mind was so possessed with the mistaken notion that he should be harshly and unkindly treated, that no possible statement of their case could have borne in his eyes any other aspect'. See *The Correspondence of William Wilberforce. Edited by his Sons, Robert Isaac Wilberforce and Samuel Wilberforce*, 2 vols (London, 1840), I, p. xv.

41   Wilberforce MS, c. 7, f. 104, Clarkson to Samuel Wilberforce, 22 May 1835.

42   Clarkson, *Strictures on a Life of W. Wilberforce*, pp. 30–46. See also Brougham Papers, HB/1062, Clarkson to Henry Brougham, 5 July 1838 and Wilberforce MS, c. 7, f. 100, William Smith to Catherine Clarkson, n. d. Clarkson was willing to concede that in all probability Wilberforce would have taken up the question of the slave trade without his intervention. But he did intervene and Clarkson maintained that at the time of their first meeting in 1787 Wilberforce still knew 'very little about the slave trade or Africa'.

43   Clarkson, *Strictures on a Life of W. Wilberforce*, pp. 63–83.

44   Oldfield, *Popular Politics and British Anti-Slavery*, pp. 88–90.

45   Discussing the activities of the London Committee of the Society for Effecting the Abolition of the Slave Trade, the Wilberforces note only that 'as their agent Mr Clarkson sought patiently for evidence in Liverpool and Bristol'. See *Life*, I, p. 152.

46   Brougham Papers, HB/1062 and HB/1057, Clarkson to Brougham, 5 July and 1 August 1838. Emphasis in original. As it happened, Brougham reviewed the *Strictures*. See *Edinburgh Review*, 68 (1838), pp. 188–90.

47   Wordsworth Library, Grasmere, Wordsworth Papers, Catherine Clarkson to Wordsworth, 30 September and 10 November 1838; William Wordsworth, *Sonnets*, London, 1838, p. 148. According to Robinson, who visited the Wordworths at Rydal Mount in December 1838, following publication of the *Strictures*, 'all here rejoice in Clarkson's triumph'. See Morley, *Henry Crabb Robinson on Books and their Writers*, II, pp. 558–62, 568.

48   Corporation of London Record Office, London, Court of Common Council Minutes, Journal 115, f. 220 (29 November 1838) and Journal 116, f. 22. Clarkson was admitted to the freedom of the City of London in 1839. For a first-hand description of the short ceremony at the Mansion House on 15 April, see Thomas Sadler, ed., *Reminiscences and Correspondence of Henry Crabb Robinson*, 3 vols (London, 1859), III, pp. 174–5. The Corporation also commissioned a bust of Clarkson by William Behnes. Adverting to this fact, James Stephen could not help observing that the 'citizens of London in their Guildhall' had 'degraded' Clarkson to the level of William Beckford, 'the insolent poltroon who stands beside him there'. See James Stephen, *Essays in Ecclesiastical Biography* (new edn, London, 1872), p. 497.

49   Thomas Clarkson, *The History of the Rise, Progress and Accomplishment of the Abolition of*

the Slave Trade by the British Parliament (new edn, London, 1839), esp. pp. 29–31; Brougham Papers, HB/36,235, Clarkson to Brougham, 24 January 1839.

50 Wilberforce MS, c. 60, f. 203, Robert Wilberforce to Samuel Wilberforce, 7 December 1842; c. 7, f. 233, Samuel and Robert Wilberforce to Clarkson, 15 November 1844. According to Clarkson, the Wilberforces made an apology, 'stating in their own words that "they had done me Injustice" but that it was owing to the advice of a third Person', presumably meaning James Stephen. See Brougham Papers, HB/48,039, Clarkson to Brougham, 4 July 1845.

51 *Eclectic Review*, 67 (1838), p. 682.

52 John Stoughton, for instance, identifies Clarkson as 'the first person who publicly appeared in England as a worker in this philanthropic cause'. See John Stoughton, *William Wilberforce* (London, 1880), pp. 65–6.

53 Henry M. Wheeler, *The Slaves' Champion: A Sketch of the Life, Deeds and Historical Days of William Wilberforce* (London, 1860), p. 111 (my emphasis); John Campbell Colquhoun, *William Wilberforce: His Friends and His Times* (London, 1866), pp. 370–3; Travers Buxton, *Wilberforce: The Story of a Great Crusade* (London, 1907), pp. 157–9.

54 Reginald Coupland, *William Wilberforce* [1923] (London, 1945), pp. 127–8, 156, 174–6.

55 John Pollock, *Wilberforce* (London, 1977), pp. 55, 225. Pollock, however, does find the 'Wilberforce controversy' distasteful. 'No defects in Clarkson,' he writes, 'could justify Robert and Samuel Wilberforce's portrayal of him, the last of the pioneers alive, as having been a sort of hack to Wilberforce and the Abolitionists'.

56 See Buxton, *Wilberforce*, pp. 158–9; Coupland, *Wilberforce*, p. 128. On a more positive note, Furneaux describes Clarkson as a 'human dynamo, a detective of incredible energy, patience and perseverance, a man of genius who had found his vocation'. See Robin Furneaux, *William Wilberforce* (London, 1974), p. 70.

57 James Elmes, *Thomas Clarkson: A Monograph. Being a Contribution towards the History of the Abolition of the Slave Trade and Slavery* (London, 1854), pp. xxvii–xxx; Anon, *A Sketch of the Life of Thomas Clarkson* (London and Wisbech, 1876), pp. 7, 28; Griggs, *Thomas Clarkson*, esp. p. 181. As Griggs puts it: 'It is not Clarkson *versus* Wilberforce but Clarkson *and* Wilberforce.'

58 Adam Hochschild, *Bury the Chains: Prophets and Rebels in the Fight to Free an Empire's Slaves* (New York, 2005), p. 4. At the same time, it is interesting to note that the book's dust jacket contains three images – those of Olaudah Equiano, James Ramsay, and William Wilberforce – but, significantly, not one of Thomas Clarkson. The British edition of *Bury the Chains* contains just two images, those of Equiano and Wilberforce, reflecting a sense that while, in the current intellectual climate, it is important to address black or African perspectives, white abolitionism – at least, for a popular audience – is still best understood through Wilberforce.

59 Wisbech and Fenland Museum, Clarkson Papers, TCC/123, pencil note in a collection of newspaper clippings, n.d.

60 Lowenthal, *The Past is a Foreign Country*, p. 347.

61 Brown, *Fathers of the Victorians*, p. 107.

62 *The Times*, 5 October 1833; *York Herald*, 5 October 1833; *Hull Advertiser*, 2, 9, 16 August 1833, 8 August 1834.

63 Brown, *Fathers of the Victorians*, p. 155. See also R. J. Hind, 'Wilberforce and the Perceptions of the British People', *Historical Research*, 60 (1987), p. 328; G. F. A. Best, 'The Evangelicals and the Established Church in the Early Nineteenth Century', *Journal of Theological Studies*, new series, 10 (1959), pp. 68–78.

64 *Life*, I, pp. 64–8, 73, 195, III, pp. 255, 320.

65 Ibid., II, pp. 74, 358, III, pp. 451–5, IV, pp. 308, 314–16. Even some of Wilberforce's warmest admirers appear to have had misgivings about his politics. Earl Fitzwilliam,

for instance, made no secret of the fact that he would not have attended the county meeting in York if it had been called to do honour to the memory of Wilberforce as a politician. When he looked at the political principles of his departed friend, he went on, 'there were points which he could not on any account approve or support'. *The Times*, 5 October 1833.

66 *Life*, III, pp. 309–11. Wilberforce's comments on these and similar issues can sometimes appear a little disarming. In 1824, for instance, he noted in his diary that he 'would zealously promote the real comforts of the poor', adding 'I love the idea of having comfortable causeway walks for them along the public roads'. See *Life*, V, p. 214. On Evangelical attitudes towards the poor, see Forster, *Marianne Thornton*, pp. 53–4; Ann Stott, *Hannah More: The First Victorian* (Oxford, 2003), pp. 182–190; Brown, *Fathers of the Victorians*, pp. 146–8, 250–52.

67 Quoted in Brown, *Fathers of the Victorians*, p. 112. See also *Athenaeum*, May 1838, p. 317.

68 Hazlitt, *The Spirit of the Age*, pp. 239–43. Emphasis in original. As Brown points out, Hazlitt's critique was based on a fundamental misconception. Religiously speaking, there was no oppression in Britain strictly analogous to African slavery. See Brown, pp. 378–9. Wilberforce's priorities only become comprehensible if we consider him as a religious reformer, whose various activities were 'inter-dependent parts of a programme designed to arrest the progress of social degeneracy, facilitate national renovation and give permanence to Britain's superiority'. See Hind, 'Wilberforce and the Perceptions of the British People', p. 323.

69 See, for instance, Liz Deverell and Gareth Williams, *Wilberforce and Hull* (Hull, 2000), pp. 59–62.

70 *Life*, III, p. 60. There are many other references to Wilberforce's independence scattered throughout this and the other volumes of the *Life*. See, in particular, *Life*, III, pp. 275–7, 307–8, 320, 528–31.

71 Ibid., I, p. 31.

72 See, for example, *Life*, II, pp. 80–1 (quotation), 273–5, III, pp. 21, 56–60, 537–9. Some critics were clearly uneasy about the extensive use made of these journals and diaries, partly on grounds of impropriety but also because the technique was thought to raise important questions about the biographer's art. Croker, for instance, decried 'the inevitable defects of either an *autobiography* or a biography written or edited by *very near relations*', adding that 'the volumes before us are in so large a proportion composed, that we cannot estimate the connecting sentences, furnished by the editors, at more than one-tenth of the whole'. *Quarterly Review*, 62 (November 1838), pp. 214–15. See also *British Magazine*, 13 (June 1838), p. 664; *Christian Observer*, 38 (June 1838), p. 570.

73 *Life*, II, pp. 21–2, 97.

74 *British Magazine*, 13 (June 1838), p. 664.

75 Ibid., II, pp. 8, 61. Even the Wilberforces, however, struggled to account for their father's failure to repudiate publicly the National Convention's decision in 1792 to confer on him the 'doubtful honour' of French citizenship. See *Life*, i, p. 368. Predictably, Croker described Wilberforce's behaviour on this occasion as 'feeble and degrading'. 'Wilberforce could not have guarded against such a gratuitous insult,' he went on, 'but he might have openly spurned and specifically rejected it.' See *Quarterly Review*, 62 (November 1838), pp. 264–5.

76 *Life*, III, pp. 76–7.

77 Ibid., III, p. 110.

78 Brown, *Fathers of the Victorians*, pp. 70–2, 97–8.

79 *Christian Observer*, 38 (September 1838), pp. 568–9. The Wilberforces were clearly embarrassed by the 'enthusiasm' of the Bible Society and, in particular, the character of

its public meetings. With this in mind, they were quick to stress that those who viewed the society in its 'consequences', should not 'forget the different positions of its founders'. 'So great was the torpor of the Church [in 1803]', they explained, 'that all more strictly regular exertions had absolutely failed, and they who devised this powerful instrument of good, are hardly to be blamed, though they have with a holy daring called up a spirit too mighty for their absolute control.' See *Life*, III, pp. 91–2.

80 Brown, *Fathers of the Victorians*, pp. 487–506; David Newsome, 'Fathers and Sons', *The Historical Journal*, 6 (1963), pp. 292–310; Furneaux, *Wilberforce*, p. 427.

81 *Life*, I, p. 248, III, p. 92 (quotation).

82 Temperley, *British Anti-Slavery*, pp. 9–18; Stephen, *Anti-Slavery Recollections*, pp. 129–58.

83 British Museum, Department of Coins and Medals, M5291/2, M6225, M6227, M6230–32, M6384; Thomas Sheppard, *Medals, Tokens, etc. Issued in Connection with Wilberforce and the Abolition of Slavery* (Hull, 1916).

84 Wilberforce MS, c. 57, f. 116, Robert Wilberforce to Samuel Wilberforce, 31 January 1835; *Life*, V, p. 170.

85 *Life*, V, pp. 129–30, 157–8, 238.

86 Ibid., pp. 262, 300, 316.

87 Ibid., p. 370.

88 Patrick Cormack, *Wilberforce: The Nation's Conscience* (Pickering, 1983), p. 46.

89 For the Conservative Christian Fellowship, see www.ccfwebsite.com accessed 25 April 2005. In 1997 the CCF established an annual address in honour of Wilberforce. Recent speakers have included Peter Lilley, William Hague, Iain Duncan Smith, and David Lidington.

90 Oliver Warner, *William Wilberforce* (London, 1962), p. 17. For Wilberforce and 'Britishness', see Chapter 4.

3

Sites of memory: abolitionist monuments and the politics of identity

In recent years there has been increased scholarly interest in public monuments and memorials, much of it focusing on war memorials, particularly those commemorating the First World War, and memorials dedicated to the victims of the Holocaust. Thanks to the work of Jay Winter and James Young, among others, we now have a much clearer understanding of the function of these objects, as well as their role in shaping popular memory.[1] Whether they commemorate loss on a grand scale, as in the case of war memorials, or celebrate heroic deeds, monument-memorials are erected not only to honour the dead but also to educate the living.[2] Monuments, like museums and historical pageantry, are sites of memory, public 'documents' that help to define the meaning of the past and, just as important, how it should be remembered. Viewed in this way, memorial activities take on a very different resonance and meaning. It is not just that we need to understand who controls or sponsors the memorialising process, although that is undoubtedly important. Monuments are also symbols of pride, and, in this sense, who or what a community chooses to commemorate is highly revealing.[3]

Monuments, in other words, help to create national 'histories', as well as national myths. In the case of transatlantic slavery, this has meant focusing on what we might call a 'culture of abolitionism', that is, the moral achievements of the 'Saints' and hence the British nation. Significantly, with the exception of the 'Pero' bridge (1999) in Bristol and now the 'Captured Africans' (2005) memorial in Lancaster, there are very few monuments in Britain that commemorate the victims of the transatlantic slave trade, or, for that matter, the thousands of white seamen who died as a result of their involvement in the trade. Instead, Britons have been led historically to place particular value on the nation's tradition of humanity, as represented by a limited number of specific (white) individuals. Wilberforce, for instance, features prominently in this discourse but so, too, does Clarkson; indeed, at one level abolitionist monuments can be read as an attempt to continue by other means a controversy that began in 1838 with the publication of *The Life of William Wilberforce*. Equally revealing is the relationship between the centre and the periphery. As we shall see, national sites of memory carry with them particular weight and authority, not least because they add lustre to local sites of memory. Priorities also can change, usually to suit present-day purposes. Here again, Clarkson's recent elevation to a figure of national importance is a perfect example of how 'interaction with a heritage continually alters its nature and context', even if that particular project speaks to values and preoccupations that, to some, notably black Britons, appear outmoded and in urgent need of repair.[4]

Significantly, Abolition (1807) and Emancipation (1834) seem to have aroused little immediate interest in memorial activities, at least at a general level. A rare exception can be found in Stroud, Gloucestershire, in the shape of the 'anti-slavery archway' built in 1834 by Henry Wyatt, of Farmhill Park, which bears two simple inscriptions: 'Erected to commemorate the Abolition of Slavery in the British Colonies, the First of August 1834'; and 'God gave Freedom. May Glory be given to God'. Important as it was, Wyatt's limestone archway was essentially a private memorial; in fact, it stood at the end of his carriage drive and was therefore visible only to visitors. Nevertheless, following the sale and redevelopment of Farmhill Park in the 1920s the monument inevitably shed some of its original meaning and took on a new significance. In fact, the value of the archway as a local and regional relic has increased with the passage of time, as witness the appeal launched in 2001, which raised over £24,000 to complete urgent restoration work. Lovingly restored, Wyatt's memorial archway stands today as a public demonstration of Stroud's anti-slavery heritage, as well as 'the connection between the past and the present'.[5]

It is instructive to compare Wyatt's anti-slavery archway with Charles Buxton's memorial drinking fountain, which was originally erected in Parliament Square at the corner of Great George Street in 1865–66, presumably to mark the abolition of slavery in the United States. The precise details are unclear, but it seems likely that Buxton took over this project from the Metropolitan Drinking Fountain Association, which, since its inception in 1859, had been campaigning to erect 'a costly and handsome fountain in Palace Yard'.[6] Dedicated to Buxton's father, Sir Thomas Fowell Buxton, and 'those associated with him: Wilberforce, Clarkson, Macaulay, Brougham, Dr Lushington and others', the monument has eight open arches, supported on clustered pillars of polished marble, arranged around a large central shaft with four massive granite drinking basins. The most distinctive feature of the fountain, however, is its ornamental spire. Rather than use lead, which invariably gave monuments 'a dark and sombre hue', or slates, which produced an effect of 'thinness', Buxton chose instead to use plaques of iron, 'with raised patterns giving shadow, while colour [was] imparted by the surfaces being enamelled'.[7]

Buxton's memorial drinking fountain, which he designed himself with the help of the architect, Samuel Saunders Teulon, was highly idiosyncratic. Strangely, it bore no visual references to British anti-slavery either in terms of statues or abolitionist motifs (the figure of the kneeling slave, for example).

6   Charles Buxton's memorial drinking fountain (c. 1865), Victoria
Embankment Gardens, London

Even the inscription at the base of the monument is curiously understated, although it is worth pointing out that the original plaques were subsequently removed; the current inscription dates from the early twentieth century.[8] None of this would have mattered so much had the drinking fountain been a private memorial, like Wyatt's anti-slavery archway. As a public monument, however, Buxton's fountain had obvious shortcomings. Yet even this Gothic curiosity could stir emotions. When in 1949 it looked as if the Government's plans to redevelop Parliament Square might result in the memorial being moved or, worse, discarded altogether, there were loud protests from various quarters. Speaking in the House of Lords, Viscount Simon declared that to his mind Buxton's drinking fountain was exactly the sort of memorial that ought to be found at 'the hub of the Empire'. 'In the circumstances,' he went on, 'the historical aspects of [the] question [were] far more important than any judgment anyone may form now on aesthetic grounds'. Echoing these sentiments, Reginald Coupland reminded readers of *The Times* that it was 'not only our own countrymen' who were concerned in honouring the memory of the 'Saints'; it was also 'the peoples of Africa who are now fellow-members with us of the Commonwealth'.[9]

In fairness, it seems unlikely that anyone seriously meant to 'destroy' Buxton's memorial, yet at the same time the Government made it perfectly clear that the drinking fountain could not be integrated into its plans for Parliament Square without ruining them 'completely'. Eventually, the two sides reached a compromise, which is how the memorial came to be re-erected on its present site in Victoria Embankment Gardens, where it forms part of a somewhat strained narrative that includes Rodin's statue of *The Burghers of Calais* (1914–15) and a more conventional monument commemorating the suffragette, Emmeline Pankhurst.[10] Buxton's drinking fountain remains an important site of memory; it is revealing, for instance, that the Anti-Slavery Society chose to celebrate its 150th anniversary in 1989 by embellishing the fountain with a special commemorative plaque. Nevertheless, a more effective memorial can be found a short distance away in Westminster Abbey, which, with some justification, has been described as the 'sanctuary of the British establishment'. Here, visitors are presented with a history of abolition that is at once familiar and reassuring. As one might expect, many of the key figures associated with British anti-slavery are commemorated in Westminster Abbey, among them William Pitt, Charles James Fox, and Granville Sharp (the 'father' of the Clapham Sect), whose simple memorial tablet is placed somewhat incongruously in Poet's Corner.[11] Important as these figures are, however, it is Wilberforce who dominates this discourse, in much the same way that he dominates other 'histories' of British anti-slavery. Indeed, Wilberforce's close identification with the 'national Valhalla' serves as yet another reminder of his heroic (even iconic) status.

Tradition has it that Wilberforce left instructions in his will that he wanted to be buried 'with the utmost privacy' in Newington churchyard. But in retrospect it seems unlikely that this was ever going to happen. Indeed, no sooner had Wilberforce died than his friends and colleagues, led by over 40 members of both houses of Parliament, prevailed upon the family to 'allow the funeral to be a public one, and the place of internment to be Westminster Abbey, that solemn habitation of "the departed great"', thus conferring on him 'the highest possible honour'. The funeral on 4 August 1833 was a grand public occasion. At 12.30, horsemen 'two and two abreast' led the procession from Cadogan Place, where Wilberforce had died, to Westminster Abbey, followed by the hearse, drawn by six richly caparisoned horses; eight mourning coaches, the first containing Wilberforce's sons; and 50 noblemen's and gentlemen's carriages. In this manner, the procession moved slowly towards the Abbey 'accompanied by immense crowds of people, who flanked it, in moving columns, on either side'.[12] Having arrived at Westminster Abbey, the mourners were joined by members of the House of Lords, led by the Duke of Wellington; the Archbishop of Canterbury and the Dean and Chapter of Westminster Abbey; and members of the House of Commons. Among the pallbearers were the Lord Chancellor, the Marquis of Westminster, His Royal Highness, the Duke of Gloucester, and Sir Robert Harry Inglis. *The Times* reported the following day that the Abbey was 'crowded by persons of distinction, amongst whom were many ladies'. Apparently, there were also several blacks in the congregation, as well as a number of American visitors, including William Lloyd Garrison.[13]

Though not a state occasion, an honour usually reserved for monarchs, Wilberforce's funeral bore all the trappings of an upper-class or state funeral – from the procession to the first-class hearse to the distinguished pall-bearers. The rituals associated with these occasions had a special resonance and meaning. As Avner Ben-Amos observes of French state funerals, the journey of the body through crowded streets 'conferred upon the deceased the sanctity of popular esteem, and turned the funeral into a momentous event that produced considerable reverberations'. In the same way, the large crowds that turned out to pay their respects to Wilberforce were a vital part of the process whereby he was transformed into one of the nation's 'ancestors'. The farewell ceremony in Westminster Abbey, which by definition was a more elite affair, played a similar role in elevating Wilberforce into the panoply of 'great men'.[14] Whether the Wilberforces had intended it or not, their decision to allow their father to be buried in Westminster Abbey immediately lifted him above his 'coadjutors' and conferred upon him a special status, that of a national hero.

The funeral service in Westminster Abbey was but one mark of the esteem in which Wilberforce was held by 'the rank, talent, and virtue of the country'. In August 1833, his friends in London, many of them MPs, agreed to raise a subscription for the 'purpose of doing honour to the memory of Wilberforce'. Part of this fund was later used to build the Wilberforce Memorial Hall in Freetown, Sierra Leone.[15] But most of it was expended on a memorial to Wilberforce in Westminster Abbey. The commission was given to Samuel Joseph (d. 1850), who had already produced a bust of Wilberforce for the Yorkshire School for the Blind in York.[16] Offered a chance to extend both his range and his skills, Joseph turned for inspiration to George Richmond's watercolour of Wilberforce (1832–33), in which the 'great emancipator' is portrayed smiling benignly from the corner of a large armchair, his body twisted and frail.[17] Joseph's attempt to imitate Richmond met with a mixed reception, however. Critics like John Scandrett Harford complained that the life-size statue, which was fixed in position in the Musicians' Aisle in 1840, gave 'undue prominence to the singularity of [Wilberforce's] figure in later years'. Others thought that Wilberforce's likeness bore rather the 'aspect of Mephistopheles [the tempting spirit of hell] than that of the serene Christian philanthropist'.[18] Up to a point, there was some justice in these criticisms: Joseph's Wilberforce is an alarmingly contorted figure whose averted gaze hardly inspires confidence.

7   Wilberforce Memorial (1840), Westminster Abbey

Yet, at the same time, there is a warmth and humour about the statue that is immediately engaging. Moreover, it succeeds in conveying something of Wilberforce's frailty, which in a curious way only adds to the measure of his achievements. Here, in other words, is a different kind of hero: slight, frail, and vulnerable, but for all that courageous and victorious.

Whatever its defects, Wilberforce's statue, like his tablet in the North Transept, helped to fix Wilberforce and abolition at the centre of the nation's history, as well as its public memory. If anything, this association between Wilberforce and Westminster Abbey became stronger as time went on. In 1939, for instance, the family donated a significant sum of money towards restoration of the Islip Chapel as a memorial to three generations of Wilberforces: William; his son, Samuel, some time Dean of Westminster (1845); and his grandson, Albert Basil Orme Wilberforce, who was Canon and Archdeacon of Westminster for nearly twenty years.[19] At the same time, other members of Wilberforce's intimate circle were also given space in the Abbey, among them

Zachary Macaulay whose marble bust in the North-west Tower is significant because it is one of the few public abolitionist monuments that recognises or incorporates a black presence, in this case a figure of a kneeling slave, together with the motto, 'Am I Not A Man And A Brother' (for the most part, abolitionist monuments tended to dissociate themselves from enslaved or freed Africans, at least in visual terms). More representative, by far, is the simple, life-size statute of Sir Thomas Fowell Buxton, which in 1844 was erected in the North Choir Aisle of Westminster Abbey by 'his friends and fellow labourers at home and abroad; assisted by the grateful contributions of many thousands of the African race'.[20]

To all intents and purposes, the integrity of this narrative, which unashamedly highlighted the role of the Clapham Sect and of Wilberforce, in particular, in abolishing transatlantic slavery, remained undisturbed until the 1990s.[21] Yet, like many histories, it was selective; more to the point, it studiously ignored Clarkson. The reasons for this oversight (if that is what it was) are not difficult to fathom. As we have seen, Clarkson was in many ways an outsider. James Stephen was more blunt. 'Far from us be the attempt to pluck one leaf from the crown which rests on that time-honoured head', he wrote in the *Edinburgh Review* in 1843. 'But with truth there may be no compromise, and truth wrings from us the acknowledgment, that Thomas Clarkson never lived in Clapham'.[22] At the same time, neither he nor his family possessed the political muscle to press his case for inclusion, even if they had wanted to; and the indications are that they did not (although it is surely significant that Clarkson's only son – in fact, his only child – pre-deceased him, thus robbing him of a political heir who might have fought to preserve his memory). Whatever the reason, Clarkson's absence from Westminster Abbey served only to reinforce his marginal status and hence his uncertain place in the nation's memory.[23]

This silence or omission did not pass unnoticed; Dean Stanley, for instance, drew attention to it in his *Historical Memorials of Westminster Abbey* (1868).[24] Yet, strangely, it was not until 1996 that Clarkson was finally granted a place in the 'national Valhalla'. Significantly, the impetus came from Wisbech, Clarkson's birthplace, where in September 1993 a special committee was organised to plan ahead for the 150th anniversary of Clarkson's death in September 1996. Though many of its activities were local in focus, from the outset the committee set out to win for Clarkson the sort of national recognition that in its view was long overdue. A number of factors appear to have been important here. One was undoubtedly the example set by the nationwide celebrations held to mark the 150th anniversary of Wilberforce's death in 1983.[25] Another was the support and encouragement of figures like Ellen Wilson Gibson, whose biography of Clarkson appeared in 1990, and Richard Clarkson, a retired aerodynamics expert and one of Clarkson's few remaining descendants. Clarkson was understandably keen to mark the 1996 anniversary in some way, having already been instrumental in helping to restore the family vault at Playford Church. Like Gibson, he was also excited by a proposal that

8 Zachary Macaulay Memorial (1842), Westminster Abbey

appears to have been in the air since 1991, and was certainly close to the hearts of the members of the Wisbech committee, namely to place a suitable memorial in Westminster Abbey.[26]

With this in mind, every effort was made to ensure that the memorial campaign was inclusive rather than exclusive, and that it linked Clarkson to the ongoing struggle against slavery and oppression, particularly in the Third World. While most members of the anniversary committee were local and had some connection with groups like the Wisbech Society, it also included two representatives from Anti-Slavery International: ASI, for its part, clearly regarded the committee's work as an important means of establishing foundations (not least, in terms of raising public consciousness about slavery) from which it might 'leap into the twenty-first century'. In the same way, the committee tried to ensure that the campaign involved other sites associated with Clarkson, notably Playford, near Ipswich. Not only did a representative from Playford sit on the committee between 1993 and 1995, but every effort was

made to liase with Ware Borough Council, which was responsible for the
Clarkson memorial in Wadesmill, and St John's College, Cambridge.[27]

Keen to make as big an impact as possible, the 150th anniversary committee pursued a number of different initiatives, among them a set of commemorative postage stamps, Wedgwood plaques, and a series of public lectures.[28] At
the heart of its endeavours, however, was the memorial idea. Initial soundings
were not favourable. For one thing, it was feared that Westminster Abbey was
already 'full' of monuments. For another, the committee's contacts indicated
that to stand any chance of success an application would require the backing
of 'eminent people', and not just 'family and friends'. Undeterred, the 150th
anniversary committee came up with the names of six 'distinguished supporters', including the Right Reverend Stephen Sykes, Bishop of Ely, the Duke of
Grafton, and Lord Tonypandy, formerly Speaker of the House of Commons.[29]
Thanks to their efforts, in May 1995 the committee was finally given the go-
ahead to place a tablet in the floor of the Musicians' Aisle, close to the statue
of William Wilberforce.[30] Almost a year later, a national appeal was launched,
headed by the Duke of Grafton and supported by Lord Tonypandy, Richard
Clarkson, and the Right Honourable Lord Wilberforce, which, in all, raised
over £14,000.[31]

Appropriately, the official unveiling of the memorial took place on 26 September 1996, the actual anniversary date. Shortly after evensong, members of
the anniversary committee met in the Lantern, where the Dean of Westminster
conducted a short dedication service, which included Wordsworth's sonnet,
'To Thomas Clarkson', as well as a reading from Clarkson's *History*. Then Professor Peter Goddard, Master of St. John's College, Cambridge, was invited to
come forward to unveil the memorial, a tablet of Cumbrian green slate with
the simple inscription, 'A Friend to Slaves / Thomas Clarkson / b. Wisbech
1760 – 1846 d. Playford'.[32] In his address, the Right Reverend Stephen Sykes
adverted to the 'dispute initiated by Wilberforce's two sons', pronouncing that
it was now 'surely at an end'. The memorial, in other words, was viewed and
presented as an act of closure. At the same time, Sykes was keen to stress the
meaning of Clarkson's achievements and the importance of his example. 'We
honour Clarkson best,' he concluded, 'when we acknowledge how much our
country owes to men and women of moral passion, when we ourselves engage
in their vision, and commit ourselves unequivocally to discern and to do the
good we have it in our power to accomplish'.[33]

Its work done, the 150th anniversary committee disbanded; in fact, its last
meeting took place on 25 March 1997. The struggle was over. Today, visitors
to Westminster Abbey will find Wilberforce and Clarkson side by side once
again, even if Clarkson does lie at the feet of his erstwhile 'coadjutor'. (An
interesting variation on the same theme can be found at St John's College,
Cambridge, where a copy of Joseph's statue of Wilberforce stands inside the
college chapel, while a statue of Clarkson is fixed in a niche outside.)[34] How
successful this attempt will prove to rewrite the public history of British anti-
slavery, at least as it is presented in the 'national Valhalla', is difficult to judge.

Rightly or wrongly, Clarkson has always been a contentious figure. If the memorial in Westminster Abbey hints at a resolution and an end to the Wilberforce controversy, this should not be taken to imply that Clarkson's rehabilitation is complete. In fact, it has only just begun.

Uniquely among British abolitionists, Wilberforce and Clarkson are also associated with a number of local sites of memory. In Wilberforce's case, the list of these sites is impressively long. Visitors will find Wilberforce plaques and memorials in London (44, Cadogan Place), Bath (Great Pulteney Street), Cambridge (St John's College), and Holwood, near Bromley, Kent, where Pitt is said to have urged Wilberforce to bring forward a motion in the House of Commons for the abolition of the slave trade.[35] A plaque marks the former site of Wilberforce's home in Clapham, itself an important site of memory; and another can be found in St Paul's Church in Mill Hill, which was built largely at Wilberforce's expense. Wilberforce is also associated with a number of other sites, many of which have either been destroyed or redeveloped: Pocklington School, Yorkshire; Lauriston House, Wimbledon; Rayrigg, Cumbria; Barham Court, Teston, Kent; Gore House, Kensington Gore; Wilford Hall, Nottingham; Marden Park, Godstone, Surrey; and Grove House, Brompton.[36]

When we think of Wilberforce, however, we tend to think of his birthplace, Kingston upon Hull, which was also his first parliamentary seat (1780–84). Despite reports of public indifference, Hull was quick to honour Wilberforce. Within weeks of his death in July 1833 a public meeting was held in the old Mansion House in Lowgate to consider erecting 'some lasting monument' to Wilberforce's memory, and a committee of all the subscribers was set up, led by the mayor, John Barkworth, and the Rev. Henry Venn, vicar of St Peter's Church, Drypool.[37] From the first, this was intended to be a 'popular' monument and, as such, a spontaneous expression of Hull's determination to commemorate Wilberforce and his achievements. As Kirk Savage has argued, what gave monuments of this kind their 'peculiar appeal' was their claim to speak for 'the people'. Hence the importance of the 'voluntary subscription'; the involvement of the subscribers in the decision-making process; and 'the rituals of corner-stone laying and dedication, where great crowds gathered and symbolically erected the monument'.[38]

The debate in Hull sheds important light on the memorialising process, not least as a contested space. As is so often the case, opinion differed over an appropriate site for the monument. In all, the committee considered three different options. The first of these, and the one favoured by the architect, W. H. Clark of Leeds, was at the very end of Queen Street, overlooking the River Humber. This idea of the monument as a beacon of liberty, visible to 'the fleets of the world' as they approached or left the town, seems to have been popular with many of the subscribers, despite the fact that it involved extra expense. Such a memorial, it was claimed, would spread the fame of Britain (and hence Hull) 'to the remotest regions of earth; not merely as a mart of wealth, the soil of industry, the seat of science, or the source of power or of glory, but as the land of freedom and religion where good deeds formed the highest claims to greatness, and where the memory of the just would be imperishable'.[39] But both the Queen Street site and a second site in Kingston Square were eventually passed over in favour of a third site opposite the Dispensary, near the Junction Dock Bridge, overlooking the old town. To Venn, at least, the merits of this alternative site were obvious. As he explained at a public meeting held in April 1834, a monument placed here 'would present itself prominently upon entering Hull from the York road and fill up the vista of Whitefriargate'. In other words, it would form a 'conspicuous object at the principal entrance into the town', and thus impose itself dramatically upon the urban landscape.[40]

Opinion was equally divided over what form the proposed monument should take, some favouring a simple column or obelisk, others insisting that the column should incorporate a statue. Here again, the debate revealed a keen awareness of the value of monuments and their role in shaping public memory. Throwing its weight behind the statue idea, the *Hull Advertiser* explained that 'the sculptured features of the illustrious dead are eloquent even in their immortality'. To contemporaries, it went on, they recalled 'hours of triumph yet "freshly remembered"'; while 'to observers of an after day, they [were] precious historical relics' that marshalled posterity into the presence of 'ancestral greatness', and gratified 'the longing common to intelligent curiosity, and not unworthy of it, to know how they looked in life, the lustre of whose achievements has irradiated the midnight of the tomb'. Wilberforce's frail and twisted form, seemingly out of all proportion to the 'majesty of spirit that dwelt within it', served also to illustrate another important truth, namely 'that the high purposes of Providence are not destined to be accomplished by the vain agencies which dazzle the bulk of mankind'.[41]

Eventually, the committee came round to the idea of a statue. They were less successful, however, in getting the Hull monument adopted as a 'county memorial'. Not to be outdone, a large county meeting held in October 1833 had decided to honour Wilberforce by setting up a school for the indigent blind in York. Part of the reasoning behind the school idea was that this (or some other 'institution of usefulness') was what Wilberforce himself would have wanted. But there was also a feeling that a column or statue was somehow inadequate, particularly in this case. As the *York Herald* put it, the Hull memorial 'will be but a mere erection of stone, in honour of a worthy individual, and grateful to the sight of those who will pass it'. The proposed county memorial, on the other hand, blended 'with those objects far higher and nobler purposes'. Its supporters would 'not only gratify the sight of the admiring strangers but relieve the wants ... of those who have no sight'. Of course, it is tempting to put down such comments to civic pride, or what might be described as a competitive humanitarian market. Nevertheless, there appears to have been widespread support for the school idea, even among the inhabitants of Hull, not least because it was felt that it would help to 'perpetuate the spirit of Wilberforce, and enable his countrymen to imitate his virtues'.[42]

As it happened, these competing claims proved highly disruptive. Backed by some of the most prominent men in the country, including the Lord Chancellor, the Archbishop of York, and Earl Fitzwilliam, the York appeal was an immediate success. By July 1834 nearly £8,000 had been donated towards the 'Yorkshire School for the Blind', in addition to which £333 had been received in annual subscriptions.[43] The Hull Memorial Appeal, on the other hand, started to falter. Whatever hopes the organisers might have had that theirs would be adopted as the 'county memorial' were quickly dashed with the appearance of the school idea; and, despite attempts to link the two appeals together, it was perhaps inevitable they should have been seen as rivals, or, at least, as 'separate and different'. Shunned by the county at large, the Hull subscription soon ran into difficulties. By April 1834 it stood at around £900, still some way short of the £1,100 then thought necessary to complete the project. Even as late as August, when Richard Bethell, MP, laid the foundation stone, the funds were described as 'still scanty'. 'The dimensions which we propose for our intended column will be of an imposing magnitude,' Venn assured the large crowd that had gathered to witness the ceremony, 'but we must depend on further subscriptions to give it the grace and ornament which it will justly deserve'.[44]

In all, it took over twelve months to complete the Wilberforce Monument: the statue was fixed in place on 12 November 1835 and the scaffolding was finally removed some weeks later.[45] Rising to approximately 110 feet and by some way the tallest and most imposing public monument in Hull, the Wilberforce Monument consisted of a fluted Doric column on a square pedestal ornamented with the arms of the town, the Dock Company, the Trinity House, and the Wilberforce family. The pedestal also contained inscriptions, which together plotted their own narrative strategy, thereby reinforcing Wilberforce's claim to be considered the 'great emancipator' and hence first among equals: 'Wilberforce / Voluntary Subscription, 1 August 1834 / First Stone Laid, 1 August 1834 / Negro Slavery Abolished, 1 August 1834'. Although it was hardly visible from the ground, except 'by a sort of under-perspective, with an upturned eye', the tapered column was surmounted by a twelve-foot statue of Wilberforce 'in his senatorial robes with a folded scroll in his [right] hand', which was fixed so that he overlooked the Old Town.[46]

In design and conception, the Wilberforce Monument echoed William Wilkins' Nelson Column (1808) in Dublin, the Lord Hill Column (1815–16) in Shrewsbury, and the Melville Column (1821) in Edinburgh, which, in turn, were all variants of the Napoleonic Vendôme Column (1810) in Paris.[47] It also anticipated Nelson's Column in Trafalgar Square (1839–40) and the towering Wellington Monument at Stratfield Saye (1866). But by and large these were military memorials that celebrated martial valour, conquest, and supreme human sacrifice. The decision to use the same design for a political figure, and especially one who had never held high political office, was therefore bold and innovative. Not only did the column form enhance Wilberforce's heroic status, by raising him high above ordinary men and women, but it also

9   Wilberforce Monument (1835), Kingston upon Hull

invited comparisons with figures like Nelson and Wellington, which was obviously the intention. Indeed, in the popular mythology surrounding
Wilberforce it is striking how often he was linked with Nelson and Wellington,
and how often his contemporaries reached for military metaphors ('warrior',
'war', 'victory') to explain his significance. Aesthetic considerations were
important here, too. Opinion was generally agreed that pillars elevated people's
thoughts, as well as their senses. The Tory diarist, J. W. Croker, spoke for
many when he argued that 'great height' was the 'cheapest way and one of the
most certain of obtaining sublimity'. 'Whatever you do be at least sure to
make it stupendously high', Croker had written enthusiastically to the secretary of the Wellington Fund in Dublin in 1814. 'Let it be of all the columns in
the world the most lofty'.[48]

  In other words, the Wilberforce Monument was designed to make an important statement, both about Wilberforce himself and, by implication, about
Hull's civic identity. Yet Venn's hopes for the monument (and the site) were
only partially realised. By the turn of the century, it 'stood amid a mass of
mainly squalid buildings and streets, of which only Savile and Chariot streets
counted as respectable'. Not surprisingly, plans drawn up around 1900 to 'turn
Hull into a place of pomp and circumstance', included two projects in the
vicinity of the monument: Victoria Square (1901) and City Hall (1903).[49] As a

result, the column became part of a formal public space that was not only designed to celebrate Hull's civic pretensions, but also its place in the national and imperial panorama: the juxtaposition of Wilberforce and a smaller, squatter statue of Queen Victoria was particularly evocative, reinforcing Hull's (and the nation's) civilising mission. Yet, as Harry Cartlidge's photographs from the 1930s make abundantly clear, the integrity of this space was severely compromised. Looking west down Whitefriargate, the Wilberforce Monument towers over the statue of Queen Victoria behind it and partially obscures City Hall; if anything, it seems strangely at odds with the buildings around it, almost as if it had been placed there by mistake.[50]

More serious still, the monument blocked communications between the eastern and western parts of the city (as it now was), creating a major bottleneck. Finally, in 1935 the City Council decided to move it to a new site on the Queen's Dock Estate, although to judge from local newspapers its removal had been a recurring topic of debate for more than a quarter of a century. The delicate task of relocating the monument was undertaken free of charge by Robert G. Tarran, a local builder and city councillor, who some years earlier had been implicated in an official inquiry into alleged irregularities over the purchase of land for housing estates.[51] Under Tarran's watchful and opportunistic gaze, the dismantling of the Wilberforce Monument instantly became a major local spectacle. From the moment work began in April 1935 ladders were fixed inside the scaffolding so that for a small charge (2s 6d during the day and 1s in the evening) visitors could climb up the monument and admire the view. Similarly, once Wilberforce's statue had been lowered to the ground, it was placed in a marquee erected on the Queen's Dock site and put on public display, together with other slavery artefacts. Local businesses were also quick to get in on the act. 'A Feat Accomplished', boasted an advertisement in the *Hull Daily Mail*. 'Electricity removes Wilberforce from his resting place in a few moments / The Slave Emancipator helped on his journey by the modern abolisher of slavery in the home and factory / Let Electricity help you in your daily work and make your life easier and happier'.[52]

Part of the excitement, of course, lay in seeing Wilberforce at close quarters for the first time. The *Hull Daily Mail* reported on 17 May 1935 that 'several hundred' people had already visited the marquee on the Queen's Dock site, including a civic party made up of the Lady Mayoress, the Sheriff and his wife, and Mrs Arnold Reckitt, one of Wilberforce's great-granddaughters. For some, it seems, the experience was both a shock and a disappointment. As one visitor put it: 'This stone giant, whose cold and soot-caked robes hang over you like a gable, and whose roll of parchment looks like a minor piece of ordnance, is not the same as the mildly dignified gentlemen we have seen so often from the street. Close to, his fixed expression gives you the idea that he hides some special private joke'.[53] While all this was going on, work was nearing completion on the new site at the Queen's Dock Estate. Significantly, the official rededication service was timed to coincide with the opening of the new Queen's Gardens on 18 September 1935. In a short ceremony presided over by Sir Alfred Gelder, chairman of the local committee responsible for the rejuvenation of the Queen's Dock Estate, Mrs Arnold Reckitt officially unveiled the monument, after which the company retired to the banqueting room at the Guildhall. In its new location, the Wilberforce Monument dominated the eastern end of the city, but did so in a manner that spatially, at least, was entirely in keeping with the 'broad lawns' and 'wide boulevards' that surrounded it. The relocation of the monument also had a wider symbolic significance. In 1835 Wilberforce had been 'so placed to fix his gaze on the Old Town'. 'His new site and his new setting', however, enabled him 'to see a little more of the extent of Hull's growth'.[54]

This is not quite the end of the story, however. In what was to be the final phase of the redevelopment of Queen's Gardens, the area around the Wilberforce Monument was transformed into College Circle, so named after the technical college that dominated the site behind it (that is, to the east of the memorial). But then in 1957 the circle, really a sort of roundabout, was filled in to make way for Wilberforce Drive, effectively stranding the monument on the 'wrong side' of Queen's Gardens.[55] As a result, it began to take on a new resonance and meaning. Today, the Wilberforce Monument dominates the piazza in front of what is now Hull College. Adjacent to it stands a teaching and administration block that, appropriately enough, is called the 'Wilberforce Building'. Perhaps more revealing still, Hull College has adopted a silhouette of the Wilberforce Monument as its official logo, a gesture that has undoubtedly breathed new life into Wilberforce's legacy, while at the same time providing the college with a ready-made 'history' or patina.

Of course, there is one other Wilberforce memorial in Hull and that is his birthplace in the old High Street, now the site of the Wilberforce House Museum. The only surviving example of a number of seventeenth-century brick-built merchants' houses, Wilberforce House originally passed into the hands of the Wilberforce family in 1732 and would remain their property until 1830 when William Wilberforce was forced to sell it to pay off the debts of his eldest son, also William.[56] Thereafter, it fell steadily into a state of decay and dilapidation until the 1890s when it was rescued by Councillor (later Alderman) John Brown, who seems immediately to have grasped its significance as a site of memory. Alert to the fact that if the house were sold it would quickly fall into the hands of 'speculative investors', Brown sought to convince his fellow councillors that 'such a fate [could] surely never be permitted', for the simple reason that Wilberforce's birthplace claimed 'a degree of veneration' that was 'not merely local, or even national, but worldwide'. Brown went further, drawing an interesting parallel between Wilberforce and other national heroes, among them prominent literary figures. As he explained in a pamphlet published in 1896: 'Stratford-on-Avon shows the house of Shakespeare, Edinburgh shows the house of Knox, Chelsea shows the house of Carlyle. Why should not Hull show the house of Wilberforce?'[57]

Others were not quite so convinced, however. In fact, it took Brown and his supporters, who included Thomas Sheppard, Curator of Hull Museums,

10 Wilberforce House Museum, Kingston upon Hull

nearly seven years to realise their ambitions for Wilberforce House. Hull Corporation finally completed the purchase of the property in April 1903, whereupon work began on essential repairs to the exterior, while nearly £800 was
spent on making good the staircase and the two front rooms. Three years
later, on 24 August 1906, the house was officially opened to the public by Cecil
George Savile, 4th Earl of Liverpool, in his capacity as a former president of
the East Riding Antiquarian Society.[58] Though dedicated to documenting
Hull's social history, Wilberforce House Museum immediately became associated with Wilberforce and with Wilberforce's struggle against transatlantic
slavery. This is not the place to discuss the museum's role as the country's first
(anti-)slavery museum, but it is worth noting in passing the acquisition of
William Day Keyworth's impressive life-size statue of Wilberforce, which had
originally been presented to the town in 1883 by Henry Briggs, one of Hull's
sheriffs. In 1912 the statue was moved from City Hall to its present location in
the front garden of Wilberforce House where it became an important site of
local memory, not least because its human scale made it altogether more ac-
cessible than the rather cold and remote figure who stands on top of the
Wilberforce Monument.[59]

Taken together, the Wilberforce Monument and Wilberforce House Museum have helped to shape Hull's public identity; in fact, the city's associations

with Wilberforce and the values he is supposed to represent are probably stronger today than they have ever been. This is perhaps most evident in Hull's close links with Sierra Leone. Wilberforce, of course, was one of the original sponsors of the Sierra Leone 'experiment' and it is fitting, therefore, that in 1982 Hull should have been twinned with Freetown (the capital of Sierra Leone), an arrangement that, in turn, led to the city's northern link road being (re)named Freetown Way.[60] Equally revealing is the city council's decision in 1995 to institute the Wilberforce Lecture, an idea that seems to have been originally mooted as far back as the 1930s.[61] As the plaques displayed proudly in Hull's Guildhall attest, the list of speakers and Wilberforce medallion winners is impressive, and includes Hugh O'Shaughnessy, formerly foreign correspondent of the *Observer*, the Nigerian novelist, Wole Soyinka, and Archbishop Emeritus Desmond Tutu, whose lecture in 1999 coincided with the celebrations held to mark the 700th anniversary of the granting of Hull's first town charter.[62]

In the same spirit, early in 2005 Hull unveiled Wilberforce 2007, a 'unique pan-city partnership' aimed at 'collectively positioning the spirit of Wilberforce across the globe and recognising that it is still alive in Hull today'. Here again, Freetown features prominently in these plans, but equally revealing are two other initiatives; one to make Wilberforce House a world heritage site, the other to set up the Wilberforce Institute for the Study of Slavery and Emancipation (WISE), with funding from Yorkshire Forward and Hull City Council. Yet what exactly is 'the spirit of Wilberforce'? A clue can be found in the terms and references of WISE, which aims to be 'one of the world's leading research centres for the cutting edge study of slavery and emancipation, keeping the Wilberforce legacy alive and acting as a platform for exploring modern human rights issues'.[63] This association between Wilberforce and human rights is echoed in the following extract from a lecture given by Sir Shridath Ramphal, Secretary-General of the British Commonwealth, at Hull University in 1983, which is preserved on a tablet in the Nelson Mandela Gardens in Hull's Museum Quarter: 'We tarnish and depreciate the memory of Wilberforce so long as slavery South Africa style flaunts its evil and defies our will to curb it, sensing our resolve to be a fragile thing'.[64] In other words, these memorials claim Wilberforce as an early human rights campaigner, whose merits and achievements are best understood in terms of the progress of 'democracy'.[65] Whether Wilberforce would have recognised himself in such a portrait is besides the point; rather, what we are witnessing here is the manipulation or rearrangement of Wilberforce's status and reputation in order to conform with 'our ideas of the moment'.[66]

Like Wilberforce, Clarkson is also associated with a number of sites of local memory. One of these is Wadesmill in Hertfordshire, the scene of his conversion to abolitionism in 1785. Clarkson had memorably described this incident in his *History* but it was not until 1833, when Clarkson revisited Wadesmill with James Merivale (later Dean of Ely), that the exact spot was located.

Speaking years later, Merivale recalled that 'he had always borne [the site] in mind', and it was largely through his efforts and those of a local landowner, James Puller, that in 1879 a stone obelisk was put up, bearing the simple inscription, 'On the spot where stands this monument in the month of June 1785 Thomas Clarkson resolved to devote his life to bring about the Abolition of the Slave Trade'.[67] Whether Puller's gesture was part of a series of coordinated commemorative acts is impossible to determine, but from this date Wadesmill became one of three sites intimately connected with Clarkson, the others being Playford, near Ipswich, and Wisbech in Cambridgeshire. In 1972 the obelisk was moved a few yards north-west of its original site on the A10 to make room for road improvements, but otherwise it remained untouched and unprotected until 1996 when Ware Borough Council arranged for the inscription to be covered with an acrylic plastic screen, and for the plaque to be replaced in bronze, as part of the celebrations to mark the 150th anniversary of Clarkson's death.[68]

Clarkson's association with Playford dated from 1816 when he and his wife, Catherine, became tenants of Playford Hall, a sixteenth-century manor house and farm owned by the Marquis of Bristol.[69] Over the years, the hall and its tenants played host to many of the leading abolitionists on both sides of the Atlantic, including William Lloyd Garrison, George Thompson, Frederick Douglass, and Henry Stanton.[70] Playford was a place of pilgrimage, a shrine where visitors came to pay their respects to Clarkson and, later, to Clarkson's memory. Harriet Beecher Stowe, for instance, visited Playford Hall in 1853 and recalled being shown into 'a large chamber overlooking the courtyard, which had been Clarkson's own room; the room where for years, many of his most important labours had been conducted'. Stowe was clearly deeply affected by the whole experience. 'When I retired to my room for the night I could not but feel that the place was hallowed,' she confessed, 'unceasing prayer had there been offered for the enslaved and wronged race of Africa by that noble and brotherly heart. I could not but feel that those prayers had had a wider reach than the mere extinction of slavery in one land or country, and that their benign influence would not cease while a slave was left upon the face of the earth.'[71]

In all, Clarkson lived at Playford for over thirty years. It was natural, therefore, that he should have chosen to be buried just a short distance away in Playford Church. As we have seen, Wilberforce's funeral had been a grand public occasion that helped to affirm his place among the nation's 'great men'. Clarkson's funeral, by contrast, was a simple affair. At a few minutes past one o'clock on Friday 2 October 1846 the hearse and four mourning coaches left Playford Hall and made their way to the church, where they were joined by a small party of mourners that included John Beaumont, Joseph Soul, Secretary of the British and Foreign Anti-Slavery Society, and George Ransome. After a short service, Clarkson's body was conveyed to the family vault on the south side of the church, where he was buried with his son, Thomas, who had died in 1837. There was no pomp, no show. It was, if anything, a village affair. 'Few of those who are accounted noble upon earth watched him to the grave,' observed one local newspaper, 'but never were remains followed to their last resting place by a sincerer band of mourners'.[72]

For obvious reasons, Playford Church would become an important site of memory, even if its remoteness from centres of power undoubtedly had a bearing on Clarkson's claim to history. Catherine Clarkson, however, seems to have resisted any attempts to embellish her husband's memory with plaques and ornaments.[73] The large granite obelisk erected in the churchyard in Clarkson's memory dates from 1857 (that is, after Catherine's death), and was the brainchild of Sir George Biddell Airy, the Astronomer Royal, and Henry Crabb Robinson, among others. Later still, Mary Clarkson, Clarkson's niece and daughter-in-law, erected a medallion and tablet inside Playford Church, which commemorates Clarkson, his wife, Catherine, their son, Thomas, and their grandson, also Thomas, who died in 1872.[74] Together, these relics serve as important reminders of Clarkson's devotion to the 'cause of Africa', and for this reason they have always assumed a significance that transcends the immediate locale. When the family vault fell into disrepair during the 1930s, for instance, the Anti-Slavery and Aborigines Protection Society and Wisbech Museum and Literary Institution both offered to help finance the restoration work, and more recently Richard Clarkson raised a large sum of money to re-paint the railings around the grave, clear the ground, and to erect three new commemorative plaques.[75]

11   Playford Church, Ipswich

The other site, of course, is Wisbech, Clarkson's birthplace. Following his death in 1846 the town considered a number of schemes to commemorate Clarkson's achievements, including restoration of the Old Grammar School, where his father, the Rev. John Clarkson, had been the headmaster.[76] But for one reason or another all of these proposals came to nothing. Finally, in 1874 or 1875 (the precise details are unclear) a local committee organised by Jonathan Peckover, among others, came up with the idea of a public monument. The timing was significant. By the 1870s the campaign to abolish slavery, first in the British Caribbean and then the United States, had come to an end. It made sense, therefore, to commemorate an event that was now located firmly in the past.[77] The monument idea also reflected Wisbech's growing importance as the commercial capital of the Fen country. During the 1860s and 1870s the town embarked on a series of public improvements, including a park (opened in 1869), a hospital (1873), and extensions to the local Working Men's Club and Institute (1872–73). Many of the men behind these different initiatives, notably the Peckovers, a Quaker banking family, were also involved with the Clarkson Memorial, and it is not too fanciful to suppose that they viewed such public images as part of a wider project aimed at fostering civic pride and, with it, civic identity.[78]

Like the Wilberforce Monument, the Clarkson Memorial was clearly intended to be a popular monument, and in a sense, of course, it was. But it is equally clear that the organisers had to work very hard to 'summon the symbolic and financial participation of a "public" that the monument would represent'; in fact, for a time the whole project ran some risk of collapsing.[79] Significantly, many of the subscribers were 'outsiders' and included figures like the Duke of Devonshire, the Earl of Shaftesbury, Lord Selborne, and the Bishop of Winchester. Comparatively few of them, it seems, came from Wisbech itself, although a lot of the expense was obviously borne by the Peckover family. Speaking at the dedication service in 1881, the Rev. James Smith alluded to this fact, expressing his hope that 'the silver of [local] tradesmen and the pences of the working classes' would be 'freely offered' to help defray the costs of the memorial. Yet for all his and the committee's efforts, it never bore a truly popular or representative character.[80]

The Clarkson Memorial was finally unveiled by Sir Henry Brand, Speaker of the House of Commons, on 11 November 1881.[81] Originally designed by Sir George Gilbert Scott, whose brother, John, was Vicar of Wisbech Parish Church, the finished work is similar in style to Scott's Martyrs' Memorial (1841–43) in Oxford.[82] But whereas the Martyrs' Memorial is hexagonal, the lower storey of the Clarkson Memorial is a simple, straight-sided square buttressed at the corners. The middle storey is also square but in this case forms an open canopy, which houses Clarkson's statue, rather in the manner of Scott's Albert Memorial (1876) in Hyde Park, London. The upper storey, by contrast, is octagonal, with trefoil arches and pillars surmounted by a pierced and crocketted spire and a large gilt cross. Planted firmly on a large, twenty-two feet square platform, with six eight-inch steps, the Clarkson Memorial is a

12   Clarkson Memorial (1881), Wisbech

fine example of what one recent scholar has described as the sort of 'half-architectural and half-sculptural Gothic public monument that became so popular in Britain during the second half of the nineteenth century'.[83]

Sixty-eight feet high and erected in the centre of Wisbech in an open space close to the market and the Town Hall, the Clarkson Memorial was clearly intended to be an important local landmark. It also made a statement of a rather different kind. In his early drawings of the memorial, Scott had depicted Clarkson as he might have appeared as a young man in his twenties or thirties.[84] But at some stage this likeness was replaced by a statue of Clarkson as a much older man, draped in a gown or what might be mistaken for senatorial robes. In his left hand he holds a scroll, and in his right the 'broken fetters of a slave'. In other words, this is unmistakably a portrait of Clarkson as 'the Great Emancipator'. Clarkson, moreover, is supported by four carved bas reliefs around the base of the memorial. One of these depicts a figure of a kneeling slave, together with the motto 'Remember them that are in bonds'; another

13 Clarkson Memorial (1881), Wisbech

depicts Granville Sharp; while a third depicts Wilberforce seated at a desk, with his right hand resting on a pile of books. Thus, Scott's memorial quite deliberately places Clarkson within an identifiable narrative structure, but in doing so leaves the spectator in no doubt who is the dominant figure.[85]

To judge from local and national newspapers, the memorial caused quite a stir and momentarily, at least, it re-opened the debate about Clarkson's place in the history of British anti-slavery. *The Times*, for instance, in its coverage of the unveiling, described Clarkson as 'the backbone of the anti-slavery cause', adding that 'he [Clarkson] might not have done without Wilberforce, but neither could Wilberforce have done without him'.[86] In the same spirit of reconciliation, the celebrations held in 1884 to mark the 50th anniversary of Emancipation commemorated the memory of all the Saints, including Clarkson. At the grand jubilee meeting on 2 August, Clarkson's bust in London's Guildhall was decorated with flowers, while in his welcoming address the Prince of Wales spoke warmly of the 'undaunted Thomas Clarkson and his great Parliamentary

coadjutor William Wilberforce'.[87] Yet there was still a sense in which he did
not quite fit. Even *The Times* was forced to concede that Clarkson was 'egotis-
tic, troublesome, a man of one idea, always on one string'.[88] As a result, the
memorial failed to build up any momentum. Once the euphoria had died down,
the indisputable fact remained that Clarkson still did not have a place in the
'national Valhalla'.

The real impact, however, was felt closer to home. Put simply, Scott's memorial redefined Wisbech's public identity. Towering over Bridge Street, it
remains a constant reminder of the town's ties with British anti-slavery, as
well as the need to recognise and honour those ties, whatever the political cost
or embarrassment.[89] If anything, Wisbech's identification with Clarkson has
intensified as the economic fortunes of the town have declined. Today, visitors to Wisbech will find a blue plaque on the site of his birthplace, the Old
Grammar School in Hill Street, and another at York Row. Similarly, Clarkson
features prominently in displays at the local Wisbech and Fenland Museum:
the current (2005) permanent exhibit fills four large cases in the main gallery,
and is complemented by an impressive education pack and outreach
programme aimed at local schoolchildren. References to Clarkson can also be
found in the town's public houses and restaurants.[90] In short, he has become
an essential part of the town's flourishing heritage industry.

Without a national focus for its celebrations, however, Wisbech was always
going to be at a disadvantage, certainly when compared to Hull. This is why
the memorial in Westminster Abbey was (and is) so important. The 150th
anniversary committee not only succeeded in restoring Clarkson's name and
reputation, but, in doing so, shifted what many locals were wont to describe as
an 'alternative' version of British anti-slavery from the periphery to the centre, creating a frame of reference (a 'theatre of memory') that set Wisbech and
Playford on a par with Hull and London. The significance of this moment,
and its relevance to historians, should not be under-estimated. If in the past
places like Wisbech have sometimes struggled to make themselves heard, and
to resist the full force of the Wilberforce 'industry', they now enjoy the reflected status of national sites of memory, with all that implies.

As we have seen, there is nothing haphazard about the memorialising process; on the contrary, who and what we choose to remember is invariably
deliberate and pre-meditated. To paraphrase Maurice Halbwachs, when a society creates or modifies its traditions, it does so to 'satisfy rational needs, and
at the very moment in which they appear'.[91] One of the key choices made in
the case of transatlantic slavery was to memorialise not the victims (that is,
black slaves) but rather their 'friends' and 'liberators' (that is, white abolitionists). Collectively, abolitionist monuments were conceived as part of a
dominant white discourse that celebrated the moral triumph of figures like
Wilberforce and hence the nation's tradition of humanitarian interventionism. Such narratives continue to have a purchase among contemporary Britons. But increasingly attention has shifted away from nationalistic histories

that celebrate Britain's imperial legacy. One manifestation of this phenomenon, at least with regard to transatlantic slavery, is the growing interest shown
in black gravestones and other sites associated with the black presence in
eighteenth-century Britain.[92] Another is the appearance of memorials that
commemorate the black diasporic experience in slavery. In Bristol, for instance, a plaque on the Industrial Museum asks us to remember 'the countless
African men, women and children whose enslavement and exploitation
brought much prosperity to Bristol through the African slave trade'. Moreover, the bridge opposite the museum is dedicated to the memory of Pero
Jones, who 'belonged' to John Pinney, probably Bristol's best-known slave
merchant. In Liverpool, meanwhile, a small plaque at Albert Dock recognises
the city's links with the slave trade, although Tony Tibbles, Curator of the
Transatlantic Slavery Gallery, prefers to call this an 'information plaque' rather
than a memorial.[93]

Equally striking is the emergence of Lancaster as a key site of black remembrance. Lancaster does not usually figure very prominently in histories
of British transatlantic slavery, but for much of the eighteenth century it was
the country's fourth largest slave port. In fact, between 1745 and 1806 over
200 slave ships left Lancaster, which, in turn, were responsible for transport-
ing some 25,000 Africans across the Atlantic and into slavery.[94] It was in an
effort to recover this history that in 2002 the City Council, Lancaster Museums Service, the County Education Service, and the campaign group Globalink
set up the Slave Trade Arts Memorial Project (STAMP). Formally launched
in 2003, STAMP has been responsible for a number of different initiatives,
including an ambitious education and outreach programme led by the performance poet, SuAndi. It has also been the driving force behind a project to
create a 'permanent commemorative art piece' on the quayside in Lancaster
that would acknowledge the city's involvement in the transatlantic slave trade.
To this end, in 2004 the Manchester-based artist, Kevin Dalton-Johnson, was
commissioned to design an appropriate memorial. Funded by Lancaster City
Council, the Millennium Commission, Arts Council North West, and
Lancashire County Council, what has become known as 'Captured Africans'
was officially unveiled on 10 October 2005 (Columbus Day) in the presence of
the mayor, some 150 school children, and the black civil rights activist, Preston
King.[95]

By his own admission, Kevin Dalton-Johnson was keen to design a memorial that would contest Eurocentric views of the slave trade.[96] Instead, 'Captured Africans' is rooted very firmly in the black experience of transatlantic
slavery. The base, for instance, has embedded in it a coloured mosaic of the
eighteenth-century Atlantic world that shows how slaves were traded on the
triangular route between Europe (Lancaster), Africa, and the Americas. Moreover, scattered across the mosaic are six iron figures – some kneeling, others
lying down – that represent the slaves and the countries they were exported
to. In other words, the memorial explicitly commemorates black loss. But, at
the same time, it is also attempts to give visual expression to the goods and

14 'Captured Africans' memorial (2005), Lancaster

trade that plantation societies in the Americas supported. Above the mosaic (the sea) is fixed a ship consisting of two pillars, one a carved sandstone block (the stern), the other a stainless steel bow section that has inscribed on it details of some twenty-five slave ships that left Lancaster between 1745 and 1806.[97] Strung between these two pillars are six acrylic blocks – the decks, if you will – each of which represents a specific cargo, organised in order of importance. At the bottom are the slaves, and here Dalton-Johnson has set in the block a plan of the slave ship *Brookes*. Then above them are arranged 'sugar', 'mahogany' (the furniture makers, Gillows, were based in Lancaster), 'rum', 'cotton', and, finally, 'wealth'. Read as a whole, therefore, 'Captured Africans' attempts not only to memorialise enslaved Africans but also to put the slave trade on show, as if it were an exhibit.[98]

Not everyone has welcomed the appearance of 'Captured Africans', some preferring to throw a veil over Lancaster's slave past, as if it were best forgotten.[99] Nevertheless, such responses and the anxieties that lie behind them should not blind us to the significance of what has been happening in Lancaster. In a city that remains predominantly white, STAMP has been instrumental in shaping a new agenda that has less to do with the moral triumph of British anti-slavery than with the voices of the forgotten, the slaves themselves. Politics play a role here, as do broadly cultural forces, not least of them being debates surrounding identity and multiculturalism. Indeed, the enterprise shown by groups like STAMP reflects not only a very different political and intellectual climate but also a very different sense of who and what constitutes the British nation. For obvious reasons, it is still too early to gauge the success of this particular memory project. What is clear, however, is that the old consensus – the one that traditionally focused almost exclusively on Britain's tradition of humanitarian interventionism – is breaking down, inviting responses that place an emphasis on remembrance rather than celebration.[100] In this sense, 'Captured Africans' is a pioneering memorial, a bold and innovative visual statement that tells us a great deal about contemporary Britain, as well as contemporary concerns.

Notes

1 Jay Winter, *Sites of Memory, Sites of Mourning: The Great War in European Cultural History* (Cambridge, 1995), esp. Chapter 4; Young, *The Texture of Memory*. See also Bruce Kapferer, *Legends of People, Myths of State* (Washington, DC, 1988); Michael Rowlands, 'Memory, Sacrifice and the Nation', *New Formations*, 30 (1996–97), pp. 8–17.

2 It is customary to make a distinction between monuments and memorials, the one commemorating heroic deeds, the other past deaths or tragic events. In general, I have observed this distinction, particularly when discussing war memorials, but, as Young points out, all memory sites are memorials of one kind or another. He goes on: 'A memorial may be a day, a conference, or a space, but it need not be a monument. A monument, on the other hand, is always a kind of memorial'. For a fuller discussion of these terms, see Young, *The Texture of Memory*, pp. 3–4.

3 Sanford Levinson, *Written in Stone: Public Monuments in Changing Societies* (Durham, NC, and London, 1998), pp. 63–5, 137.

4 Lowenthal, *The Past is a Foreign Country*, p. 263.

5 www.anti-slaveryarch.com; www.digitalstroud.com; www.thisisstroud.com/stroud/archive/2002/01/31/features accessed 16 February 2005. These web sites also include details of the celebrations held to commemorate the 'rededication' of the anti-slavery archway, including a play, 'Freedom's Arch', which was performed at Archway School in March 2002. The quotation comes from David Drew, MP for Stroud, speaking in the House of Commons on 14 October 2004. See *Hansard*, sixth series, vol. 425, col.168WH (14 October 2004).

6 Simon Bradley and Nikolaus Pevsner, *The Buildings of England: London 6: Westminster* (London, 2003), p. 707; *The Times*, 27 January 1866, 22, 24 December 1949; *Illustrated London News*, 10 March 1866, pp. 241–2. There was also a personal connection here. The founder and first president of the Metropolitan Drinking Fountain Association was Samuel Gurney, MP for Penryn (1857–65) and, like Buxton, a prominent abolitionist.

7 *Illustrated London News*, 10 March 1866, p. 242.

8   *The Times*, 22, 24 December 1949.

9   *The Times*, 12, 13 December 1949. The Government proposed two alternative sites, including the one at Victoria Embankment Gardens, but quickly this whole controversy developed into a debate over who should decide the ultimate fate of the memorial, Parliament or the Minister of Works. Significantly, the Government lost this particular battle, although patently it got its way over the redevelopment of Parliament Square. For details, see *Hansard*, fifth series, vol. 165, cols. 1421–41, 1626–32 (13, 15 December 1949); *Hansard*, fifth series, vol. 470, cols. 2815–30, 3039–42 (14, 15 December 1949).

10 Bradley and Pevsner, *The Buildings of England*, p. 707; *The Times*, 14, 15, 16 December 1949.

11 Honour, *The Image of the Black in Western Art*, i, pp. 99–100.

12 *The Times*, 2, 5 August 1833; Joseph John Gurney, *Familiar Sketch of the late William Wilberforce* (Norwich, 1838), pp. 45–6.

13 *The Times*, 5 August 1833.

14 Ben-Amos, *Funerals, Politics, and Memory in Modern France, 1789–1996*, pp. 328–42.

15 *The Times*, 5 August 1833; John Scandrett Harford, *Recollections of William Wilberforce, Esq. MP for the County of York during nearly Thirty Years: with brief Notices of some of his personal Friends and Contemporaries* (London, 1865), pp. 323–8. Plans for the Wilberforce Memorial Hall in Freetown were approved in July 1860 and the foundation stone was laid in 1864.

16 Anon, *The Manor House, York: The Yorkshire School for the Blind* (Hull, 1883), p. 1; Richard Ormond and Malcolm Rogers, eds., *Dictionary of British Portraiture: Late Georgians and Early* Victorians, 2 vols. (New York, 1979), II, p. 223. The marble bust is now in the City Art Gallery, York.

17 Harford, *Recollections of William Wilberforce*, p. 257; Richard Walker, *Regency Portraits*, 2 vols. (London, 1985), II, pp. 555–6. Wilberforce's physical image, represented in many forms, shifted significantly over the years, and warrants closer study. Some of the earliest images of Wilberforce, notably John Rising's painting of 1790, are recognisably society portraits. Heckel's portrait of 1794 strikes a different note, however, as do many of the paintings and prints of Wilberforce dating from the 1810s and 1820s. Suddenly, Wilberforce's face becomes fuller, his jaw-line less well defined. His mouth, moreover, is invariably closed almost in a straight line. In other words, this is a much stiffer and more serious image, accentuated (more often than not) by Wilberforce's upright pose. Richmond's painting signals a further (and final) transformation: here, as in Sir Thomas Lawrence's 1828 portrait, Wilberforce is represented as a benign, 'saintly' figure, trapped inside a frail body. This is also the image that Joseph sought to represent, and in many ways it remains central to our image of Wilberforce today. See Walker, *Regency Portraits*, plates 1380, 1382, 1384, 1385, 1386. For an interesting comparative perspective, see Bernard Bailyn's fascinating study of the 'history' of Benjamin Franklin's public image, in Bailyn, *To Begin the World Anew: The Genius and Ambiguities of the American Founders* (New York, 2003), pp. 60–99.

18 Harford, *Recollections of William Wilberforce*, p. 257. Pevsner thought 'the face so violently characterized that it is almost a caricature'. See Nikolaus Pevsner, *London*, 2 vols (third revised edition, London, 1973), I, p. 452.

19 Westminster Abbey Muniments, WAM 62113, 62117, 62118–19, 62123.

20 Neither of these figures is buried in Westminster Abbey: Macaulay is buried at the now disused ground in Mecklenburg Square, London; Buxton is buried at Overstrand, Norfolk. Significantly, one of those involved in the subscription raised for Macaulay's memorial was James Stephen, who also supplied the inscription. See *Dictionary of National Biography*.

21 The size and composition of the Clapham Sect is a subject of considerable historical debate, but the names of Sharp, Wilberforce, and Macaulay are among those memorialised on the south wall of Clapham parish church. Buxton was not a member of the 'Party' but was unmistakably an Evangelical. See Brown, *Fathers of the Victorians*, pp. 326, 389–90, 406, 410.

22 Stephen, *Essays in Ecclesiastical Biography*, p. 538.

23 Trouillot, *Silencing the Past*, p. 47.

24 Arthur Penrhyn Stanley, *Historical Memorials of Westminster Abbey* (London, 1868), pp. 265–6.

25 See Chapter 4.

26 Wisbech and Fenland Museum, EO3/14/1, Thomas Clarkson 150th Anniversary Committee Book, entry for 10 September 1993; Wisbech Society, 58th Annual Report, Wisbech, 1997, p. 13. The anniversary committee was led by Margaret Cave, who later became Mayor of Wisbech.

27 Thomas Clarkson 150th Anniversary Committee Book, entries for 21 June and 22 November 1994, 21 March, 30 May, and 7 December 1995, 16 January and 20 February 1996.

28 Ibid., 7 December 1993, 15 March, and 22 November 1994, 24 January, 30 May, 5 September, and 23 October 1995. Again, not all of these projects got off the ground. The Post Office, for instance, finally rejected the idea of commemorative postage stamps, and the plaque idea was abandoned once Wedgwood made it clear that they would only produce them as a 'private venture' and not as a 'company project'.

29 Ibid., 15 March and 23 November 1994; Wisbech Society, 58th Annual Report, p. 13. The other three 'distinguished supporters' were Lord Archer of Sandwell, Professor Hinde, Master of St. John's College, Cambridge, and Dr John Lonsdale, Reader in African history at Cambridge University.

30 Thomas Clarkson 150th Anniversary Committee Book, 30 May 1996. It appears that not all of the committee were happy with the site chosen by the Abbey, some preferring Poet's Corner, near to Granville Sharp's memorial. See Committee Minutes, 30 May and 5 September 1995. Wilberforce, it should be added, was not the issue here. The objections seem to have had more to do with access and visibility.

31 Ibid., 7 December 1995, 20 February, 12 August, and 5 November 1996; Wisbech Society, 58th Annual Report, p. 13.

32 Wisbech and Fenland Museum, EO3/14/2, Thomas Clarkson 150th Anniversary Committee, Miscellaneous Printed Papers, Order of Service, Westminster Abbey, 26 September 1996. The memorial tablet was designed and executed by Linda Kindersley of the David Kindersley Workshop, Lion Yard, Cambridge. See *Cambridge Weekly News*, 25 September 1996.

33 'Address given by the Right Reverend Stephen Sykes, Bishop of Ely, at the Unveiling and Dedication of a Memorial to Thomas Clarkson at Westminster Abbey on 26 September 1996', Wisbech Society, 58th Annual Report, pp. 15–17.

34 The sculptor's model of Joseph's statue of Wilberforce was given to St John's College in 1890 by R. P. Hookham of Noke, Islip, who at one time had hoped to place it in his local parish church. The statue was at first placed in the college library but was later moved to the chapel. Personal communication from Malcolm Underwood, St John's College, Cambridge.

35 Ian Ousby, *Blue Guide England* (London, 1995), pp. 203, 288; Leonard W. Cowie, ed., *William Wilberforce, 1759–1833: A Bibliography* (Westport, CT, 1992), p. 132. The site at Holwood Hill, the so-called 'Emancipation Oak', is marked by an inscription upon a stone seat.

36 Cowie, *William Wilberforce*, pp. 130–5; Robert Isaac Wilberforce and Samuel

Wilberforce, *Life of William Wilberforce*, V, pp. 299–312; www.stpaulschurch millhill.co.uk/wilberforce.html accessed 8 April 2005.

37   *Hull Advertiser*, 16 August 1833. Venn was the son of the Rev. John Venn, vicar of Holy Trinity Church, which was the parish church of the Clapham Sect. He later became Secretary of the Church Missionary Society.

38   Savage, *Standing Soldiers, Kneeling Slaves*, p. 6.

39   *York Herald*, 5 October 1833.

40   *Hull Advertiser*, 19 December 1833, 14 March, 4 April 1834; *Hull Packet*, 21 March, 4, 11 April 1834; *Hull Times*, 18 May 1935. Liz Deverell and Gareth Watkins speculate that the Monument Bridge site was also attractive because it was close to the site of Beverley Gate, where in 1642 the people of Hull had refused entry to King Charles I, but this historical connection does not appear to have been mentioned or considered at the time. See Deverell and Watkins, *Wilberforce and Hull*, pp. 68–70.

41   *Hull Advertiser*, 16 August 1833. The decision to add a statue was not taken until 1 May 1835, when a meeting of all the subscribers agreed to levy an additional 25 per cent on their subscriptions to cover the extra cost (about £300), but to judge from local newspapers many observers assumed all along that the monument would consist of a pillar and statue. See *Hull Packet*, 1 August 1834; *Hull Rockingham*, 18, 25 April, 2 May 1835.

42   *Hull Advertiser*, 13 September, 4 October, 13 December 1833, 10 January 1834; *Yorkshire Gazette*, 21 September 1833; *York Herald*, 14 December 1833.

43   *York Herald*, 26 October, 7 December 1833; *Hull Advertiser*, 17 January, 11, 19 July 1834. The Yorkshire School for the Blind, at King's Manor, formerly the residence of the abbot of St Mary's, was opened in 1835 and finally ceased operations in 1964. Significantly, the school was not named for Wilberforce; the 'Wilberforce Memorial' merely refers to the charity that sponsored and ran the school. See *Victoria County History: City of York* (London, 1961), pp. 459–60. The Wilberforce Home for the Multiple-Handicapped Blind, York, dates from the late 1960s and was also supported (in part) by the Wilberforce Memorial.

44   *Hull Advertiser*, 13 December 1833, 4 April, 8 August 1834; *York Herald*, 14 December 1833. The choice of Bethell was interesting. According to *The Times*, both the mayor and his predecessor in office, John Barkworth, refused to lay the foundation stone. No reason was given, but it is seems likely that both men disapproved of the Monument Bridge site. See *The Times*, 9 August 1834; *Hull Times*, 18 May 1935.

45   *Hull Rockingham*, 14 November 1835; J. J. Sheahan, *History of the Town and Port of Kingston upon Hull* (Beverley, 1866), pp. 672–5.

46   Sheahan, *History of the Town and Port of Kingston upon Hull*, p. 674; Jack Allerston, *Statues, Busts and Ornamentation of Hull* (Hull, 1984), p. 4; *The Builder*, 14 August 1852.

47   Alison Yarrington, *The Commemoration of the Hero, 1800–1864: Monuments to the British Victors of the Napoleonic Wars* (New York and London, 1988), pp. 15–23, 135–166, 253–4. As Yarrington points out, the original source for all of these memorials was Trajan's Column (AD 113) in Rome, which commemorates Trajan's two campaigns in Dacia (Romania) in AD 101–3 and AD 107–8. It is also worth noting that the completion of the Wilberforce Monument in Hull coincided with the unveiling of the Duke of York Monument (1834) in London.

48   Bernard Pool, ed., *The Croker Papers, 1808–1857* (London, 1967), pp. 21–2.

49   Edward Gillett and Kenneth A. MacMahon, *A History of Hull* (Oxford, 1980), pp. 366–7.

50   *Harry Cartlidge, 1893–1987: Hull Photographer* (Hull, 1998), pp. 48–9.

51   Gillett and MacMahon, *A History of Hull*, pp. 397–9.

52   *Hull Daily Mail*, 9, 17 April, 1, 17, 27, 30 May 1935.

53   *Hull Daily Mail*, 13, 15 April , 1, 27, May 1935.

54   *Hull Daily Mail*, 9 April, 19 June, 20 August, 19, 20 September 1935

55 *Flashback*, 23 September 1995. These alterations can also be plotted on Ordnance Survey maps. See, in particular, the maps for 1956 and 1965.

56 Deverell and Watkins, *Wilberforce and Hull*, pp. 73–4.

57 John Brown, *Wilberforce House, High Street, Hull: A Memoir and a Memorial* [1896] (Hull,1985), pp. 26–8.

58 Deverell and Watkins, *Wilberforce and Hull*, pp. 74–6; *Hull Corporation Minutes, 1903–04*, 2 vols (Hull, 1904), II, p. 83 (Minutes of the Property Committee, 24 April 1903); *Hull Corporation Minutes, 1904–05*, 2 vols (Hull, 1905), II, pp. 120 (Minutes of the Museums and Records Sub-Committee, 12 April 1905), 144 (Minutes of the Museums and Records Sub-Committee, 1905); *Hull Corporation Minutes, 1905–06*, 2 vols (Hull, 1906), II, pp. 9 (Minutes of the Museums and Records Sub-Committee, 30 November 1905), 109 (Minutes of the Museums and Records Sub-Committee, 19 April 1906). Quite apart from public disquiet over the cost of acquiring Wilberforce House, the legal problems surrounding the purchase created lengthy delays. Moreover, before they could legally acquire the property, Hull Corporation had to adopt the Museums and Gymnasiums Act of 1891. See *Hull Corporation Minutes, 1901–02*, 2 vols (Hull, 1902), II, pp. 27 (Minutes of the Property Committee, 20 December 1901), 70 (Minutes of the Property Committee, 11 April 1902).

59 Deverell and Watkins, *Wilberforce and Hull*, p. 73; T. Tindall Wildridge, *The Wilberforce Souvenir* (Hull, 1884), pp. 18–19. A painted plaster replica of Keyworth's statue, formerly the property of Wilberforce Lodge No. 2134 of Free and Accepted Masons, can be found on the ground floor of the Guildhall in Lowgate.

60 Deverell and Watkins, *Wilberforce and Hull*, p. 77.

61 *Hull Daily Mail*, 21 July 1933.

62 Deverell and Watkins, *Wilberforce and Hull*, pp. 77–80.

63 For WISE and Wilberforce 2007, see the press release, dated 15 February 2005, at www.hull.co.uk/newsDetail.aspx accessed 16 February 2005.

64 Sir Shridath Ramphal was given an honorary Doctor of Letters by Hull University in 1983 as part of the 150th anniversary celebrations held to mark the 'end' of slavery in the British West Indies. That same year he gave a public lecture at the University's Middleton Hall as part of a series on the abolition of slavery, from which this extract is taken.

65 Significantly, the Wilberforce medallion is given to 'those individuals who in the opinion of the City Council have made a significant contribution to furthering the cause of Human Rights and Democracy'.

66 Halbwachs, *On Collective Memory*, p. 183. This point is explored at greater length in Chapter 4.

67 *Wisbech Telegraph*, 12 November 1881; *East Anglian Daily Times*, 28 November 1956; *Hertfordshire Mercury*, 16 August 1985.

68 It is striking, for instance, that the Wadesmill memorial and the much larger Clarkson Memorial in Wisbech were unveiled within two years of each other. This may have been coincidence, but equally it may have hinted at something else, namely an appropriate interval or distance between Clarkson's death and the act of remembering his death. See *The Times*, 12 November 1881.

69 Gibson, *Thomas Clarkson*, pp. 155–7. Playford Hall remains in private ownership and for this reason, among others, has never become a popular site of memory.

70 Benjamin Quarles, *Black Abolitionists* (New York, 1969), pp. 130–31; William S. McFeely, *Frederick Douglass* (New York, 1991), pp. 142–3.

71 Harriet Beecher Stowe, *Sunny Memories of Foreign Lands*, London, 1854, II, pp. 77–8. Stowe was entertained by Catherine Clarkson, then in her eighty-fourth year, and her daughter-in-law, Mary Clarkson.

72   *Suffolk Chronicle*, 6 October 1846; *Gentleman's Magazine*, 1846, p. 545.

73   Stowe visited Clarkson's grave during her visit to Playford in 1853. She noted that it was 'marked by a simple white marble slab' and 'carefully tended, and planted with flowers'. See Stowe, *Sunny Memories*, p. 75.

74   *East Anglian Daily Times*, 28 November 1956; *Evening Star*, 9 July 1982.

75   Wisbech and Fenland Museum, Minute Book of Wisbech Museum and Literary Institution, entries for 7 November and 3 December 1932; *The Times*, 17, 21, 22, May 1935; *East Anglian Daily Times*, 21 May 1935 and 15 July 1982.

76   *The Times*, 12 November 1881. There was even a proposal to dedicate 'a marble vase' (a blank cenotaph) in front of Wisbech General Cemetery to Clarkson's memory. See Wisbech and Fenland Museum, Wisbech General Cemetery, Minutes of the Board of Management, entries for 9 and 14 October 1846, 14 October 1847. The proposal was rejected.

77   As Lowenthal rightly observes: 'the memorial act implies termination. We seldom erect monuments to ongoing events or to people still alive'. See Lowenthal, *The Past is a Foreign Country*, p. 323.

78   Frederick John Gardiner, *History of Wisbech and Neighbourhood during the last Fifty Years* (Wisbech, 1898), pp. 185, 190, 220–1, 280–1. There was also a personal connection here. Clarkson had been personally acquainted with Jonathan Peckover's grandfather, also Jonathan, and had corresponded with him up to and including 1808. See Madeline G. H. Reynolds, *The Peckovers of Wisbech* (Wisbech, 1994), pp. 3, 7–9, 15; Wisbech and Fenland Museum, Clarkson Papers, TCC/1–2, Thomas Clarkson to Jonathan Peckover, 24 February 1807 and 3 June 1808.

79   Savage, *Standing Soldiers, Kneeling Slaves*, p. 6; *The Times*, 12 November 1881.

80   *The Times*, 12 November 1881; *Wisbech Advertiser*, 9 November 1881. Significantly, the British and Foreign Anti-Slavery Society refused to contribute to the Clarkson Memorial, on the grounds that they had 'no funds at their disposal for such objects'. Rhodes House Library, Oxford, MSS Brit. Emp. S20 E2/10, BFASS Committee Minutes, entries for 5 February and 1 October 1875.

81   *Wisbech Telegraph*, 12 November 1881.

82   The Martyr's Memorial, in turn, was based on the Waltham (Hertfordshire) Eleanor Cross, which dated from the thirteenth century. See Nicola C. Smith, 'George Gilbert Scott and the Martyrs' Memorial', *Journal of the Warburg and Courtauld Institute*, 42 (1979), pp. 195–206; David Cole, *The Works of Sir Gilbert Scott* (London, 1980), pp. 15–17.

83   Smith, 'George Gilbert Scott and the Martyrs' Memorial', pp. 203–6. Work on the Clarkson Memorial was overseen by Scott's son, John Oldrid Scott. For details, see Royal Institute of British Architects Library, London, John Oldrid Scott Papers, ScJo/1/1, p. 86 and ScJo/2/1, p. 33.

84   *The Builder*, 33, 9 October 1875, pp. 909, 911, 19 November 1875, p. 650, 26 November 1875, p. 683.

85   This effect is heightened by the size and scale of the statue, which at seven feet tall is larger than life-size.

86   *The Times*, 12 November 1881.

87   *The Times*, 2 August 1884.

88   *The Times*, 12 November 1881.

89   See Chapter 4.

90   There is also a 'Clarkson Arms' public house in Wisbech, which can be found on Lynn Road, opposite the junction with Clarkson Avenue. It need hardly be added that Clarkson also features prominently in the promotional literature issued by the local tourist board.

91   Halbwachs, *On Collective Memory*, p. 183.

92   See Alan Rice, *Radical Narratives of the Black Atlantic* (London, 2003), pp. 213–17.

93   Ibid., pp. 203–5.

94   For Lancaster and the slave trade, see Nigel Tattersfield, *The Forgotten Trade: Compris-ing the Log of the* Daniel and Mary *of 1700 and Accounts of the Slave Trade form the Minor Ports of England, 1698–1725* (London, 1991), pp. 324–5; David Eltis, *The Trans-Atlantic Slave Trade: A Database on CD-ROM* (Cambridge, 1999).

95   *Lancaster Guardian*, 14 October 2005.

96   www.lancaster.gov.uk/whatson/NewsRM.asp?id=SXDF14-A7805D92&cat=529 ac-cessed 12 September 2005.

97   The idea here seems to have been to provide viewers with a representative sample of slave voyages, although, as some critics have pointed out, the result is a somewhat distorted view of the full extent of Lancaster's involvement in the transatlantic slave trade. See *Lancaster Guardian*, 14 October 2005.

98   www.lancaster.gov.uk/whatson/NewsRM.asp?id=SXDF14-A7805D92&cat=529 ac-cessed 12 September 2005.

99   For local responses to 'Captured Africans', see *Lancaster Guardian*, 7, 21, 28 January, 4, 18 February, 28 October 2005. I am most grateful to Paul Collins of the *Lancaster Guardian* for drawing this material to my attention.

100   The same emphasis was evident in many of the 'celebrations' surrounding the recent bicentenary of Trafalgar (1805), most notably in the decision to remember all of those who had died in the conflict, and to avoid expressions of patriotic militarism. Hence the decision to re-enact a battle between the 'reds' and 'blues' rather than between the British and French/Spanish fleets.

4

Abolitionist rituals: celebrations and commemorations

One function of public monuments, of course, is to provide a focus for commemorative acts. In the case of British transatlantic slavery, these acts have tended to centre round a number of key dates and anniversaries: 1807, 1833, and 1834 (then, as now, little attention seems to have been paid to the end of 'apprenticeship' in the British West Indies in 1838). But, as we shall see, not all of these anniversaries have been marked in quite the same way. In fact, the commemorative process has proved highly selective, privileging certain dates and individuals – even certain places – while others have been neglected or ignored. Moreover, it is clear that priorities have changed, and continue to change, in response to fresh stimuli and competing demands; indeed, new 'insertions' are not only possible but in some cases actively supported and encouraged. Yet, in other respects, the commemorative process has proved remarkably consistent, not least in its determination to evade white complicity in the transatlantic slave trade – and slavery's role in building Britain's national wealth – and to focus, instead, on the moral triumph of abolition. The result has been the creation of a usable past (a specific 'history') that reflects honour on the British nation, as well as its commitment to freedom, justice, and equality.

Significantly, (anti-)slavery ceremonials in Britain have never been recurrent or 'calendrical' in character, as they were for a time in the United States and as they continue to be in parts of the Caribbean.[1] Instead, they tend to fall at less regular intervals, usually 25 or 50 years apart, thereby ensuring change as well as continuity. The first of these milestones came on 1 August 1859, the 25th anniversary of the date on which the Emancipation Act of 1833 had actually gone into effect in the British colonies.[2] While this anniversary does not appear to have been celebrated in the country at large, even in places like Hull, it was marked by a public meeting in London at the Music Hall in Shore Street, Bedford Square, presided over by Lord Brougham. Many of the leading figures in the British and Foreign Anti-Slavery Society were present, as were George Thompson, Frederick William Chessom, Governor Hincks of the Windward Islands, and several American abolitionists, among them Amos Walker, Ellen Craft and Sarah P. Remond. As Seymour Drescher rightly observes, 'the gathering was only a faint echo of the intense mass meetings of popular antislavery in its heyday'.[3] Nevertheless, by placing peculiar emphasis on the 'Saints' and a 'culture of abolitionism', it established a 'tradition' that, as we shall see, anticipated the celebrations held in 1884 and again in 1933–34.

The tenor of the Shore Street meeting was unashamedly Eurocentric. While conceding that many planters had suffered and would continue to suffer in the British Caribbean, Lord Brougham nevertheless maintained that Emancipation ('the mighty experiment') had been a great success. As a general rule, he declared, 'there has been no diminution in the growth of sugar, and no want whatever of men to work at proper wages'. To this extent, the abolitionists' faith in the superiority of free over slave labour had been fully vindicated. George Thompson was more emphatic still. To his mind, the 'argument drawn from political economy had been settled long, long before. Adam Smith, [Jean-Baptiste] Say, and a host of others, had demonstrated that with reference to sugar growing, as to every other human occupation, free labour was better than forced'. Yet, in saying this, Thompson was also careful to lay stress on the moral argument for Emancipation. 'Even should our political economy be false,' he argued, 'the principle on which the anti-slavery cause was based would stand unshaken, for that principle was that emancipation from bondage was the right of the slave, and that his enslavement was a crime to be abolished, not an evil to be mitigated'. Echoing these sentiments, the London *Morning Star* heralded Emancipation as 'one of the greatest events in the history of England' and one that 'exalted this nation high above the other civilized nations of the earth'.[4]

Over the years, this moral argument would come to dominate public discourse on Emancipation (and hence transatlantic slavery). What is perhaps more striking is that in 1859 abolitionists were still willing to engage with their critics over the economic outcome of Emancipation, even though the benefits of free labour in the British Caribbean were doubtful.[5] The point is worth making, if only because it helps us to appreciate the significance of the celebrations held in 1884 to commemorate the 50th anniversary of Emancipation. To mark this event, abolitionists organised another public meeting, this time at London's Guildhall, which was presided over by the Prince of Wales. But, on this occasion, economic arguments for Emancipation were conspicuous by their absence. Instead, the speakers, who included Lord Derby, Earl Granville, and the Archbishop of Canterbury, highlighted the moral achievement of British anti-slavery. The Prince of Wales captured the general mood of the gathering when he explained that the purpose of the Great Commemorative Ceremony was 'to rekindle the enthusiasm of England and to assist her to carry on this "civilizing torch of freedom" until its beneficent light shall be shed over all the earth'.[6]

By the 1880s, in other words, a new consensus had emerged. Calmly and deliberately, the clamour over the economic benefits of Emancipation, and the £20m paid in compensation to colonial planters (itself a matter of acute embarrassment to many abolitionists), was set aside and forgotten. In its place, Britons substituted an imperialistic discourse – sometimes referred to as the 'New Imperialism' – that celebrated the nation's moral leadership and, in doing so, legitimised its claim to continue to protect those who were considered too weak to protect themselves. 'The object of the great meeting held in the Guildhall yesterday is, happily, one in which all Englishmen, and, indeed, all Christian men, are at one', editorialised *The Times*, reflecting the expansionist mood of the 1880s. 'There is no nobler chapter in the history of English freedom than that which ended fifty years ago in the emancipation of every slave within the Imperial dominions of the British Crown'.[7] Here were Britons in heroic mode: independent, freedom loving, idealistic, and brave. As Raphael Samuel and others have argued, such 'histories', as well as the silences that accompany them – in this case, the long history of British involvement in transatlantic slavery – are an integral part of the creation and re-creation of the nation as an idealised community. Not only do they provide a focus for group loyalties, but they also provide 'plots to structure our individual memories and a larger context within which to interpret our new experiences'.[8]

The 1884 meeting was to prove the last of the great anti-slavery meetings, and certainly the last presided over by a member of the Royal Family. By 1907, the 100th anniversary of the abolition of the slave trade, the mood had changed perceptibly. Significantly, the executive committee of the British and Foreign Anti-Slavery Society appears not to have anticipated the centenary, and was frankly embarrassed by the polite nudges it received from groups like the Church Missionary Society and the London Secretaries Association.[9] The response was lukewarm. Travers Buxton, Secretary of the BFASS, pointed out that it was 'always difficult to arrange a public meeting unless one has well known names as speakers, and is prepared to spend a considerable amount in advertising'. Moreover, the actual anniversary date (25 March) fell in Holy Week. Nevertheless, Buxton was clearly aware of the need to do something about the centenary, and immediately referred the matter to Sir Tomas Fowell Buxton (1837–1915), the BFASS president.[10]

Buxton, however, decided against celebrating the centenary, at least in any deliberate or conspicuous fashion. As he explained in a letter to *The Spectator* in April 1907, 'the present condition of things in Africa generally is not such as to justify joyful celebrations as though the victory were won. The evils are, of course, less open and glaring than they used to be, but the dangers are more subtle and more difficult to attack'. What Buxton had in mind was the situation in the Belgian Congo, which, thanks to the efforts of E. D. Morel and the Congo Reform Association, had emerged as the 'most glaring instance of present-day slavery'. But neither was Britain 'entirely free from reproach in its dealings with the natives in [her] African Colonies and Protectorates'. On the contrary, Buxton claimed that there had been a lamentable 'retrogression in the policy of this country towards the native races, and that we have rather gone backward than forward during the last ten years'. Even the abolition of the legal status of slavery in the coastal strip of the British East African Protectorate, he argued, had been 'evaded and delayed'.[11]

It was these reflections that prompted Buxton to propose a different kind of celebration. As Travers Buxton explained in a circular letter to BFASS committee members in January 1907: 'In view of the large public meeting on the Congo question which it is now proposed to hold in the coming session of Parliament, it seems that the most practical way in which our Society can celebrate the centenary of the 1807 Act would be for our Committee to render all the assistance it can towards making that meeting a success and for our people to take a definite part in it.' It would be 'foolish', he added, to 'try to set up another anti-slavery public meeting', particularly when the Congo agitation had reached such a critical stage.[12] Nevertheless, 'assistance' of this kind carried with it obvious risks. Some clearly questioned whether Morel's Congo movement and anti-slavery were actually the same thing. Others were more anxious that the centenary might be displaced or ignored altogether. Even Travers Buxton was forced to admit that the 'prominent introduction of the centenary [in the coming Congo meeting] would weaken the case'; and, indeed, the London Council of the Congo Reform Association seems to have been adamant that the meeting 'should not be called a commemoration of the centenary, but should be distinctly for rousing public opinion on the Congo scandals'.[13]

As it happened, the Congo meeting was subsequently postponed, which left the BFASS in the worst of all possible positions.[14] Ironically, it was a group of African students studying in London, led by A. B. C. Merriman-Labor, who came up with a viable alternative. Merriman-Labor's idea was a simple commemorative service in Westminster Abbey, and with this in mind he approached Travers Buxton, who, in turn, put him in touch with the Dean of Westminster. As a result, on 25 March a 'little ceremony' was held in the Abbey during which wreaths bearing the inscription 'From grateful Africans' were laid on the monuments of Wilberforce, Buxton, Zachary Macaulay, and Granville Sharp. Though clearly intended as a personal tribute by and for Africans, the congregation included the radical imperialist, Sir Charles Dilke, as well as representatives from the Society of Friends, the British and Foreign Anti-Slavery Society, the Congo Reform Association, the Church Missionary Society, the Wesleyan Missionary Society, and the Aborigines Protection Society. According to Merriman-Labor, over 300 people attended the ceremony, which, fittingly, was conducted by Dean Joseph Robinson, assisted by Wilberforce's grandson, Archdeacon Albert Basil Orme Wilberforce.[15]

Affecting though these scenes were, the truth is that the 1907 centenary passed with barely a murmur. 'If the British public are not so ready as the French to celebrate the recurrence of their great dates,' observed *The Spectator*, 'they are still not exactly backward in doing so. Yet the centenary of the abolition of the slave trade has not been generally acclaimed, or even remembered, in the Press, although no date is more important in the march of civilization'.[16] It was the same thing in the provinces. 'Yesterday was the centenary of the abolition of the slave trade', lamented the *Eastern Morning News and Hull Advertiser*. 'We looked about in the city which was so proud to boast of Wilberforce as one of its sons for some outward indication of this, but there was not one thoughtful pair of hands to place at the foot of his monument the simplest and cheapest token of remembrance'.[17] More disturbing still, the day had been allowed to pass 'without even the fact being recorded within the smallest compass of space in the bulk of the English press'. The one notable exception was the *Manchester Guardian*, which marked the 1907 centenary with a lengthy editorial on Wilberforce ('the apostle and evangelist of Emancipation'), as well as a photo-spread two days later featuring both Clarkson ('the pioneer of the Abolitionist Movement') and Wilberforce (its 'chief advocate in Parliament').[18]

Perhaps just as striking is the lack of interest taken in the centenary by the Government or government agencies, something that was evident again in 1933–34 and 1983 when the focus, of course, was Emancipation.[19] Critics were inclined to attribute this silence to public indifference or, at least, to a sense that 'everybody's business [was] nobody's business'. The real problem, however, lay with the BFASS, which for its own reasons distanced itself from the 1907 centenary and refused to give it nationwide publicity. As the *Eastern Morning News and Hull Advertiser* put it: 'Had a committee been appointed to celebrate the day, we feel sure the gratitude which still lingers in the minds of the people for Wilberforce would have formed ample public expression.'[20] The mistake was to prove a costly one. By taking the position it did, the BFASS allowed the abolition of the slave trade (1807) to slip out of public consciousness, so much so that it passed unnoticed again in 1957 and was gradually displaced by Emancipation (1833–34) as the key anniversary date.

Whereas abolitionists had been at best ambivalent in their response to the 1907 centenary, they awaited the celebrations in 1933–34 with eager anticipation. One obvious reason for this was that the anti-slavery movement had been given a tremendous boost in 1932 by the decision of the League of Nations to set up 'expert machinery', in the shape of seven advisers, for the purpose of securing 'the suppression of slavery in all its forms' throughout the world. For abolitionists, and for the Anti-Slavery and Aborigines Protection Society, in particular, the League's action created an opportunity not only to celebrate 1833 but also to educate public opinion in 'Great Britain, the Dominions, and the Dependencies' in the work that remained to be done. Despite battling against a background of economic depression, unemployment, and poverty, the Anti-Slavery Society set itself the ambitious target of recruiting 1,000 'Celebration members', as well as 10,000 'Associate celebration members', who it was hoped would bring in £20,000.[21]

To help them realise these ambitions, the Anti-Slavery Society availed itself of the services of Emmeline Harris, daughter of Sir John Harris, the Society's parliamentary secretary, whose job it was to set up local committees, which, in turn, would be responsible for organising centenary celebrations. Harris seems to have begun this work in the summer of 1932, when she toured through Essex and East Anglia, and she was active in Manchester, Liverpool, and Sheffield as late as 1934.[22] Working closely with local branches and officers of the League of Nations Union, Harris met with an immediate response. Her father reported to the London Committee of the Anti-Slavery Society in June 1932 that local centenary committees had been organised in Cromer, Coventry, Newcastle-upon-Tyne, Bournemouth, Newport (Gwent), Bristol, York, Hull, Cardiff, Bath, Worthing, Brighton, Eastbourne, Reading, Colchester, Norwich, Birmingham, Yarmouth, St. Albans, Salisbury, Tunbridge Wells, and Chichester.[23] Undoubtedly, there were others, but sadly the records of the Anti-Slavery Society are incomplete.

The main task of these committees was to organise local events to mark the centenary of Emancipation. But at the same time they were advised and encouraged to exploit the potential of the centenary as a propaganda tool. The Bath committee, for instance, which met three times in 1932, worked tirelessly on two fronts. One of these involved targeting local clergy, which in practice meant getting them to preach special sermons and to devote space to the centenary in parish magazines. The other involved local schools. For obvious reasons, the members of the Anti-Slavery Society were keen to see the subject of the centenary taken up in elementary and secondary schools, and in Bath at least they were successful. In December 1932 a conference of headmasters and headmistresses, convened by the Mayor, William Grenfell, not only agreed to devote a lesson or lessons to the centenary, but also adopted a series of recommendations that included an essay-writing competition and the distribution of special (illustrated) commemorative folders to local schoolchildren.[24] Such initiatives were deemed vital to the future of the anti-slavery movement. As Sir John Harris put it in July 1933, 'without an International Conscience the international machine [would] fail to accomplish at an early date the task before it'.[25]

For the most part, the various local committees were left to their own devices. But the Society in London, or 'Headquarters', as it was sometimes referred to, also provided vital support, in the shape of 'speakers' notes' and lantern lecture slides. Props like these were to prove invaluable in arousing public opinion against slavery and the slave trade. Travers Buxton reported in April 1932 that 30 lantern lectures had been delivered in the past six months, and, to judge from the published lists of bookings, they remained popular throughout the centenary period (1933–34). In addition, the Society made available a range of books and pamphlets. The commemorative issue of the *Anti-Slavery Reporter and Aborigines' Friend*, published in July 1933, listed no less than fourteen recommended titles, including eight pamphlets. Some of these titles were reprints of earlier works (Travers Buxton's *William Wilberforce* is a case in point), but others, like John Harris's *A Century of Emancipation* (1933), were specially commissioned for the centenary.

In a novel departure, the Anti-Slavery Society also produced a special

15   Anti-slavery pageant (c. 1933)

centenary pageant play, usually referred to as 'Slavery' or 'Towards Freedom'.[26] The pageant, which in its final form consisted of eight short scenes linked together by two figures representing 'Liberty' and 'Public Opinion', opened with a 'Roman Slave Auction' and carried the history of slavery and abolition through to the American Civil War (represented, in this case, by a scene from John Drinkwater's play, *Abraham Lincoln*), before closing with two modern scenes, a 'Slave Market in Mecca, 1932' and 'Nations and their Record (Nepal, Burma, Sierra Leone, Tanganyika, Abyssinia, Arabia, China, Liberia)'. The clear intention of the pageant was to take stock of 'the progress made towards our proper state of universal freedom', while at the same time reminding audiences of the work that yet remained to be done. 'You have loosed your slaves, you now know the joys of freedom', 'Liberty' tells Nepal, Burma, and Tanzania towards the end of the final scene of the pageant. 'Now must we all in this great year bring slavery to an end for ever. How can we do it? The League of Nations is helping us – the sons of free men should help us – all should help us to bring the light of freedom to those that sit in the darkness of bondage.' Britons, too, shared a responsibility to end slavery. Turning finally towards the audience, 'Liberty' declares: 'YOU must help us to free the slaves of Arabia, you must help us free the slaves of China and Liberia … Abolish Slavery! Free the slaves!'[27]

Internal evidence suggests that the pageant play was first performed before an invited audience, chiefly consisting of members of the Anti-Slavery Society, at the Rudolf Steiner Theatre in London in October 1932. Extensively revised by Geoffrey Edwards, who also added some extra scenes, it was put on again in London in December 1932 and March 1933, and then made available for national distribution, the idea being that local centenary committees and other interested parties could hire the text of the 90-minute pageant, as well as the costumes, on what were evidently regarded as advantageous terms: two guineas and ten per cent of the takings, or 25 per cent of gross takings.[28] As these few details suggest, the Anti-Slavery Society agonised over the pageant play and, in particular, its tone and accessibility. To judge from the comments of those who saw the play in London, the 'plan' was thought by some to be 'rather awkward', while others felt that the slave market scene, complete with dancing girls, veered too much towards entertainment. As one of them put it, judging the effect of the scene on the 'strong Christian minded boy of eighteen', 'very few of the audience have been East and seen girls dancing like that'.[29] Decency, or, rather, indecency, was only part of the problem here. Understandably, critics wanted the pageant to drive home 'the lessons of slavery', even if that meant undermining its dramatic effect. Striking the right balance between the desire to instruct and entertain proved difficult, even elusive, but one of the chief merits of the pageant was its adaptability. Local dramatic groups clearly cut or added scenes, as they saw fit, while in schools it was not unusual for teachers and their pupils to extract and perform a single scene from the play by way of recognising the centenary.[30]

What we are dealing with here, in other words, is a highly orchestrated campaign that was designed to arouse public opinion against the international slave trade, and to carry the movement beyond the forthcoming centenary. The celebrations proper began in March 1933, although for obvious reasons most of the events were planned for July, the anniversary of the passage of the Emancipation Bill. Perhaps the most spectacular of these were the weeklong celebrations held in Wilberforce's birthplace, Kingston upon Hull, but there were also similar meetings and services in London, Salisbury, Bedford, Bournemouth, Chichester, Bristol, Bath, Tunbridge Wells, Brighton, Kettering, and Saffron Walden.[31] To coincide with the centenary, moreover, the BBC broadcast a series of talks on slavery and the slave trade that aimed to highlight the nation's 'tradition of humanity'. Appropriately, the series began on 24 April with a talk on 'Slavery and the Slave Trade up to 1833' by Sir John Harris, and over the next eight weeks this was followed by contributions from, among others, Reginald Coupland ('The Emancipation of the Slaves, 1833' and 'Livingstone and the Arab Slave Trade'), Lady Simon ('Slavery and the Treatment of Slaves To-day'), and Margery Perham ('The Results of Abolition in West Africa'). Harris then returned on 26 June to give a 'summing up of slavery talks'.[32]

In many parts of the country, the celebrations continued into November and December. Indeed, the centenary is best understood as a rolling programme of events that was intended to mark Emancipation (1 August 1834), as well as the passage of the Emancipation Bill in 1833. The August anniversary was marked by special services at St Botolph's Church, Bishopsgate, attended by Sir John and Lady Simon and Dr Harold Moody, President of the League of Coloured People, as well as at Southwark and Carlisle. London blacks, meanwhile, held their own celebrations in Barking Road Church, Poplar, during which the congregation, 'most of whom were coloured men from the West Indies, rose and recited a part of the Declaration of the House of Commons declaring the slaves free and slavery for ever abolished'.[33] Two other events are worthy of note. One of these is a private gathering held at Northrepps Hall, the 'old home' of Sir Thomas Fowell Buxton, in September 1934, to mark the centenary of Emancipation. The other is the Lord Mayor's reception at the Mansion House in November, which formally brought the celebrations to a close.[34]

Estimates of this kind are necessarily tentative, but it seems likely that over 250 commemorative events were put on between March 1933 and November 1934.[35] This figure includes civic meetings, as well as special church services. It also includes 17 performances of the pageant play and a larger number of lantern lectures (43 in all), although in each case the precise figure was probably significantly higher. Just as remarkable as the size and scale of these celebrations was their range and diversity. It is perhaps not surprising that the largest number of events was held in and around London, but there were also extensive celebrations in the north-east (Yorkshire and Northumberland) and the north-west (Lancashire and Cheshire). Very few English counties, in fact, failed to mark the centenary in some way. No less striking is the number of events held in Scotland, Wales and Ireland. In Scotland, there were services and meetings in Edinburgh, Perth, Glasgow, and Aberdeen, not to mention Lochgelly, Stepps, Airdrie, Girvan, and Wigtown. Meanwhile, in Ireland there were public meetings in Belfast and Dublin, and in Wales in Cardiff and Barry.[36] The truly national character of these celebrations is reinforced by the surviving list of lantern lecture bookings. Roughly half (10) of the bookings made in the first half of 1934, for example, came from outside England, eight of them from Scotland and a further two from Wales (Skewen and Cardigan).[37]

The success of the centenary celebrations can, in part, be attributed to the support that the Anti-Slavery Society received from religious bodies. Anticipating the centenary, in July 1932 the Archbishops of York and Canterbury, together with the leaders of the Free Churches, issued an appeal to clergy and ministers, urging them 'to refer to abolition during service on one Sunday in July 1933', and the Archbishop of Canterbury made a similar appeal in 1934.[38] How many clergy responded to these calls is impossible to say, but certainly there were special services at Westminster and St Paul's, Southwark, Chichester, Bristol, Liverpool, Edinburgh, and Dundee. In addition, many other religious organisations associated themselves with the centenary, among them the Church Missionary Society, the General Assembly of Unitarian and Free Christian Churches, and the Church of Scotland. Besides offering their congratulations, either to the League of Nations or to the Anti-Slavery Society, or both, each of these bodies pledged themselves to 'direct public attention to the widespread evils of slave-owning, slave-raiding, and slave-trading', mindful that they were following in a 'great national tradition'.[39]

The Anti-Slavery Society also forged important links with the British Left. Chief among its allies was the League of Nations Union (LNU), which, with over 3,000 local branches and close ties to organised religion and schools and universities, was the largest and most influential organisation in the British peace movement.[40] An important figure here was Sir John Harris, who besides being parliamentary secretary of the Anti-Slavery Society was also a member of the LNU's executive committee. It was hardly surprising, therefore, that the Union supported the centenary or that it encouraged its branches to cooperate with the Anti-Slavery Society, 'provided that none of the expenses attaching to such celebrations should be made a charge on the Union's funds'.[41] Harris, who worked tirelessly throughout the centenary celebrations, addressed ten LNU branch meetings between 1933 and 1934, the proceeds being divided equally between the two organizations.[42] More ambitious still was the programme of events organised by the Bournemouth branch of the League in July 1933. Here, the day's proceedings at the Winter Gardens began with a 'Pageant of Peace', performed by 200 Sunday school children, followed by a performance of the slavery pageant and then, in the evening, by a public meeting addressed, in this case, by Lady Harris.[43] Several branches of the League, in fact, put on special performances of the pageant, including Comrie, which claimed to be the first Scottish branch to perform 'Slavery', and Waterloo, Crosby, Seaford and Litherland. Elsewhere, the League of Nations Union and the Anti-Slavery Society joined forces to organise large public meetings to mark the centenary, as in the case of the Sussex county meeting held at the Dome in Brighton in February 1934.[44]

Clearly, the League of Nations Union was an important ally, providing abolitionists with organisational support as well as access to its various publications. *Headway*, for instance, the LNU's monthly newspaper, carried news of branch meetings devoted to the centenary, and in July 1933 opened its pages to Sir John Harris, who contributed an article on the centenary, 'The Challenge of Slavery'.[45] The Anti-Slavery Society also cooperated with the Post-War Brotherhood, an international movement whose aim was 'to make the world safe for the League of Nations'.[46] These different groups not only shared a commitment to peace and to peacekeeping, but also a concern for the poor and the oppressed. Men and women who spoke idealistically of the 'communalization' of land and the protection of 'native peoples' in what we would now call the Third World naturally embraced the centenary celebrations with enthusiasm. What made their support all the more significant was the fact that the British peace movement was at its peak during the years 1933–35. Indeed, it is a measure of the strength of anti-war feeling that at its annual conference in Hastings in 1932 the Labour Party adopted a resolution that, in the event of war, it would initiate a general strike to prevent Britain's participation.[47]

Such alliances undoubtedly alienated some sections of the British press. Lord Beaverbrook's *Daily Express*, which vehemently opposed the Peace Ballot of 1935, limited its coverage of the centenary celebrations to a highly inflammatory piece by the novelist, Evelyn Waugh, questioning the wisdom of

Emancipation, and drawing attention to the social, political, and economic 'problems' it had created, both in Africa and the West Indies.[48] Yet it would be misleading to regard the centenary as merely a preoccupation of the British Left. To judge from the available data, roughly ten per cent of the 250 events put on between 1933 and 1934 were organised by the League of Nations Union, and the figure is only marginally higher if we include groups like the Society for Equal Citizenship and the Women's Citizen's Council. More revealing still is the number of events organised by the Rotary Club, local branches of the Women's Institute, and even in one case (Richmond, Surrey) the Women's Conservative Association.[49] Indeed, the overwhelming impression is that the centenary celebrations appealed to a wide spectrum of the British public, cutting across the lines of gender, religion, and politics.

Impressive as the celebrations were in 1933–34, it is pertinent to ask how they functioned, that is, as a form of organised remembering? First and foremost, the centenary evoked a common past and a common tradition of humanity. In this sentimental discourse, Emancipation was invariably seen as a 'disinterested act' – a 'gift' that, above all else, reflected credit on Britain's sense of justice and fair play: rarely, if ever, did these events acknowledge black perspectives; rarely, if ever, did they acknowledge the role that transatlantic slavery had played in Britain's commercial and imperial expansion. *The Times*, quoting Lecky, described Emancipation as among the three or four 'perfectly virtuous acts recorded in the history of nations'. Emancipation, echoed the Bishop of Winchester, was 'one of the most striking applications of the Christian teaching of the value of each individual life'.[50] Proof, if proof were needed, was to be found in the career of William Wilberforce, who seemed to contemporaries to exemplify what could be done by 'moral power inspired by religion'. The Attorney-General, Sir Thomas Inskip, went a step further when he hailed Wilberforce as the 'begetter of the principle, happily revived in recent years, that [Britain] was the trustee for helpless millions', adding significantly that this principle was the 'true basis of the Empire'.[51]

In other words, the celebrations in 1933–34 constructed a vision of the past that was worthy of commemoration and, at the same time, useful to the present as well as to the future. The 'materialism' of the 1930s seems to have engendered a renewed interest in 'great human ideals'. 'Where the men of 1833 cried out against forced labour,' observed *The Times*, 'we are oppressed by the no less grievous evil of forced idleness, and have no such golden ideal as liberty to draw us on and out of the morass. In domestic affairs, where all seems reduced to a balancing of expedients in a perplexity divorced from moral significance, it would seem hopeless even for a WILBERFORCE to try to introduce the idealism that makes politics heroic'.[52] If there was a fascination in this, as well as a hint of frustration – what we might call a politics of nostalgia – there was also something else: a reminder and a challenge. 'Just as the conscience of England was aroused by Wilberforce', Lord Irwin told a congregation in York Minster, 'it was now necessary to arouse and stimulate the international conscience of mankind'. Many in the peace movement, of course, spoke the same language, but for abolitionists such sentiments had a particular resonance and meaning. As Sir John Harris put it, there was no more fitting method of celebrating the work of men like Wilberforce than 'to follow in their footsteps and in the same fervent spirit to complete the work both of abolition and emancipation'.[53]

Abolitionists drew one further lesson from the past. The struggle, they conceded, had been a long and arduous one. Wilberforce and his fellow workers, moreover, had been 'opposed by the two most formidable adversaries of all political idealism – avarice and fear'. Yet they had never faltered.[54] With some reason, abolitionists warned that the campaign to end slavery throughout the world would almost certainly require the same courage and the same 'fervent spirit'. As Charles Roberts, Chairman of the Anti-Slavery Society, admitted to a meeting in Carlisle: 'If you ask me how slavery is going to be abolished in countries which are not under our own control, such as Arabia, Persia, or Abyssinia, I do not think anyone can tell you, but somehow it will be done … if we have the same faith and the same practical enthusiasm that distinguished the early emancipators we shall get over the difficulties of the present time'.[55] *The Times* agreed, pointing also to a wider lesson: 'If at times the securing of the peace of the world seems an enterprise as Quixotic as the abolition of slavery seemed when WILBERFORCE was young, those are the times when we can comfort ourselves with the memory of one Quixote who died triumphant.'[56]

The Anti-Slavery Society invested a great deal of time and energy in the centenary celebrations. Many of its officers, including Lady Simon and Sir John Harris, also took a prominent part in the proceedings, addressing meetings across the length and breadth of the country. Harris alone gave as many as 50 speeches between 1933 and 1934, and his wife, Lady Harris, gave over 20. In addition, the Society spent heavily on the celebrations. The pageant play, for instance, cost over £500 to produce, on top of which the Society bore a share of the cost of a special parliamentary luncheon held at the Hotel Victoria on 17 July 1934, as well as contributing £40 towards the City of London celebrations at the Mansion House the following November.[57] If that was not enough, the Society appears to have agreed to share equally in any deficits run up by local committees, as it did in the case of a meeting held in Eastbourne. What this meant in hard financial terms was that the Centenary Fund never reached anything like its projected target. In fact, when the fund finally closed in January 1935 the balance stood at just £754.[58]

Yet it would be wrong to dwell on the financial failings of the centenary. As we have seen, the celebrations in 1933–34 were intended to raise public awareness about slavery, and in this they largely succeeded. One reason they did so was by recovering a version of the past that was immensely reassuring. It was not just that the achievements of figures like Wilberforce were so remarkable, or that in pursuit of them abolitionists had been required to overcome obstacles every bit as daunting as the depression of the 1930s. As Reginald Coupland explained to a centenary meeting in Hull, abolition also demonstrated that idealism was 'not after all a romantic illusion', or 'a solace for the soft-hearted and soft-headed'. 'It may be that politics is often no more than a mask for the strife of rival interests', Coupland conceded, fixing his sights on post-war cynics. 'But the lives and works of Wilberforce and the "Saints" are certain proof that not merely individuals but the common will, the State itself, *can* rise on occasion to the height of pure unselfishness'.[59]

Interestingly, one effect of the celebrations in 1933 and 1934 was to attach greater significance and meaning to William Wilberforce, and hence his place in the nation's collective memory. In part, this was an accident of history. Wilberforce's death in July 1833, just a month before the Emancipation Bill was finally passed into law, served to blur the distinction between the public and the private. As a result, the two events became almost indistinguishable in the public mind: celebrations of the one tended naturally to run into the other, if only because that way they were easier to organise and manage. But arguably the tendency to equate Wilberforce with Emancipation was less obvious in 1859 than it was in 1933 or, for that matter, 1983. Put a different way, the commemorative process has tended to attach greater relevance and importance to Wilberforce as time has gone on, and as each generation has been forced to revise which heroes it notices and how to interpret them.

Significantly, the earliest anti-slavery celebrations made little effort to distinguish between the 'Saints'. Lord Brougham, for instance, in his address to the 25th anniversary meeting in 1859, not only paid homage to Clarkson, Wilberforce, and Buxton but also noted the achievements of James Stephen (the 'pioneer' of emancipation), Zachary Macaulay, and Joseph Sturge.[60] It was the same thing in 1884. In his opening address to the Great Commemorative Ceremony held at London's Guildhall, the Prince of Wales spoke warmly of Wilberforce but did so in a manner that made it clear he had been Clarkson's 'Parliamentary coadjutor'. He also paid tribute to Zachary Macaulay, whose 'war' against apprenticeship had led to the Act of 1838 and, with it, 'complete emancipation'. Lord Erskine ranged more widely still, noting the contributions of Granville Sharp, Thomas Fowell Buxton, and Lord Brougham, as well as those of Fox, Pitt, and Burke. Admittedly, Wilberforce was mentioned by name by most of the speakers at the Guildhall celebrations, but more often than not he appeared as one of a triumvirate: 'Wilberforce, Clarkson, Buxton'.[61] There was little or no attempt to single out Wilberforce for special notice, and just as telling was the obvious attention paid to Buxton, as Wilberforce's successor as leader of the anti-slavery campaign in the House of Commons.

Even during the muted celebrations surrounding the 1907 centenary of the abolition of the slave trade, Wilberforce's name was usually mentioned in the same breath as Clarkson's.[62] Twenty-five years later the focus was very different. The 1930s seemed ripe for the return of heroes. Beset by rising unemployment and growing social unrest, many Britons, particularly those who were just too young to have served in the First World War, began to call for a new standard of morality. Some even talked vaguely of the need for a 'revolution' to cure 'the English sickness'.[63] Given these hopes and anxieties, it is hardly surprising that the 100th anniversary of Wilberforce's death in July 1933 was the occasion for nationwide celebrations. Fittingly, the evening services at Westminster Abbey on 23 July were devoted to 'the centenary of Wilberforce'. There were also special services at other sites associated with his memory: at Keston Parish Church, for instance; at St Paul's Church on the Ridgeway, Mill Hill; and, finally, at St Luke's Church in Battersea, where a 'crowded congregation' was addressed by Sir John Harris.[64]

More impressive still were the celebrations held in Kingston upon Hull. The weeklong series of events began with a civic procession (on 23 July), and was followed by the opening of the Wilberforce Centenary Exhibition at the Mortimer Galleries in Hull City Hall and an open-air ceremony held at the foot of the Wilberforce monument (on 28 July), which was attended by over 20,000 people. Other events included a garden party on 27 July to meet members of the Wilberforce family and a one-off performance of *Wilberforce*, a radio

16　Centenary celebrations of the death of William Wilberforce,
Kingston upon Hull, 1933

chronicle play, which was broadcast by the BBC (again on 27 July) through the North Regional area from its studios in Leeds. The ceremonial civic tribute on 28 July, which featured a 'fanfare of trumpets', the simultaneous unfurling of the flags of 50 nations, and 'a salute by aircraft', was also broadcast live 'with a running commentary' by the BBC. Meanwhile, in Cambridge the celebrations took the form of a luncheon in St John's College, when the Master and Fellows entertained over 150 guests, including Lord Cecil and several members of the Wilberforce family.[65]

Not to be outdone, *The Times* published its own tribute on 29 July, in the shape of an article by George M. Trevelyan, Regius Professor of History at Cambridge University. While conceding that 'for some years before he died he [Wilberforce] had been living in the most honoured of retirements', Trevelyan nevertheless hailed Wilberforce as a 'warrior' whose tireless energy had lifted mankind to a higher plane. 'The combination of such selfless devotion to a cause has seldom gone with such cool temper and judgment', he wrote, stamping his considerable authority on the centenary celebrations. 'It was a difficult path to tread, and he trod it with the sure foot of absolute sincerity and single-mindedness, and ended by being the leader of the whole nation without distinction of party or of sect.' Perhaps just as important, Trevelyan stressed the essential 'Englishness' of Wilberforce's 'life story'. Emancipation, he explained to his readers, like the slave trade agitation before it, 'was pre-eminently a result of our free institutions, our freedom of speech and association, and all that habit of voluntaryism and private initiative which distinguished the England of Pitt and Fox, Castlereagh and Canning, from the Europe of Napoleon and Talleyrand'.[66]

Here, in others words, was a man (and a cause) worthy of study and emulation; in fact, Wilberforce's legacy was quite deliberately manipulated or 'rearranged' in order to meet contemporary demands, as well as contemporary preoccupations. It is telling, for instance, that eulogists like Trevelyan made little or no reference to Wilberforce's deep political conservatism, or, indeed, to his support for measures like the notorious Six Acts. Instead, Wilberforce was celebrated chiefly as an apostle of freedom, or else as a social reformer worthy to be ranked alongside figures like the Earl of Shaftesbury.[67] This tendency to equate Wilberforce with freedom, justice, and equality – with what we might term 'liberalism' – became a signature of the 1933 celebrations and beyond. As *The Times* put it, in a typically glowing tribute: 'He, if any man, was worthy to establish the Victorian faith in a continuous progress of humanity in and to freedom, and to vindicate for politics the sublimity that they had possessed in the eyes of PLATO'.[68]

Inevitably, many of the events organised in 1933 to commemorate 'the centenary of Wilberforce' doubled as celebrations of the passage of the Emancipation Act. Lord Cecil, for instance, made no secret of the fact that 'they were [in Cambridge] to celebrate the centenary of Wilberforce *and* the abolition of slavery so far as this country and the Dominions were concerned'.[69] The process could also work the other way. To take an obvious example, on 23 July a special service was held at St Paul's Cathedral to 'commemorate the centenary of the abolition by the British Parliament of slavery '. But, here again, the preacher, the Archdeacon of London, linked the celebration to the death of Wilberforce; in fact, he went a stage further by adding a third centenary, that of the birth of Charles George Gordon (1833–85), governor-general of the Sudan.[70] In this way, the two events became indistinguishable; indeed, many observers might have been forgiven for thinking that Wilberforce alone was responsible for Emancipation. As if to emphasise the point, Westminster Abbey marked the day the Emancipation Act had received the royal assent, 28 August 1833, by placing flowers at the foot of Wilberforce's statue.[71]

Even at an official level there was a tendency to blur the distinction between Wilberforce and Emancipation. On the whole, abolitionists tended to be even-handed in their approach to the centenary celebrations. So, while they were quick to recognise Wilberforce's achievements, they also were careful to give Buxton his due. Particularly striking in this regard is the Anti-Slavery Society's decision in 1931 to commission a biography of Buxton, 'linking it with the subsequent work of the Society' – what, in effect, became John Harris' *A Century of Emancipation*.[72] Similarly, Lady Simon was careful to highlight Clarkson's 'unselfish and life-long devotion' to the abolition of slavery and the slave trade, adding that the 'alliance between Clarkson and Wilberforce [was] one of the closest and longest in the history of co-operative public spirit'. Simon's lecture notes, which happily survive, make it very clear that for abolitionists, at least, Wilberforce was not the sole focus of the anniversary celebrations. For this very reason, the Anti-Slavery Society reacted nervously to the demands of the local Hull committee, who obviously felt that the metropolitan group 'should make more of Wilberforce and his Hull association' in its national programme, and even insisted on 'separating' the celebrations in Hull from those in other towns, at least for promotional purposes.[73]

Nevertheless, this delicate balancing act could sometimes prove difficult to sustain. Take the special pageant play commissioned by the Anti-Slavery Society to commemorate the 1933 centenary. As already noted, the pageant consisted of eight different scenes, which ranged chronologically from AD 500 to 1932. Only four of these scenes dealt specifically with British themes, however, and no less than half of them were devoted to Wilberforce, the others being an 'Elizabethan scene' and Lord Mansfield's decision in the Somerset case of 1772. Scene four, for instance, depicted Wilberforce's 'conversion' to abolition at Holwood Park, near Bromley, Kent, while scene five took as its subject Wilberforce's last illness in 1833. Admittedly, both scenes included other prominent figures in the movement, among them Pitt and Lord Grenville (scene four) and Buxton (scene five). But, as a representation of British anti-slavery, the pageant play came dangerously close to reinforcing what was rapidly becoming a standard or orthodox view of events between 1787 and 1833, namely that in the struggle that brought slavery to an end Wilberforce ranked alone. 'For fifty years he laboured, for fifty years he spent himself for others,' 'Liberty' tells 'Opinion' in the dialogue that links scenes four and five, 'he caused the abolition of the slave trade, but it was not until he had entered the Valley of the Shadow that the Bill for the Emancipation of the Slaves came before the House of Commons.' Wilberforce's last words in scene five pick up the same theme. 'I give thanks to God for bringing me to this great cause,' he confides to his son, Henry, 'the long fight is over.'[74]

Many sections of the British press were similarly drawn to Wilberforce and his peculiar role within the anti-slavery movement. *The Times*, for instance, marked the 1934 centenary by publishing a lengthy editorial celebrating the achievements of all the 'Saints', among them Clarkson, Buxton, and Zachary Macaulay. In doing so, however, the newspaper was at pains to point out that it was 'improbable that their object would have been attained in their own generation if they had not won the support and accepted the leadership of a man of genius'. But what did that genius consist of? Part of the answer, of course, lay in Wilberforce's skills as an orator; indeed, *The Times* described Wilberforce as 'one of the most effective Parliamentary campaigners of his age'. More controversially, perhaps, he was also credited with having 'invented a whole new technique of political agitation'. *The Times* went further, claiming that in 'international esteem [Wilberforce] was more famous than Pitt or Wellington'. In these and other ways, Wilberforce was elevated above his 'co-adjutors'. It was not just that he came to be acknowledged as the dominant force in British anti-slavery. At a period when men and nations 'presumed to think of liberty as but a means to an end', or 'something that [might] be safely bartered for wealth, for security, for efficiency, or for national dominance', Wilberforce was also recognised and cherished as one of the 'supreme leaders of human progress'.[75]

Wilberforce's ability to speak to contemporary concerns was apparent again in 1959, at the height of the Cold War, when the nation paused to celebrate the bicentenary of his birth. As the *Methodist Recorder* put it in a lengthy editorial, 'in a day when many refugees still live in an uncertain hinterland, when forced labour camps still exist, and when new discoveries made possible, not only the H-bomb with its possibilities of wholesale physical destruction, but processes by which human personality is distorted so that the very self seems to be obliterated', it was well to consider the achievements of those, like Wilberforce, who had pledged themselves to the defence of freedom, and who held human personality 'sacred'.[76] As had been the case in 1933, Hull was at the forefront of the bicentenary celebrations. On 24 August, the actual anniversary date, the Bishop of Hull led a small procession to Wilberforce House Museum, where the Deputy Mayor, the headmaster of Hull Grammar School, and members of the local auxiliary of the British and Foreign Bible Society laid wreaths at the foot of Wilberforce's statue. Later in the year, there was also a civic dinner and a special 'united' church service at Hull's Holy Trinity Church, both of which were timed to coincide with the opening of exhibitions in local museums; and, to mark the anniversary, the singer and activist, Paul Robeson, visited Hull in April 1960, when he gave a gala concert at the City Hall.[77] But, just as important, the bicentenary of Wilberforce's birth was celebrated at the national level as well. Following the ceremony at Wilberforce House Museum on 24 August, a small civic party consisting of the Deputy Mayor, the Sheriff, and the Town Clerk travelled by train to London, where they joined members of the Anti-Slavery Society, the Church Missionary Society, and the British and Foreign Bible Society in Westminster Abbey for another wreath-laying ceremony, this time at the site of Wilberforce's grave.[78]

By the time the 150th anniversary of Wilberforce's death came around in 1983, the rituals associated with these occasions had become all too familiar. On 26 July the Prince of Wales attended a National Service of Thanksgiving in Westminster Abbey. To mark the occasion, Wilberforce's name was also included in the *Alternative Services Book*, where, as the only MP, he joined the company of 'a long list of saints, martyrs, bishops and doctors of the universal church, together with outstanding Christian characters'.[79] Meanwhile, Anti-Slavery International organised and coordinated an ambitious programme of over 40 events to coincide with the anniversary. For obvious reasons, Hull was the focal point of these celebrations. Throughout June and July 1983, the city and university hosted a series of 150th anniversary events that included lectures, exhibitions, plays, dance performances, concerts, parades, and 'a National Service of Thanksgiving'.[80] But there were also large-scale commemorative events in other parts of the country. In Bristol, for instance, there were two exhibitions, one ('Bristol and the Abolition of Slavery') in the City Museum, Clifton, and the other, organised by the Anti-Slavery Society, in the City Library on College Green. At Clapham, too, there was a Wilberforce exhibition and, on 29 July, the Right Honourable George Thomas, former Speaker of the House of Commons, addressed an ecumenical service at Clapham's Holy Trinity Church.[81]

As had been the case in 1933, there was little effort to distinguish between the celebrations surrounding Wilberforce's death and those surrounding the passage of the Emancipation Act. In fact, the programme of events organised by Anti-Slavery International quite deliberately linked the two celebrations, sometimes giving Emancipation precedence and sometimes Wilberforce. Leading articles in *The Times* also tended to run the two events into each other. Patrick Cormack, for example, Conservative MP for Staffordshire South, used the 150th anniversary of Wilberforce's death to attack the persistence of slavery, or, at least, the exploitation of labour, in Haiti, China, and the Philippines.[82] This is not to deny that other figures were remembered and commemorated during the 1983 celebrations.[83] But none of them dominated the proceedings in quite the same way. As his entry in the *Alternative Services Book* made abundantly clear, Wilberforce had now moved into a completely different realm of public memory, and one significantly denied to any of his fellow abolitionists, namely the realm of 'saints' and 'outstanding Christian characters'.

Not everyone was quite so uncritical, however. In Hull, for instance, several of the plays put on as part of the celebrations commemorating the 150th anniversary of Wilberforce's death sought to problematise Wilberforce. One of these, *Slaves*, performed by the Theatre Community Workshop at Spring

Street Theatre, explored the 'dramatic contrasts in the time of Wilberforce' and, in particular, the failure of the government 'to relieve the adverse social conditions of the poor of England'.[84] Equally striking is the tone of *Wilberforce; or, the Liberator Reflects*, an operetta by Derek Scott and Steve Davis, which was performed at the University of Hull in May 1983. The libretto followed what by now was a familiar course, charting Wilberforce's life at Cambridge and then his decision to take up the slave trade issue in Parliament. But the second act strikes a rather different note. No sooner has the slave trade been abolished than Wilberforce's opponents return 'seeking revenge'. Moreover, they find satisfaction 'in an oblique manner when they discover that Wilberforce realises he has done more than abolish the slave trade; he has helped to create a frightening new era' – frightening, that is, to the country's landed interests. The point is picked up in two choruses, 'The Bible writes' and 'There was a time', both of which address the plight of the poor, whose concerns are 'still with us'. 'Worst of all, [Wilberforce] has to face the poor folk who saw him as their hero and then in disillusionment stoned his house in London'. In other words, we are confronted here with a very different portrait of Wilberforce as a Tory with strong beliefs in authority and a fear of extending power to the working classes.[85]

Though hardly popular entertainments, pieces like these revealed an increasing willingness to question the breath of Wilberforce's political vision, something that would have seemed unthinkable in the 1930s. Then the accent had been on reclaiming Britain's imperialistic mission and, with it, a sense of the nation's tradition of humanitarian interventionism. The dislocations of the 1980s, however, elicited a very different set of responses. The second half of the twentieth century witnessed not only a decline in Britain's global influence but also a redefinition of what it meant to be British. If anything, the 'race' riots of the early 1980s (there were riots in Bristol in 1980 and again in Liverpool and Manchester in 1981) intensified this process, fuelling a growing awareness that the nation was 'somehow inadequate'. As Caryl Phillips so aptly puts it: 'In the 1980s and early 1990s, Poll Tax rioters, Clause 28 "Queers", Brussels bureaucrats, and the perpetrators of "race" riots, all fed Britain's sense of herself as a nation in crisis. There was a perceived need to co-opt "trouble-makers" from the fringes, and make them feel a part of the centre'.[86] It was in this context, therefore, that some Britons began to re-examine Wilberforce's legacy, just as some began to re-examine the impact of blacks on British society, an historical, cultural, and sociological inquiry that – as we shall see – led to a much greater emphasis on black or 'African' perspectives, particularly in museums.[87]

Inevitably, the double celebrations held in 1983 cast a long shadow over the 150th anniversary of Emancipation in 1984. By and large, the centenary passed unnoticed. *The Times*, for instance, reported on special anniversary meetings in Jamaica and Guyana, but made no mention of similar meetings in Britain. It did, however, carry a photograph depicting African and Caribbean costumes shown in London on 23 August 'to commemorate the 150th year of emancipation'. This silence was not deliberate or premeditated, at least not in the sense of 'a self-decided attitude taken by a whole community'.[88] Rather, it signified a subtle shift in the commemorative process, whereby 1834 (Emancipation) increasingly gave way to 1833 (the passage of the Emancipation Bill) as the key anniversary date. In turn, the emphasis on 1833 served to conflate Wilberforce and Emancipation. As we have seen, this association was already explicit by 1933 and it continued to dominate abolitionist rituals down to 1983. In this way, 'Wilberforce' and 'Emancipation' became interchangeable terms. Whereas in 1884 it had still been possible to talk of a triumvirate, 'Wilberforce, Clarkson, Buxton', by 1933 the emphasis had shifted to Wilberforce, to the obvious exclusion of Clarkson and, to a lesser extent, Buxton.

If the commemorative process has tended to privilege Wilberforce above all other abolitionists, his ascendancy has not gone unchallenged. On the contrary, in recent years there has been a concerted effort to restore Clarkson's reputation, led principally by the inhabitants of Wisbech. For obvious reasons, Wisbech has always been an important site of abolitionist memory. As one might expect, the town marked the 1933 centenary, albeit in a relatively low-key manner, and in 1960 put on a much more ambitious programme of events to celebrate the bicentenary of Clarkson's birth (the model presumably being the celebrations held in Hull the year before to celebrate the bicentenary of Wilberforce's birth).[89] The celebrations began in March with a wreath-laying ceremony at the Clarkson Memorial, followed by a commemorative service at Wisbech Parish Church, and finally ended in June with an open-air service organised by Wisbech Council of Churches. To coincide with these events, the borough council planned a host of other activities, including lectures, concerts, and an essay competition for schoolchildren. There was also a Clarkson exhibition at the local museum, and, picking up on the same theme, Wisbech entered a tableau in the annual Cambridgeshire and Isle of Ely Agricultural Show, which bizarrely depicted Clarkson and behind him 'a bunch of slaves driven into captivity by a villainous Arab slaver, complete with a vicious cat-o'-nine tails'.[90]

Clearly, some of these events were not a success; others, it seems, never got beyond the planning stage. Correspondents in the local press complained that 'important people who were to have spoken about Clarkson have never arrived, spectacular exhibits have never materialised'.[91] But this was to miss the point. Against the backdrop of decolonisation and growing political concern about apartheid in South Africa, the organisers (chiefly the members of the borough council) set out not only to celebrate Clarkson's life but also to help 'further' relations between themselves and 'coloured people'. With this in mind they tried, usually without success, to bring African lecturers and performers to Wisbech, hoping as a result to raise consciousness about black achievements and to highlight black 'problems'. In other words, the council and its supporters attempted to reinvigorate Clarkson's legacy by stressing its relevance

to contemporary concerns. Lord Hemingford of the African Bureau, who spoke at the special commemorative service in March, made the same point, stressing that Clarkson's message (his 'tradition of humanity') was as relevant in 1960 as it had been during his own lifetime.[92]

The 150th anniversary of Clarkson's death in 1996 prompted another series of commemorative celebrations. But this time there was an important difference. Not content with celebrating Clarkson's local associations with Wisbech, the organisers set out to honour him at a national level as well. As we have seen, the campaign to place a Clarkson memorial in Westminster Abbey was central to this process; indeed, the ceremony on 26 September 1996 represented an important stage in the rehabilitation of Clarkson's status and reputation. Around this event, the Wisbech committee organised a series of celebrations that helped to create a continuum between the centre and the periphery. The programme began in June with a 'Clarkson Open Day' at Playford. This was followed in mid-September by a 'Clarkson Week-End', a tour that among other sites took in Wadesmill, Westminster Abbey, the Anti-Slavery International offices in Brixton, and St John's College, Cambridge. Here again, Playford featured prominently in the celebrations. Having planted honeysuckle around Clarkson's grave in Playford Church, as Mary Clarkson and her son had done many years before, residents of Wisbech and Playford joined forces to present a 'Thomas Clarkson at Playford Anthology' in the village hall, before repairing to Playford Hall where a commemorative oak tree was planted. Finally, during the week of the unveiling itself, special services were held at Wisbech (22 September) and again in Playford (29 September), which brought the celebrations to an end.[93]

These different ceremonials served to set Clarkson's considerable achievements in some sort of context; Wisbech and Playford not only defined who Clarkson was but also provided a frame of reference, organising the celebrations in Westminster Abbey into a coherent narrative. Just as important, the 150th anniversary committee succeeded in creating a focus for future national celebrations, and, in doing so, made it easier for Wisbech to compete with Hull and the challenge posed by the Wilberforce 'industry': it is interesting to note that the bicentenary of Clarkson's birth in 1960 received little or no attention at a national level. Of course, this does not mean that Clarkson has been fully restored or rehabilitated. But it does mean that in future he will be harder to ignore. Adam Hochschild's *Bury the Chains* (2005) is but one recent example of how pressure from both within and outside the academy can shift perspectives and, in doing so, alter or rearrange our understanding of British transatlantic slavery/abolition, however imperfect that understanding might be.

At the same time, the political capital invested in figures like Clarkson, and the continuing relevance of the 'Wilberforce controversy', tell us a great deal about the commemorative process. For the most part, (anti-)slavery ceremonials, certainly those held between 1859 and 1983, were conceived as nationalistic rituals. Drawing on and supported by imperialistic notions of 'stewardship', they were intended to reaffirm Britain's status as a civilised,

Christian nation. Wilberforce is a key figure here. As we have seen, Wilberforce's high idealism, and his reputation as a 'statesman-saint', came to embody Britain's much-vaunted 'tradition of humanity', particularly during moments of crisis and self-doubt.[94] Wilberforce's pre-eminence, moreover, reinforced the essential whiteness of these occasions. While blacks occasionally appear in nineteenth- and twentieth-century (anti-)slavery ceremonials, usually as guides or entertainers, they are rarely considered as *objects* of commemoration.[95] In fact, British involvement in the transatlantic slave trade – or, 'what came before' – has, until now, been largely absent from the public discourse on Emancipation. These, then, are highly elaborate rituals. Read carefully, they reveal not only how nations construct versions of the past but also how they employ them for 'self-understanding and to win power and place in an ever-changing present'.[96]

Today, such 'histories' are liable to provoke alarm and consternation. They can also seem woefully inadequate. Some sense of how far we have come, particularly since 1983, emerges from the 2004 Commons debate on the (then) forthcoming bicentenary of the abolition of the slave trade. In a wide-ranging discussion, MPs touched on a number of themes, among them the need to keep in mind the ongoing struggle against 'forced and bonded labour, the worst forms of child labour, child soldiers and early and forced marriages'. But, at the same time, there was understandable concern to improve awareness of British involvement in the transatlantic slave trade, however uncomfortable that knowledge might be. To take one example, Gary Streeter, Conservative MP for South-West Devon, told the Commons that there 'must be an acknowledgement of the part that the country played in this appalling atrocity; that what we did was wrong; that it is a scar on our history, and is only partially redeemed by the fact that we led the way in the abolition of the trade and then the abolition of slavery'. Similarly, Jeremy Corbyn (Islington North, Labour) urged his fellow MPs to remove themselves from 'the English and European feeling of self-satisfaction that we did a good job for the world 200 years ago. The reality is that Britain and Europe made a vast amount of wealth from the slave trade, and that wealth is still with us'. Many other MPs voiced similar sentiments, fuelling a sense that 2007 was an opportunity not simply to 'do justice' to transatlantic slavery but also to 'ensure that we learn the lessons of the past'.[97]

Debates of this kind have typically focused on a number of key issues. One is the demand for the government to make an apology for British involvement in the transatlantic slave trade. Another is a call for reparations, a highly sensitive issue that threatens to divide opinion on both sides of the Atlantic, despite official recognition, in the British case, at least, that 'appropriate reparations' should be made for slavery, 'both historically and as it exists now'.[98] There is also considerable support for a national slavery remembrance day. Speaking to this proposal, Louise Ellman, Labour MP for Liverpool, Riverside, has stressed the need for a permanent commemoration; not just something that lasts one or two days but a lasting memorial, along the lines of

Holocaust Memorial Day, that would recognise the inhumanity of transatlantic slavery, 'celebrate slaves' rebellions and the resistance that played such an important part in their emancipation', and emphasise the links between slavery and racism, 'much of which still persists'.[99] Similar initiatives are under way in different parts of the country. Liverpool, for instance, already has its own 'Slavery Remembrance Day', celebrated each year on 23 August, which, significantly, commemorates the successful uprising by slaves in Saint Domingue in 1791, and the National Maritime Museum in London holds an annual *Freedom* festival, also in August.[100]

None of this is to suggest that figures like Wilberforce are about to be displaced or erased from the nation's collective memory. But, as the bicentenary of the abolition of the slave trade approaches, there is clearly a growing sense, both inside and outside parliament, that the old frame of remembrance must be dislodged, so as to recover a version of the past that was in danger of being lost, if it existed at all; as Iwona Irwin-Zarecka has suggested, in such circumstances it is perhaps more appropriate to talk of filling a 'memory void'.[101] For obvious reasons, preparations for the 2007 anniversary have given this debate an added sense of urgency. The real challenge, however, will be not so much to confront the horrors of the Middle Passage, or the indignity of slavery in the Americas, but to do so in a way that takes cognisance of the specific, British roots of abolitionism, as well as Britain's tradition of humanitarian interventionism. Negotiating these competing demands will require the utmost skill, sensitivity, and political know-how. Otherwise, there is a serious danger that the celebrations in 2007 will become seriously fragmented, or, worse, result in the sort of uneasy compromises that ultimately satisfy no one.

Notes

1 Connerton, *How Societies Remember*, pp. 44–5. Connerton is primarily concerned with repetitive or recurrent ceremonials (birthdays, for instance), which, he argues, 'do not simply imply continuity with the past but explicitly claim such continuity'. For obvious reasons, anti-slavery ceremonials do not fit into the same category. Nevertheless, they remain important rituals, not least because they are 'formalised acts' that 'give value and meaning to the life of those who perform them'. For celebrations in the United States and the Caribbean, see Chapter 6.

2 Significantly, abolitionists do not appear to have celebrated the 25th anniversary of the passage of the Emancipation Act in 1858. Emancipation (1834) was clearly considered the more important anniversary, as it was in 1884.

3 Wheeler, *The Slaves' Champion*, pp. 148–9; C. Peter Ripley, *The Black Abolitionist Papers, vol. 1, The British Isles, 1830–1865* (Chapel Hill, NC, 1985), p. 460. Drescher, *The Mighty Experiment*, pp. 209–11.

4 *The Times*, 3 August 1859; Wheeler, *The Slaves' Champion*, p. 160.

5 Surveying the quarter century between 1834 and 1859, *The Times* concluded that there 'still remains sufficient evidence that free labour is not so advantageous as slavery to the owner of property'. 'What we see around us confirms this theory', the paper went on. '[There is] no doubt that slavery in the United States has extended, is extending,

and will extend. It is remunerative, and as long as it is so there is not the smallest chance for the Abolitionists'. *The Times*, 20 October 1859. For an excellent discussion of the ongoing debate over free and slave labour, and the impact of social science on British anti-slavery, see Drescher, *The Mighty Experiment*.

6   Drescher, *The Mighty Experiment*, pp. 225–7; *The Times*, 2 August 1884.

7   *The Times*, 2 August 1884. Kathryn Castle and others have identified a very similar emphasis in late nineteenth-century children's books and magazines. Here again, there is a tendency to highlight Britain's role in the abolition of slavery and the slave trade, and to link the nation's history of humanitarian interventionism to its role as a protector of 'weaker mortals'. See Kathryn Castle, *Britannia's Children: Reading Colonialism through Children's Books and Magazines* (Manchester, 1996), pp. 64–9; John Ahier, *Industry, Children and the Nation: An Analysis of National Identity in School Textbooks* (London, New York, and Philadelphia, 1988), pp. 158–63.

8   Raphael Samuel, *Theatres of Memory* (London, 1994); Geoff Eley and Ron Suny, eds., *Becoming National: A Reader* (Oxford, 2000), pp. 22–4; David Glassberg, *American Historical Pageantry: The Uses of Tradition in the Early Twentieth Century* (Chapel Hill, NC, 1990), p. 1 (quotation).

9   Rhodes House Library, Oxford, BFASS Papers, MS Brit. Emp. S18 C87/118, Rev. John H. Ritson to Travers Buxton, 22 December 1906; MS Brit. Emp. S18 C88/114, Rev. John Sharp to Travers Buxton, 17 January 1907; MS Brit. Emp. S19 D1/3, Travers Buxton to Rev. J. H. Ritson, 24 December 1906.

10 BFASS Papers, MS Brit. Emp. S19 D1/3, Travers Buxton to Sir Thomas Fowell Buxton, 31 December 1906 and 4, 8 January 1907.

11 *The Spectator*, 13 April 1907, p. 571. For the Belgian Congo, see E. D. Morel, *Red Rubber: The Story of the Rubber Slave Trade flourishing on the Congo in the Year of Grace 1906* (London, 1906); Adam Hochschild, *King Leopold's Ghost: A Story of Greed, Terror, and Heroism in Colonial Africa* (Boston, 1998).

12 MS Brit. Emp. S19 D1/3, Travers Buxton to BFASS committee members, 9 January 1907. See also MS Brit. Emp. S19 D1/3, Buxton to Henry Fox Bourne, 10 January 1907 and Buxton to Rev. J. H. Ritson, 16 January 1907.

13 MS Brit. Emp. S19 D1/3, Travers Buxton to Rev. John Sharp, 15 February 1907. In the opinion of Henry Fox Bourne, who was Secretary of the Aborigines Protection Society, the purpose of the Congo meeting was 'to embarrass the proposals for the taking over [of] the Congo by Belgium and to force on it if possible some arrangements by which "British interests" in the Congo would be developed and supported'. 'In this project I cannot concur,' he went on, 'and it is a serious trouble to me that there is now so much risk for a movement which our Society started on purely philanthropic grounds being diverted in favour of British aggrandisement'. See MS Brit. Emp. S18 C76/119, Henry Fox Bourne to Travers Buxton, 11 January 1907.

14 MS Brit. Emp. S20 E2/12, BFASS Committee Minutes, entry for 1 March 1907.

15 MS Brit. Emp. S19 D1/3, Travers Buxton to A. B. C. Merriman-Labor, 12, 15 March, and 9 April 1907; *Anti-Slavery Reporter*, March–May 1907, pp. 41–2; A. B. C. Merriman-Labor, *Britons through Negro Spectacles or A Negro on Britons* (London, 1909), pp. 153–6.

16 *The Spectator*, 30 March 1907, pp. 490–91.

17 *Eastern Morning News and Hull Advertiser*, 26 March 1907. Responding to this criticism, in October 1907 the Parks and Burial Committee of Hull Corporation 'requested' the Parks Superintendent to 'decorate the Wilberforce Monument on the 24th August in each year, being the anniversary of Wilberforce's birth'. See *Hull Corporation Minutes, 1906–07*, 2 vols (Hull, 1907), II, p. 215 (meeting of 1 October 1907).

18 *Manchester Guardian*, 23, 25 March 1907.

19 By contrast, the present Government has identified itself strongly with the forthcoming

bicentenary of the abolition of the slave trade. Speaking in the House of Commons on 14 October 2004, Fiona Mactaggart, Parliamentary Under-Secretary of State for the Home Department, declared that 'as Members of Parliament we have a responsibility to ensure that the bicentenary is effectively commemorated'. See *Hansard*, sixth series, vol. 425, col. 147WH (14 October 2004) and subsequent debate.

20   *Eastern Morning News and Hull Advertiser*, 26 March 1907.
21   MS Brit. Emp. S25 K21/4, 'Statement issued by the Committee of the Anti-Slavery Society and Aborigines Protection Society, 1932'. It should be noted that in 1909 what had formerly been the British and Foreign Anti-Slavery Society (BFASS) had amalgamated with the Aborigines Protection Society to form the Anti-Slavery and Aborigines Protection Society, hereafter the Anti-Slavery Society.
22   MS Brit. Emp. S19 D2/25 and D2/27, Emmeline Harris to Travers Buxton, n.d. and 21 June, 1933; MS Brit. Emp. S20 E2/17, Rhodes House Library, Oxford, Anti-Slavery Society, Committee Minutes, 1931–34, entries for 2 July and 5 November 1931, 7 January, 4 February, 3 March, and 2 June 1932, and 4 January 1934.
23   Anti-Slavery Society, Committee Minutes, entry for 2 June 1932.
24   MS Brit. Emp. S19 D2/27, Robert Gillie to Travers Buxton, 12 November 1932 and W. T. Grenfell to Buxton, 25 November 1932 (enclosing minutes of Bath Anti-Slavery Society). See also Grenfell to Buxton, 16 December 1932 and 18 January and 13 February 1933.
25   *Headway*, 15 (July 1933), p. 131. See also MS Brit. Emp. S25 K21/4, 'Statement issued by the Committee of the Anti-Slavery and Aborigines Protection Society, 1932'
26   A rare example of *Slavery: A Centenary Pageant Play*, published by the Anti-Slavery and Aborigines Protection Society in 1933, can be found at Wilberforce House Museum, Kingston upon Hull, Wilberforce and Anti-Slavery Collection, Box 14A,Wilberforce Centenary, 1933. See also Anti-Slavery Society, Committee Minutes, entries for 2 July 1931 and 4 February, 2 June, 7 July, 4 August, 6 October, 3 November, and 8 December 1932. The entry for 4 February notes that the libretto 'was to be written by Captain Reginald Berkeley', but I have been unable to verify this.
27   MS Brit. Emp. S25 K21/4, printed programme, 'Third Presentation of the revised Centenary Pageant Play by the Hampstead Imperial Players and the Field Flower Players, Rudolf Steiner Theatre, 13 March 1933'; *Slavery: A Centenary Pageant Play*, pp. 30–1.
28   Anti-Slavery Society, Committee Minutes, entries for 6 October, 3 November, 8 December 1932, 2 February 1933; *Anti-Slavery Reporter and Aborigines' Friend*, 22 (January 1933), p. 132. Significantly, the second performance of the pageant play was given before delegates to the General Council of the League of Nations Union. See *Headway*, 14 (December 1932), supplement, *League of Nations Union News*, p. iv, and 15 (January 1933), p. 17.
29   MS Brit. Emp. S19 D2/26 and 27, Samuel Maltby to Travers Buxton, 10 December 1932 and B. Godfrey Buxton to Buxton, 14 March 1933. Echoing these sentiments, a critic in the *Reading Mercury* observed that the 'chief dramatic weakness' of the pageant 'lay in the characters of "Public Opinion" and "Liberty"', adding that this was not the fault of the actors, but 'rather the author (unknown), since he used them to underline each episode, as if doubting the ability of drama to convince on its own'. See *Reading Mercury*, 14 October 1933.
30   MS Brit. Emp. S19 D2/27, Florence Ames to Travers Buxton, 20 February 1933; *Salisbury Times*, 7 July 1933; *Isle of Ely & Wisbech Advertiser*, 22 November 1933. In Salisbury the pageant was abridged and performed as four scenes, as follows: 'Queen Elizabeth', 'Wilberforce', 'Lincoln', and 'The Progress of Freedom'.
31   *Anti-Slavery Reporter and Aborigines' Friend*, 23 (July 1933), p. 60.

32 Ibid. It appears that Lady Simon's name was only added to the list of speakers after representations had been made from the Anti-Slavery Society to the BBC. See Anti-Slavery Society, Committee Minutes, entries for 2 March and 6 April 1933.
33 *Anti-Slavery Reporter and Aborigines' Friend*, 24 (October 1934), p. 107; *The Times*, 1 August 1934; *Daily Telegraph*, 1 August 1934.
34 *The Times*, 3 September 1934;
35 All of these figures are based on the minutes and correspondence of the Anti-Slavery Society, the *Anti-Slavery Reporter and Aborigines' Friend*, and local and national newspapers.
36 *Anti-Slavery Reporter and Aborigines' Friend*, 23 (July 1933), pp. 55–6, 78 (Edinburgh, Cardiff, Barry, and Belfast); (October 1933), pp. 100, 107 (Edinburgh, Lochgelly, and Glasgow); 24 (January 1934), pp. 143, 179 (Glasgow, Edinburgh, Aberdeen, Airdrie, Stepps, and Wigtown); (April 1934), pp. 31, 35 (Girvan and Perth); Anti-Slavery Society, Committee Minutes, entry for 7 December 1933 (Dublin and Belfast).
37 Ibid., January 1934, p. 179.
38 Anti-Slavery Society, Committee Minutes, entries for 4 June, 2 July 1931, 7 April, 2 June, 7 July, and 4 August 1932; *The Times*, 29 July 1932; *Anti-Slavery Reporter and Aborigines' Friend* (October 1934), p. 105.
39 *Anti-Slavery Reporter and Aborigines' Friend* (July 1933), pp. 66–8.
40 For the activities of the League of Nations Union and its organizational strength, see J. A. Thompson, 'The League of Nations Union and Promotion of the League Idea in Great Britain', *Australian Journal of Politics and History*, 18 (1972), pp. 52–61.
41 Lionel Robbins Library, London School of Economics, League of Nations Union Papers, microfilm edition, reel 4, LNU Executive Committee Minutes, 21 April 1932. See also LNU Papers, reel 1, Minutes of the General Council of the League of Nations Union, 20, 21, 22 June 1933; Anti-Slavery Society, Committee Minutes, entry for 5 May 1932.
42 Anti-Slavery Society, Committee Minutes, entries for 1 October 1931, 8 December 1932, 4 May 1933.
43 *Bournemouth Daily Echo*, 17 July 1933.
44 *Headway*, 15 (August 1933), p. 166, November 1933, p. 222, December 1933, p. 246, and 16, February 1934, p. 38.
45 *Headway*, 15 (July 1933), pp. 131–2. It also seems likely that the Anti-Slavery Society borrowed many of the LNU's opinion-building techniques, including the use of lantern slides, lecture notes, and pageants. The LNU, in turn, appears to have been alert to the fact that the centenary celebrations would give encouragement to 'those who in this generation hope to abolish international war'. See LNU Papers, reel 14, League of Nations Union, Education Committee Minutes, 4 November 1932.
46 *The Times*, 16 September 1919.
47 Andrew Thorpe, *Britain in the 1930s* (Oxford, 1992), p. 28.
48 *Daily Express*, 15 July 1933.
49 Again, these details are extracted from the correspondence and minute books of the Anti-Slavery Society, the *Anti-Slavery Reporter and Aborigines' Friend*, and national and local newspapers.
50 *The Times*, 30 July and 1 August 1934.
51 *Anti-Slavery Reporter and Aborigines' Friend* (October 1934), p. 106.
52 *The Times*, 29 July 1933.
53 *Anti-Slavery Reporter and Aborigines' Friend* (July 1933), pp. 53, 56.
54 See, for example, *The Times*, 24 July 1933.
55 *Carlisle Journal*, 10 November 1933.
56 *The Times*, 29 July 1933.

57 *Anti-Slavery Reporter and Aborigines' Friend*, 23 (April 1933), p. 34; Anti-Slavery Society, Committee Minutes, entries for 8 December 1932, 2 August and 6 December 1934.

58 Anti-Slavery Society, Committee Minutes, entries for 2 March 1933, 6 December 1934, and 3 January 1935.

59 Coupland, *The Empire in These Days*, p. 268. Emphasis in original.

60 *The Times*, 3 August 1859; Wheeler, *The Slaves' Champion*, pp. 151–3, 161–3. Significantly, Brougham described Clarkson as 'the pioneer of the great cause of abolition', a view echoed by George Thompson.

61 *The Times*, 2 August 1884.

62 *Manchester Guardian*, 25 March 1907.

63 Samuel Hynes, *The Auden Generation: Literature and Politics in England in the 1930s* (London, 1976), pp. 98–131.

64 *The Times*, 24, 25 July 1933.

65 *The Times*, 29, 31 July, and 2 August 1933; *Hull Daily Mail*, 21–31 July 1933. For details of the radio chronicle play, see Thomas Sheppard, *William Wilberforce: Emancipator of Slaves, 1759–1833* (Exeter, 1937), pp. 53–60; Wilberforce House Museum, Wilberforce and Anti-Slavery Collection, Box 14A, Wilberforce Centenary, 1933.

66 *The Times*, 29 July 1933.

67 *The Times*, for instance, noted that 'in the same year that WILBERFORCE was carried to Westminster Abbey, LORD SHAFTESBURY took up his work against the sordid miseries that had been bred of liberty and *laissez faire* in the factories and the mines'. See *The Times*, 29 July 1933.

68 *The Times*, 29 July 1933.

69 *The Times*, 2 August 1933. My emphasis.

70 *The Times*, 24 July 1933.

71 *The Times*, 28 August 1933.

72 Anti-Slavery Society, Committee Minutes, entries for 2 July, 6 August, 1 October 1931, 7 July, 4 August, 6 October 1932, 2 March 1933. Another example of the Society's evenhandedness is the care taken to give Buxton and Wilberforce equal billing in the *Anti-Slavery Reporter and Aborigines' Friend*. So, while Wilberforce's portrait appeared on the cover of the October 1933 edition, Buxton's appeared on the cover of the January 1934 edition.

73 MS Brit. Emp. S25 K7, Miscellaneous Papers; MS Brit. Emp. S19 D2/26, H. R. Wright to Travers Buxton, 15 and 17 February 1933; Anti-Slavery Society, Committee Minutes, entries for 2 February and 2 March 1933.

74 Perhaps in reaction to this, some of the revised versions of the play performed in the provinces appear to have included an extra scene depicting 'Thomas Clarkson in Liverpool, 1787'. See, for instance, *Reading Mercury*, 14 October 1933.

75 *The Times*, 1 August 1934.

76 *Methodist Recorder*, 3 September 1959. It was not unusual for figures like Wilberforce and Thomas Jefferson to be appropriated by Cold War rhetoricians. Only the week before, President Eisenhower had reaffirmed the steadfast purpose of the English-speaking peoples to defend 'freedom, liberty and the dignity of man'.

77 *Hull Daily Mail*, 27 July and 21, 24, and 25 August 1959; Deverell and Watkins, *Wilberforce and Hull*, plate 73.

78 Westminster Abbey Library and Muniments, WAM 64204–6, Sub-Dean of Westminster Abbey to J. Haydon W. Glen, Town Clerk of Hull, 7 July, 1959; B. D. Nicholls, Information Officer, Church Missionary Society, to Sub-Dean of Westminster Abbey, 23 July 1959; Note by Dr A. Fox, Sub-Dean of Westminster Abbey. The address was given by Lord Hemingford. See MS Brit. Emp. S.19. D.11/11/1.

79   *The Times*, 27, 30 July 1983.

80   Wilberforce House Museum, Wilberforce and Anti-Slavery Collection, Box 20, 150th Anniversary, 1983, official programme for celebrations in Hull.

81   Wisbech and Fenland Museum, Wisbech, EO3/14/2, Thomas Clarkson 150th Anniversary Committee, Miscellaneous Printed Papers, '1833–1983 Wilberforce Anniversary', Official Programme. Significantly, the 1983 anniversary does not seem to have been commemorated in Wisbech. For Hull, see Chapter 5.

82   *The Times*, 29 July 1983.

83   Buxton, for instance, was recognised at a short service in Westminster Abbey on 28 August 1983 to commemorate the royal assent given to the Emancipation Bill on 28 August 1833. See *The Times*, 24 August 1983.

84   Wilberforce House Museum, Wilberforce and Anti-Slavery Collection, Box 20, material relating to the 150th anniversary, 1983, flyers and synopsis of *'Slaves'*.

85   Ibid., synopsis of 'Wilberforce ; or, the Liberator Reflects'.

86   Caryl Phillips, foreword, in Reyahn King, ed., *Ignatius Sancho: An African Man of Letters* (London, 1997), p. 9 (quotation) and following.

87   See Chapter 5.

88   Luisa Passerini, 'Memories between Silence and Oblivion', in Katherine Hodgkin and Susannah Radstone, eds., *Contested Pasts: The Politics of Memory* (London and New York, 2003), p. 244.

89   Wisbech and Fenland Museum, Minute Book of Wisbech Museum and Literary Institution, entries for 1 May and 12 June 1933; *Isle of Ely & Wisbech Advertiser*, 7 June 1933.

90   Wisbech and Fenland Museum, Wisbech Museum and Literary Institution, Museum Day Book, January to October 1960 (newspaper clippings); *Isle of Ely & Wisbech Advertiser*, 30 March 1960; MS Brit. Emp. S19, D11/11/1.

91   Museum Day Book, October 1960.

92   Ibid., January 1960. For Hemingford's speech, see *Isle of Ely & Wisbech Advertiser*, 30 March 1960.

93   Thomas Clarkson 150th Anniversary Committee Minutes, entries for 7 December 1995, and 20 February 1996; Thomas Clarkson 150th Anniversary Committee, Miscellaneous Printed Papers; *The Times*, 22 May 1935.

94   I am thinking here of the 1930s, but for some the 1960s were also a period of crisis, and not just because of the Cold War. A case in point is the playwright, Alan Thornhill, whose *Mr Wilberforce, MP* (1965) was clearly an attempt to restore to Britain a sense of 'moral leadership'. 'Admiration for past greatness does not justify acceptance of present smallness', he explained in the preface to the printed text. 'Today we face the unpalatable truth that our nation, linked for generations with standards of character and excellence that led the world, is increasingly recognised as an exponent of laxness, godlessness and the second rate'. See Alan Thornhill, *Mr Wilberforce, MP* (London, 1965), p. vii, and Appendix.

95   See Chapter 6.

96   David W. Blight, *Beyond the Battlefield: Race, Memory and the American Civil War* (Boston, 2002), p. 1.

97   *Hansard*, sixth series, vol. 425, col. 149WH (Streeter), col. 151WH (Corbyn), and col. 143WH (Fiona Mactaggart, Slough, Labour), 14 October 2004.

98   Ibid., col. 152WH (Corbyn), col. 162WH (Mike Hancock, Portsmouth, South, Liberal Democrat), col. 168WH (Oona King, Bethnal Green and Bow, Labour), and col. 171WH (Mactaggart). For an illuminating insight into the reparations debate in the United States, especially as it has impacted on American universities, see Frances Fitzgerald, 'Peculiar Institutions: Brown University looks at the Slave Traders in its Past', *The*

New Yorker, 12 September 2005, pp. 68–77.

99 Hansard, sixth series, vol. 425, col. 159–162WH; Guardian Unlimited, 14 October 2004, www.guardian.co.uk/race/story/0,11374.1327387,00.html; Black Information Link, 9 November 2004, www.blink.org.uk/print.asp?key=4852.

100 *Hansard*, sixth series, vol. 425, col. 159–162WH; *NMM Community News* (Autumn/ Winter 2004). 23 August is also the date chosen by UNESCO as the International Day for the Remembrance of the Slave Trade and its Abolition. See Chapter 6.

101 Irwin-Zarecka, *Frames of Remembrance*, p. 117.

5

Sites of memory: transatlantic slavery and the museum experience

In recent years the heritage industry has become perhaps the most fertile ground for inquiries into our understanding of and engagement with British transatlantic slavery. Whereas thirty or even twenty years ago there were only a handful of museums and galleries devoted to transatlantic slavery, today there are major permanent slavery exhibitions in Bristol, Hull, Liverpool, and London, and plans are currently under way to create a National Museum and Centre for the Understanding of Transatlantic slavery. (It is also worth noting that similar initiatives are underway in France and the Netherlands.)[1] Expansion of this kind has, of necessity, required curators and scholars to look again at how they present and interpret transatlantic slavery. At the same time, 'new articulations of space, object, and subject [have created] the conditions for the emergence of new technologies' and new ways of looking at things.[2] We should not view these changes uncritically, however. If, on the one hand, the urgency for museums and galleries to consult as well as to inform their 'customers' has proved beneficial, on the other, the attempt to accommodate sometimes very different perceptions of slavery and the slave trade has hardly been unproblematic.

Collecting and presenting artefacts connected with slavery and the slave trade has a long history dating back to the early abolitionist movement and beyond. One thinks, for instance, of Thomas Clarkson's 'Africa box', which contained examples of African produce (cotton, spices, gum rubber, and different kinds of wood) and was designed to convince sceptics that there was, after all, an economic alternative to the transatlantic slave trade.[3] More arresting still were the whips, shackles, and irons collected and displayed by abolitionists. Both Clarkson and Wilberforce owned – or, at least, had access to – items of this description, some of which obviously found their way into local museums, and, as we know, David Livingstone collected slavery artefacts, among them a wooden yoke that he is supposed to have removed from the neck of a slave.[4] Abolitionism also generated its own artefacts. Probably the best known, and certainly most ubiquitous, of these was Josiah Wedgwood's jasper medallion of a kneeling slave (1788), together with the motto 'Am I not a Man and a Brother?' But, in truth, the early abolitionist movement produced a range of artefacts – cameos, tokens, medals, and medallets – all of which proved highly collectable. The nineteenth century would witness further innovations, particularly in the area of ceramics. Anti-slavery jugs, plates, cups, and even dinner services were all familiar sights during the 1830s and 1840s, as were prints, broadsides, and doilies.[5]

Nevertheless, the collection of these artefacts was largely uncoordinated. All of this changed with the appearance of the Wilberforce House Museum (1906). Under the expert eye of Thomas Sheppard, Wilberforce House collected enthusiastically, if unsystematically, on a number of fronts: items related to Wilberforce (books, prints, letters, furniture); items connected with the African slave trade (shackles, whips, branding irons); and items connected with abolition (prints, cartoons, medals, and figurines). Sadly, many of the museum's records were destroyed during the Second World War, but it seems likely that the bulk of the collection dates from Sheppard's years as curator of Hull Museums (1901–41).[6] As Britain's first, and for many years only, slavery museum, Wilberforce House was also perfectly placed to participate in and to benefit from the commemorative process. In 1933, for instance, Hull Museums marked the centenary of Wilberforce's death with a special exhibition at the Mortimer Galleries in the City Hall, an event that was chiefly remarkable for the acquisition of a life-size wax figure of Wilberforce, donated by Madame Tussaud's, which was displayed, appropriately, with 'period settings', and later transferred to Wilberforce House Museum where it became a part of the permanent collection.[7]

Hull and Wilberforce House did not have things all their own way, however. Significantly, Wisbech Museum also celebrated the 1933 centenary, in this case with a special exhibition that included Clarkson's 'Africa box' (acquired in 1870), as well as a considerable collection of portraits, lithographs, books, and autograph letters covering the greater part of Clarkson's working life. Although most of these items do not appear to have been on permanent display, there is no mistaking Wisbech Museum's determination to 'specialise' in objects connected with the anti-slavery movement, or, in pursuit of that objective, its eagerness to solicit 'gifts or loans' that 'would make its already rich collection more complete'.[8] Over the years, the rivalry between Hull and Wisbech would become, if anything, more intense, drawing, as it did, on perceived injustices – at least, on the part of the authorities in Wisbech – and a lingering sense that Clarkson had been 'written out' of the official history of British anti-slavery. As we have seen, the bicentenary of Wilberforce's birth in 1959 was marked by a series of events in Hull's museums. Not to be outdone, the following year Wisbech Museum celebrated the bicentenary of Clarkson's birth with a special exhibition that featured items borrowed from Hull Museums, the National Portrait Gallery in London, and members of Clarkson's own family.[9]

In short, the first half of the twentieth century witnessed the emergence of two rival collections that, crucially, presented two very different 'versions' of British anti-slavery. Just as important, in highlighting the achievements of figures like Clarkson and Wilberforce, these museums enabled Britons to view slavery through the moral triumph of Emancipation. Africa, according to this narrative, was a place where Europeans got 'slaves'. Similarly, whips, shackles, and instruments of torture were either divorced from their original context, or else displayed in such a way as to give meaning to the *abolitionists'* struggle. At Wilberforce House Museum, for instance, slavery relics were placed indiscriminately alongside anti-slavery medals and cameos, 'beautiful statuettes in Crown Derby biscuit ware of Wilberforce and Hannah More', seals, tobacco boxes, Wilberforce's court dress, a large family bible, and a set of Sierra Leone postage stamps issued to commemorate the centenary of the death of Wilberforce.[10] Here again, what is interesting about this narrative is what it left out. Significantly, the permanent exhibition at Wilberforce House made no mention of black 'agency' or, indeed, the meaning of the black experience. Instead, its curators fell back on a discourse that interposed a safe distance between Britain and colonial slavery, in the process shifting African perspectives to the margins.

Where blacks appeared at all, they tended to fill supportive or 'theatrical' roles. Perhaps reflecting the mood of the 1930s, Thomas Sheppard planned the centenary exhibition in Hull in the manner of an 'entertainment'. Besides the familiar slave relics (whips, shackles, irons) and the 'stage tableau of Wilberforce', there were 'recitals of Negro spirituals' and 'native sketches' performed by 'celebrated coloured artists from Jamaica and West Africa'. As if this were not enough, 'Edward Stubbs and his orchestra' were also hired to play 'fantasies of plantation songs, spirituals, and slave songs'.[11] No doubt the organisers intended these innovations to dignify the black experience and to bring 'authenticity' to the 'noble work that ended the terrible traffic in human beings'.[12] Yet, in reaffirming popular, music-hall images of blacks as minstrels and 'entertainers', performances of this kind served also to underline the superiority of white (Christian) civilisation. In the Hull case this effect was heightened by advertisements placed in local newspapers, which highlighted the various 'acts' on show at the Mortimer Galleries in a banner-style layout that was reminiscent of cinema and theatre advertisements. 'Do not miss this', the byline proclaimed, 'the chance of a lifetime to see in review the visible relics of a barbarous age'. Even the opening hours, 2.30 to 10.00 p.m. each weekday, with regular performances of the 'Negro spirituals' at 2.15, 4.15, 8.00 p.m. and 9.00 p.m., seemed to blur the distinction between 'popular' and 'respectable' entertainments.[13]

Whatever their limitations, the displays at Hull and Wisbech dominated public discourse on transatlantic slavery, such as it was, for over 75 years. Then, in the early 1980s, perspectives and priorities started to change. In 1983 Wilberforce House Museum opened two new exhibits, 'The Slave Trade' and 'Wilberforce and Abolition', to coincide with the 150th anniversary of Wilberforce's death. A decade later, Wisbech and Fenland Museum mounted a new, permanent Clarkson display, the first of its kind. But of far greater significance, not least because of its size and scale, was the opening of 'Against Human Dignity', the Transatlantic Slavery Gallery at Merseyside Maritime Museum, Liverpool (1994). This was followed by 'A Respectable Trade? Bristol and Transatlantic Slavery', which was originally exhibited at Bristol City Museum and Art Gallery in March 1999 and later moved to Bristol Industrial Museum, although it is important to note that the current display is only half its original size. These exhibitions also coincided with other local initiatives, including slave trade trails (Bristol) and educational packs for children (Wisbech). Perhaps just as important, the National Maritime Museum included a section on transatlantic slavery in its controversial 'Trade and Empire' gallery, which was opened to the public in 1997 and reopened in 2001, following extensive refurbishment (much of it in response to hostile criticism of a tableau depicting a manacled black hand emerging from a hatch beneath a white British lady drinking tea); while a similar display, albeit on a much smaller scale, can be found at the newly established British Empire and Commonwealth Museum, again in Bristol (2001).[14]

These exhibitions, of course, were conceived in a very different political and intellectual climate. The language of diversity, and more inclusive notions of 'Britishness', placed new demands on museums and galleries, as they did on schools and colleges. National Lottery funding, launched in 1994, also underlined the message, amplified by many black and Asian community groups, that museums had a 'public duty to make provision for all parts of society', which meant 'taking care to mount exhibitions and displays that [interested] as broad a range of groups as possible'.[15] These pressures, not to mention new technologies and new approaches to the interpretation of texts, led in the 1980s to a radical reappraisal of the role of the museum in modern society and, with it, the emergence of the notion of the 'universal' museum. As Eilean Hooper-Greenhill explains: 'Today's "universal" museum is one where all the various needs of visitors can be satisfied: a museum with well-displayed and enlivened collections, with a shop in which desirable and well-packaged objects can be purchased, with several places to eat according to one's taste and pocket, with a rest area, and with space for the children to be cared for and to play. Open, intelligent spaces offer increased access to subject and object.'[16]

Museums, in short, have had to redefine themselves. In many museums and galleries today visitors will find, and expect to find, discovery rooms, hands-on exhibits, film, dioramas, interactive video, and audio recordings. Similarly, greater emphasis is placed on 'enactive' and 'experimental' modes of learning, whereby visitors acquire knowledge through demonstrations, role-playing, or, more often, the handling of objects. 'New' museums are also more 'user friendly' in the sense that they quite openly seek and encourage the involvement of their 'customers'. This means not only targeting certain audiences, particularly those (minorities, for instance) that might have been neglected or omitted in the past, but also seeking their active participation in the planning and organisation of museum displays. Whereas in the past the museum or art gallery was 'very much the territory of the professional staff, with the "public" allowed in on sufferance, if their behaviour was appropriate, [now] the "client" demands active rights and expects good service'. In some cases – at Leicester New Walk Museum, for instance – community groups have been invited to exhibit their own 'histories', either making use of pre-existing collections or displaying their own objects. As a result, the curator ceases to be in control, 'and instead of one point of view, many voices are encouraged to speak'.[17]

For obvious reasons, the representation of transatlantic slavery invited just this sort of open, 'democratic' process. In Liverpool, for instance, one of the first things the organisers of the Transatlantic Slavery Gallery did was to adopt a mission statement. As the curator, Anthony Tibbles, explains: 'We took steps to explain our role and the way we saw the gallery developing and crucially the role others could play in that process.' To this end, the National Museums and Galleries in Merseyside appointed an outreach worker for the proposed gallery, whose job it was 'to go out into the community, and in particular the Black community, to stimulate interest in the gallery and to develop activities and programmes that would extend the traditional role of the museum'.[18] Similarly, the exhibition originally put on at Bristol City Museum and Art Gallery was the culmination of a 'three-year programme of public consultation and discussion developed under the aegis of the Bristol Slave Trade Action Group'; and, more recently, the National Maritime Museum in London has conducted a series of consultative meetings with local community and action groups ahead of the bicentenary of the abolition of the slave trade in 2007.[19]

In each case, this process has prompted and, to some extent, legitimised a re-thinking of our approach to transatlantic slavery. But, at the same time, slave museums and galleries have been influenced by recent trends in academic scholarship and, in particular, the challenge thrown down by so-called 'revisionist' accounts of plantation life in the Americas. The last quarter of the twentieth century witnessed a remarkable outpouring of books and articles on transatlantic slavery, nearly all of which rejected the traditional model of slave brutality, or 'victimization', in favour of what is sometimes referred to as slave 'autonomy', a term that since the 1970s has become synonymous with slave culture, community and resistance. Determined to unravel and document 'the world the slaves made' (the emphasis is important), scholars on both sides of the Atlantic increasingly turned their attention to what had hitherto been neglected areas of slave life: religion, folklore, music, dance, material culture. This inquiry was also driven by a more flexible approach to and interaction with new sources and 'new' methodologies, among them literary theory, anthropology, and historical archaeology. The result was a revolution in slave studies that, in many ways, reflected developments in other fields, notably women's history. Suspicious of what in the past had undoubtedly been an over-reliance on European or 'white' perspectives, scholars of transatlantic slavery called instead for much greater emphasis on black 'agency' and, just as important, African 'voices'.[20]

Dovetailing neatly with shifting political agendas, 'revisionist' arguments have played an important part in shaping representations of transatlantic slavery. This is perhaps most evident at the Transatlantic Slavery Gallery in Liverpool, where the exhibition 'goes straight to Africa and only later picks up the European involvement – the traders and their ships'. As Anthony Tibbles explains, the intention is to show that 'other things went on [in Africa] and that there were influences other than European'.[21] To illustrate this point, extensive use is made of a range of artefacts, among them intricately carved wooden stools, musical instruments, and stunning gold rings and pendants. Similar displays can be found at Hull and at the Industrial Museum in Bristol, where, again, attention is drawn to the richness and diversity of African cultures, both before and during the era of the transatlantic slave trade.[22] Less successful perhaps, and certainly more problematic, are the attempts made by these various displays to visualise indigenous African peoples. Merseyside Maritime Museum, at least, has the advantage of one of the Benin Bronzes, on loan from the Museum of Mankind, which date from the sixteenth and seventeenth centuries and depict Bini guards in armour and musicians with gongs and pipes. But the display at the Industrial Museum in Bristol is forced back on a modern re-creation, in the shape of a life-size model of a native African in 'period' dress, although the precise date is indeterminate. Paradoxically, the assumption here seems to be that Africa is 'exotic' and 'alien'. As Marcus Wood puts it: 'There is the peculiar sense that these exhibits are timeless, that they represent not how people in Africa lived at the time of the slave trade ... but how people in Africa have always lived and still live.'[23]

If Africa has been 're-imagined' by these different exhibitions, so, too, has the transatlantic slave trade. Particularly striking in this regard is the much greater emphasis placed on the organisation of the 'triangular trade', or the 'great circuit', as it is sometimes referred to, and its relevance to British concerns. At the Industrial Museum in Bristol, for instance, imaginative use is made of local trade cards and advertisements to show how 'everyone' was involved in the trade, and a short distance away at the British Empire and Commonwealth Museum similar use is made of information boards on 'Bristol manufacturers and the slave trade'.[24] Slavery here is not something distant or removed from the British experience; rather, it is seen as an integral part of the growth of local economies and the prosperity of ports like Bristol and Liverpool. Indeed, it is one of the strengths of the exhibition at the Industrial Museum in Bristol that it links slavery to everyday 'objects': to streetnames, buildings, fashionable suburbs, and even local schools. (Conversely, one of the criticisms initially levelled at the Transatlantic Slavery Gallery in Liverpool was that it failed to make enough of the local 'connection'.)[25] Put a different way, the Bristol example demonstrates how European perspectives – in this case, Bristol's role in the transatlantic slave trade – can be re-fashioned in order to encourage a more critical evaluation of the past, as well as of issues like 'race' and national identity.

17   Mock-up of the interior of a slave ship, Wilberforce House Museum,
Kingston upon Hull

But it is not just the organisation of the transatlantic slave trade that has
preoccupied curators. Much more challenging has been the representation of
the Middle Passage. To quote Anthony Tibbles: 'Everyone recognised the cen-
trality of the Middle Passage – it was the one common experience of all Africans who were enslaved and was of profound psychological significance'. The
question was how to capture or simulate this experience – to make it 'authentic'. Influenced by curatorial theories emphasising 'client participation', and
the popularity of 'living' sites like the Jorvik Viking Centre in York, curators
up and down the country came up with the idea of a cross-section of the interior of a slave ship.[26] The first of these was devised and installed at Wilberforce
House Museum in Hull, following its extensive refurbishment in 1983. Here,
in what is a walk-through display, visitors are confronted by eight black plaster models (all men) tightly packed into the hold of a slave ship. Significantly,
the figures are arranged in such a way as to suggest torment or, at least, extreme discomfort. There is also a soundtrack – apparently made by the museum staff – which features coughs, moans, and the sound of splashing water,
and, above them, snatches of a dialogue: 'another one dead there ... get it out
of the way, get it over the side ... get out of my way, you bloody animal'.[27]
    A very similar mock-up can be found at the Transatlantic Slavery Gallery
in Liverpool, but this time there are no figures and while there are some

atmospheric noises, mainly the crashing of waves, the 'principal sound is al-
ternate readings from the log of John Newton ... and readings from the memoirs of [Olaudah] Equiano'. Meanwhile, images of shackled human beings are
projected against the interior of the hold, creating a sense of movement as
they roll over or sit against each other.[28] Less sensationalised perhaps than
the mock-up at Wilberforce House, the display nevertheless conveys something of the horrors of the slave trade, even at the risk of seeming cold and
sanitised. Finally, there is the mock-up at the Industrial Museum in Bristol.
Here, visitors are presented first with a giant reproduction of the well-known
abolitionist print, *Description of the slave ship Brookes*, which, in a novel departure, has affixed to it a series of individual life histories. A short distance away
is the painted white interior of the hold of a slave ship. Again, there are no
figures; instead, the interior is stark and bare. But, in an effort to offset the
lifelessness of the display, clever use is made of sound recordings featuring
extracts from black slave narratives, as well as an extended clip from Stephen
Spielberg's film, *Amistad*.

Three-dimensional displays of this kind have become an integral part of
the client-centred approach of many 'new' museums.[29] Nevertheless, their
use, particularly in the case of something as politically sensitive as transatlantic slavery, has raised understandable concerns. Visitors' responses to the Transatlantic Slavery Gallery in Liverpool, for instance, suggest that while many
find the interior of the slave ship 'moving' and 'atmospheric', others regard it
as 'far too clean, empty, [and] not nearly hard hitting enough'. Equally revealing

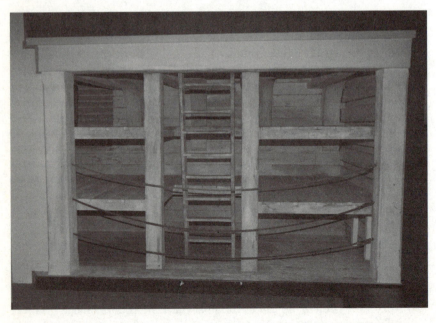

18   Mock-up of the interior of a slave ship, Industrial Museum, Bristol

are the responses of children. Here again, some like the ship reconstruction; others, however, find it frightening. (Anticipating such reactions, the mock-up at the Industrial Museum in Bristol actually warns children, and their parents, that they might find the scenes from *Amistad* 'distressing'.) New articulations of space, object, and subject, therefore, can give rise to 'potentially conflictual points of view'. Some of the risks and benefits involved are perhaps best summed up in the words of an 11-year-old visitor to the Transatlantic Slavery Gallery in Liverpool, who admitted that he got 'scared inside the cabin of the ship because it was so realistic. It must of [sic] been horrible in real life ... It made me feel terrible and ashamed of coming from England'.[30]

Such responses are, in many ways, a vindication of what these mock-ups are trying to achieve, namely to simulate the experience of the middle passage. But, at the same time, ship reconstructions, however tastefully they are presented, run the risk of trivialising the transatlantic slave trade, not least by suggesting that by walking through and around them we can find out 'what it was really like'. The presumption here is that we can 'know' the past by experiencing or re-experiencing it. Even if this were possible, where are the limits? Are those who find the Liverpool display 'clean' and 'empty' suggesting, as an alternative, total immersion in the slave experience, involving *all* our senses; and, if so, would this constitute 'knowledge' or merely pander to a kind of voyeurism that, by its very nature, demands thrills and entertainment? Inevitably, displays of this kind also raise awkward ethical questions. Perhaps, as Marcus Wood suggests, 'there are subjects and objects which cannot fit within the educational framework of current museum culture'? This is not an argument for doing nothing, or simply saying that transatlantic slavery, like the Holocaust, defies description. But, by the same token, we do need to think critically about our ability to use ship reconstructions 'as a means of entering into and living vicariously in a past time', just as we need to ask ourselves whether, in cases such as these, 'absolute empathy' is either possible or desirable?[31]

Less controversial, perhaps, is the way these different galleries and museums deal with plantation life in the Americas. Here again, particular emphasis is placed upon the 'indignity' of transatlantic slavery. At Liverpool, for instance, visitors are confronted with leg irons and punishment collars, starkly mounted upon cut-out reproductions of human figures, as well as graphic accounts of slave sales, the process of 'seasoning' in the Caribbean, and labour on plantations. The display also 'confirms the widespread sexual abuse of black women by white men'.[32] Running against or alongside this narrative, however, is an insistence that slaves were not 'passive victims' but historical actors in their own right. Accordingly, attention is drawn to acts of resistance, some of them overt (rebellions, for instance), others, like keeping African heritage alive through words, names, music, and beliefs, more accurately described as 'passive'. Hence the importance attached to the relatively small number of surviving slave artefacts, many of them from the American South: wooden bread bowls, stools, rolling pins, and musical instruments. At a number of museums, notably the Transatlantic Slavery Gallery in Liverpool, work songs and traditional African music are also used to stress the 'continuity of African traditions amongst slaves and former slave communities' through to the present day.[33]

Displays of this kind are clearly intended to present museum visitors with a new reality of the (slave) past. Nevertheless, the results are uneven. At the Industrial Museum in Bristol, for instance, there is an obvious tension between text and object that arises, in part, because, without appropriate artefacts or other visual devices, the theme of resistance is difficult to curate. More to the point, plantation displays, however they are conceived, run the risk of being overshadowed by what precedes them. Slave ship reconstructions inevitably raise expectations, just as they involve choices on the part of museum curators. (In this connection, it is interesting to note that only Wilberforce House Museum has thus far attempted to 'concretize' slave life in the Americas, by including in its display a mock-up of a 'slave hut in the West Indies'.)[34] New technologies, in other words, can sometimes distract or overwhelm visitors, in this instance serving to reaffirm the importance of the transatlantic slave trade and the Middle Passage, in particular, as a site of national memory. Not surprisingly, the element of the Transatlantic Slavery Gallery in Liverpool mentioned most by visitors is the slave ship reconstruction; by contrast, relatively few of them mention facts about enslaved Africans or, for that matter, slavery itself.[35]

In these different ways, museums and curators have set out to re-fashion our approach to transatlantic slavery. As the mission statement issued by the Transatlantic Slavery Gallery in Liverpool declares: 'The aim of the gallery is to increase public understanding of the experience of Black people in Britain and the modern world through an examination of the Atlantic slave trade and the African diaspora.'[36] For obvious reasons, this has involved shifting attention away from European perspectives and towards an 'African' point of view. It has also meant spelling out the long-term effects of slavery, as well as its blighting effects on black communities, here and across the Americas: significantly, all of these exhibitions have sections on the economic and psychological impact of slavery, which also attempt to problematize the African diaspora and relate it to contemporary concerns. In much the same way, nearly all of them stress the legacy of resistance. At the Industrial Museum in Bristol, for instance, conscious links are made between slave rebellions and strikes, trade boycotts, and 'campaigns for civil rights and independence in the former colonies'. Equally, visitors to the museum are reminded that the idea that 'Black is Beautiful' is 'also a form of resistance, whose roots go back to leaders such as Marcus Garvey and Leopold Senghor'. 'At the time of the Millennium', the text goes on, 'peoples of the African Diaspora are reclaiming their own history and, through artistic, spiritual and other means, are redefining their own cultural identities.'[37]

If these exhibitions carry social and political messages, they also make demands on our emotions. Indeed, one of the most significant features of the

'new museology' is that curators are quite often looking to prompt and cali-
brate just these sorts of responses, although in the case of transatlantic slavery
this aim is perhaps more understandable than in most. Research commissioned by the Transatlantic Slavery Gallery in 1995 notes with approval that
the gallery evoked a range of powerful emotions, including sadness (62 per
cent of those interviewed), shame (40 per cent), and guilt (31 per cent) – interestingly, shock (25 per cent) and humility (19 per cent) registered less frequently among respondents. Equally pertinent, visitors were also found to
have experienced some more 'positive' emotions, principally 'fascination' (47
per cent) and 'enjoyment' (17 per cent); perhaps, less surprisingly, only 6 per
cent of those interviewed claimed that they had been 'inspired' by what they
had seen. The report concludes: 'In our view, it is unusual for any exhibition
to evoke such strong, but appropriate, emotions. This should be considered a
strength of the gallery.'[38] Comments of this kind tell us a great deal about the
role of 'new', 'universal' museums. Visitors, it is implied, need to be moved in
some way, an emphasis that, if anything, encourages the drive to 'make the
past come alive'.[39]

But we might legitimately ask: 'come alive' for whom? Most of these galleries and museums were devised with the intention of catering, in part, to the
intellectual and emotional needs of minorities – principally, blacks. Yet the
results have been disappointing. The survey conducted in Liverpool in 1995
revealed that, even during half-term, the gallery was not attracting a high
proportion of such visitors; in fact, only two per cent of those interviewed
were 'Black Caribbean', while a further two per cent were either 'Black (other)'
or Asian. In other words, the racial profile was (and remains) heavily skewed
towards whites. The reasons are not difficult to fathom. Despite the lengthy
consultation process, many local blacks clearly feel that, for whatever reason,
the Transatlantic Slavery Gallery does not speak to them, or to their concerns;
some, according to Marcus Wood, refuse to enter the gallery because they
were *not* consulted.[40] No doubt, curators would protest that such responses
are an unavoidable part of the process, and, in a sense, they would be justified
in doing so. But, at the same time, we need to be alert to the extent to which
these museums and galleries still speak to – and are informed by – the white,
liberal imagination, and are really about 'our' needs, 'our' guilt, and 'our' sense
of the past. Put another way, the real issue here might not be the consultation
process itself, but who controls that process and, ultimately, who determines
what is and is not included.[41]

As one might expect, these different trends have also led to a reappraisal of
British anti-slavery ('abolition'). Here again, museum curators have been at
pains to incorporate black voices into their displays, even at the expense of
traditional, white perspectives. Perhaps the most radical and far-reaching example of this revisionist tendency can be found at the British Empire and
Commonwealth Museum in Bristol, where, in a wide-ranging exhibition, slavery is referred to twice, the first time in an introductory section entitled,

'Trading Fortunes (1480–1800): Plantations in the Americas'. The display makes a number of points, not least that transatlantic slavery was cruel, violent, and oppressive. But, at the same time, visitors are told that 'slaves rebelled frequently in every sugar colony', thus retaining their 'humanity and individuality'. In fact, so successful were these rebellions that they 'brought the sugar colonies to their knees. In Britain the public refused to defend the planters any longer, and Parliament outlawed slavery'. The exhibition returns to this theme later in a brief section entitled 'The Humanitarian Impulse'. While conceding that 'anti-slavery humanitarians' roused public opinion against the slave trade, the accompanying text makes it clear that these men and women only made slavery 'unacceptable in Britain'. The real work, it is implied, took place in the Caribbean where frequent slave revolts drew attention to the evils of slavery, as well as the cost of putting them down.[42]

Several things are interesting about this exhibition. One is the determination to contest European perspectives on British anti-slavery: hence the emphasis on black agency. Another is the tendency to speak in terms of generalities ('anti-slavery humanitarians', 'rebellious slaves') rather than specifics; indeed, this is a narrative in which white, male figures like Clarkson and Wilberforce are conspicuous by their absence. As one might expect, the artefacts on display are equally impersonal. The section on the 'Humanitarian Impulse', for instance, is illustrated by three objects: an anti-slavery banner, a print of a Royal Navy cutter engaged in the suppression of the slave trade, and an enormous wooden slave yoke. Some distance away, as the exhibition moves on to 'Education and Medicine in Africa', visitors are confronted by another display case. Inside, are laid out a series of medals commemorating Emancipation (1834) and a collection of items from an anti-slavery dinner service, which to judge from the inscription, was produced to mark Thomas Clarkson's appearance before the World Anti-Slavery Convention in 1840. But, strangely, there is no legend or accompanying text. Instead, the artefacts are left to speak for themselves, as if they required no interpretation, or could safely be ignored.[43]

Elements of this revisionist tendency can be found in most of Britain's slave museums and galleries. Keen to avoid relying too much on European perspectives, curators are inclined, instead, to focus on black agency: 'revolts on board ship, the large scale uprisings in the Americas, the passive resistance of go slows', and, no less important, the role of blacks in the abolitionist movement.[44] A key figure here is Olaudah Equiano, whose *Interesting Narrative*, published in 1789, remains probably the most complete account we have of an eighteenth-century slave's life. (By contrast, surprisingly little attention has been paid to the scores of black American abolitionists who visited Britain between 1830 and 1861, among them Frederick Douglass, Moses Roper, and William Wells Brown.)[45] For obvious reasons, curators have been quick to exploit Equiano's potential as an authentic black 'voice', so much so that his *Interesting Narrative* has become an important site of abolitionist memory, whether accessed via the printed text, or, as we have seen, via carefully selected audio readings. It also helps that we think we know Equiano; in fact, Equiano's 'dignified and empowering' image has become so ubiquitous that it has begun to take on a life and a history of its own, not only displacing many white, male images (Wilberforce, for instance) but also serving frequently as a convenient visual shorthand for the black presence in eighteenth-century Britain.[46]

Greater attention to figures like Equiano, who was practically unknown until he was rediscovered by scholars in the 1960s, has opened up new ways of thinking about British anti-slavery that, at the same time, reflect political, ideological, and broadly cultural forces, as well as current academic scholarship. Having said that, very few institutions take the same uncompromising approach as the British and Empire Commonwealth Museum. At the Transatlantic Slavery Gallery in Liverpool, for instance, European perspectives are reflected in a broad range of abolitionist artefacts, among them commemorative medals, plates, cups, sugar bowls, electoral tallies, and a pair of Staffordshire figures celebrating the end of slavery.[47] Much the same thing is true at the Industrial Museum in Bristol, where, in keeping with the overall design and conception of the exhibition, abolitionism is woven into the story of Bristol's role in the eighteenth-century slave trade. In what is an awkwardly constructed space, portraits of Olaudah Equiano and leading local white abolitionists jostle with an impressive array of European artefacts: cameos, tokens, medals, lead tobacco boxes, a wooden model of the slave ship *Brookes*, and, somewhat incongruously, Staffordshire figurines of 'Uncle Tom and Eva'.[48]

While most slave museums acknowledge the value of abolitionist artefacts as memory tools, however, very few of them distinguish between different types of objects (medals and cameos, for instance) or take the trouble to explain their meaning. These silences are revealing. If anything, the reaction against the European pre-occupation with the 'Saints' and, with it, the cult of personality, has placed even greater emphasis on the ability of abolitionist artefacts to provide a gateway to our knowledge of British anti-slavery. But can objects bear the weight of these expectations, especially when, as in the case of the displays in Bristol, they are unmediated? As James Young and others have pointed out, objects can mislead; they can also 'change their meaning not just over the years as different historiographical and institutional currents pick them out and transform their significance, but from day to day as different people view them and subject them to their own interpretation'.[49] When we look at a display case of abolitionist artefacts, what do we experience: shame, guilt, sadness, or perhaps something else – wonder and admiration? Properly to understand these objects we need to know who produced them, and how they were used and in what circumstances. This means, among other things, responding to contemporary debates about fashion, taste, and consumption; when all is said and done, Wilberforce's cameo is still a beautiful object. But it also means humanising abolitionist artefacts, and giving them a sense of purpose, which inevitably brings us back to the role of the 'Saints' and the dynamics of popular abolitionism.[50]

In much the same way, images can change their meaning, depending on what we bring to them and what we can be made to see. Equiano is a case in point. Visual images of Equiano are problematic for two reasons. In the first place, it now seems likely that the exquisite oil portrait in the Royal Albert Memorial Museum and Art Gallery in Exeter, copies of which can be found in Liverpool and at the Industrial Museum in Bristol, is not Equiano at all, but Ottabah Cugoano, or possibly even one of the black 'toys' described by Marcus Wood in *Blind Memory*.[51] More reliable, it would seem, is the three-quarter-length engraving included as the frontispiece to the first edition of Equiano's *Interesting Narrative*, in which a rather serious looking Equiano gazes out confidently at the reader. Arresting though this image is, however, it conveys a very Europeanised idea of what a writer or scholar should be. Equiano's self-assured pose, his fashionable attire, even the Bible open in his hand, are all familiar tropes, designed, in this case, not only to establish Equiano's respectability – after all, the *Narrative* was intended as a piece of abolitionist propaganda – but also to lend his testimony authority and legitimacy. Imagining Equiano, in other words, demands that we look beyond the formal image and think critically about its construction, just as it demands that we think critically about 'race' and identity and the role of blacks in eighteenth-century British culture and society.[52]

By and large, curators have responded only fitfully to challenges of this kind. Rather, the emphasis has been on inclusivity, which in practice has meant adjusting to the demands of an ever-widening range of people. Here again, the results have been uneven. If the best of these displays successfully challenge comfortable ideas and, on occasion, provoke passionate responses, others lack coherence or can appear to be trying to do too many different things at once. Representing British anti-slavery from below is also problematic, especially when objects are removed from their original context and little attempt is made to explain how abolitionism was organised, that is, as a grass-roots movement. At the Industrial Museum in Bristol, for instance, visitors are told that Bristol was 'the first provincial city to set up a committee for the abolition of the slave trade', and yet the relationship between the centre (London) and the periphery (Bristol) is left largely unexplained. Equally striking, is the seeming reluctance of all of these museums and galleries to discuss anti-slavery in terms of parliamentary debates and procedures, or competing political and economic interests, not least of which was the powerful West India lobby, whose influence both inside and outside parliament proved a critical factor in the ongoing struggle against transatlantic slavery. Too often, it seems, history and context are sacrificed in favour of critical positions that block off alternative, European perspectives.

What has happened at Bristol, Liverpool, and, to a lesser extent, the National Maritime Museum in London inevitably invites comparison with Wisbech and Hull, although it is worth pointing out that Wilberforce House Museum pioneered many of the innovations that have since become familiar in British slave museums. Following its refurbishment in 1983, the slavery material at Wilberforce House, which is also home to Hull's social history collection, was rearranged into two discrete displays, 'The Slave Trade' and

'Wilberforce and Abolition', which can be viewed either separately or to-gether.[53] Filling two of the upstairs rooms, 'Wilberforce and Abolition' sets out to trace Wilberforce's career, at the same time interleaving it with a series of abolitionist landmarks, which are organised under a number of headings: 'Beginnings of Anti-Slavery', 'Slave Trade Abolition', 'Emancipation and Death'. As this suggests, the display is arranged chronologically, although the layout of the main room, which has been adapted to accommodate a mock-up of Wilberforce in his study, means that visitors can circulate in two different directions. There are no videos or hands-on activities for children and, by contrast with 'The Slave Trade' next door, the whole exhibit is staid and, in places, lacking in imagination. There are no videos or hands-on activities for children and, by contrast with 'The Slave Trade' next door, the whole exhibit is staid and lacking in imagination (although at the time of writing plans are already under way to redesign the galleries ahead of the 2007 anniversary).

Not surprisingly, the figure that emerges from this display is curiously cold and distant. While we learn a great deal about Wilberforce's life history, for instance, we learn very little about his character, his beliefs, or, indeed, his conversation. Even the vexed question of Wilberforce's politics warrants only the comment that 'like most men of property Wilberforce wanted to uphold the rule of law in the face of popular unrest. He was against reformers who did not share his Christian beliefs'. Wilberforce, as a result, never fully 'comes to life'; in fact, the whole display is now beginning to look rather tired and out-dated, especially when compared with exhibitions like the 'Nelson – The Man and the Hero' gallery at Portsmouth Historic Dockyard, where a wide range of new technologies, including a specially commissioned video, hands-on ac-tivities for children, and computer interactives, are used effectively to get at the question: 'What was Nelson really like?' Wilberforce, by contrast, is held at arm's length. Rather like his life-size wax figure, which is sealed behind a perspex screen, in effect accentuating the distance between object and viewer, he remains somehow remote and, ultimately, unknowable.[54]

Where the display does score heavily, however, is in its attempts to set Wilberforce's abolitionism in some sort of context. The section on 'The Be-ginnings of Slavery' starts, appropriately enough, with the Clapham Sect and figures like Granville Sharp and James Ramsay. Perhaps just as important, the display also acknowledges the pioneering work of Thomas Clarkson, who, in the accompanying website, is described as 'among the first abolitionists of slavery'. Throughout, there is clearly a determination to be 'balanced' and 'objective', and visitors are left in no doubt that Wilberforce was drawn to 'an already-established Society for [Effecting] the Abolition of the Slave Trade'.[55] Having said that, the display is arguably less successful in explaining the dy-namics of popular abolition, even at a local (Hull) level, or the relationship between figures like Wilberforce and the movement outside parliament. More-over, unlike many newer slave museums and galleries, 'Wilberforce and Abo-lition' pays little attention to black perspectives, or to black activists, and rarely moves beyond the narrow world of the 'Saints'. In other words, the display adopts a fairly traditional, European stance, albeit one that, in its efforts finally to put the 'Wilberforce controversy' to rest, invites visitors to regard British anti-slavery as something more than a movement in which Wilberforce dominated.

Visually, 'Wilberforce and Abolition' draws heavily on Wilberforce House Museum's rich collection of abolitionist artefacts, as well as a range of more personal items, including books, furniture, and Wilberforce's court dress. Also, at the heart of the exhibit, there is the mock-up of the interior of Wilberforce's study, which, in a manner reminiscent of many folk museums, attempts to reveal the 'private' Wilberforce, surrounded by some of his most treasured possessions. Interpreting such a wide range of objects means inevitably that some parts of the display work better than others. Comparisons are perhaps invidious, but some of the most effective sections are those dealing with highlights of Wilberforce's career, such as the 'Great Yorkshire Election' of 1807, where the artefacts speak directly to the subject. Less convincing, however, are those sections dealing with 'Abolition' and 'Emancipation', partly because they fail to distinguish between different types of artefacts, but also because the displays' narrative strategy dictates that what did not directly affect or involve Wilberforce is left out; so, for instance, the exhibit deals only superficially with events leading up to the passage of the Emancipation Act, largely because during those years (1826–33) Wilberforce was out of the political limelight.

Equally striking is the fact that the display makes little attempt to bring the story up to date – remember that 'Wilberforce and Abolition' was commissioned to mark the 150th anniversary of Wilberforce's death in 1983 – or to engage critically with the legacy of slavery, as is the case in Bristol and Liverpool. By contrast, 'Wilberforce and Abolition' ends abruptly with 'Emancipation and Death', which does, admittedly, contain references to 'new abolitionists', among them John Brown and Harriet Beecher Stowe; and a brief statement to the effect that 'the evils of slavery did not end with Abolition. Colour prejudice, built up by centuries of black slavery, is still with us today'. None of this would matter quite so much, except for the fact that visitors to Wilberforce House Museum are greeted by two display boards, one announcing that Hull is twinned with Freetown in Sierra Leone, and the other pointing out that Hull was the first local authority to support Jubilee 2000, the organization campaigning in the United Kingdom for the cancellation of Third World debt. The visitor is therefore 'introduced to the museum with a sense of contemporary social history'. Yet, as John Beech observes, this accent on the continuing legacy of slavery stands in 'stark contrast' to the displays upstairs, where there 'is virtually no attempt to continue the story of the fight [against slavery] after 1833.[56]

If Wilberforce House Museum seems rather staid and conventional in its handling of British anti-slavery, so, too, does its closest rival, Wisbech and Fenland Museum. As we have seen, Wisbech had been drawn into competition with Hull from as early as 1933, but, interestingly, it was not until the

1990s that the local museum successfully organised a permanent Clarkson exhibition, originally entitled 'Thomas Clarkson, Slavery and the Slave Trade'. Opened in 1993, the display occupied most of the foyer and included material on Clarkson, his brother, John, as well as 'Africa' and 'New World Slavery'. Three years later, the curator, David Devenish, also organised a special (temporary) exhibition to coincide with the 150th anniversary of Clarkson's death, which was put on in the museum's newly-built Hudson Gallery, and featured no less than 21 exhibits, ranging from 'The Triangular Trade' to 'Folklife', 'Sugar', and 'Thomas Clarkson's Chair'. During the summer and early autumn of 1996, in other words, there were effectively two Clarkson displays at Wisbech and Fenland Museum, a circumstance that reflected not only the enthusiasm of local activists, among them Devenish and Margaret Cave, but also the importance attached to the 150th anniversary celebrations. Some time later, however, both displays were dismantled and reorganised into a much smaller permanent exhibition, which now fills four display cabinets in one of the main halls of the museum.[57]

What is interesting about these different initiatives is that they were obviously conceived as part of an ongoing struggle to defend Clarkson, not least against Wilberforce and his supporters. For Devenish, in particular, this appears to have been an overriding concern. Reviewing the refurbished display at Wilberforce House Museum, for instance, he notes that 'the display follows the "orthodox" or "received" view, in other words the one propounded by the very filial Wilberforce brothers'; and, elsewhere, he poses the rhetorical question: 'To what extent should a Curator impose his own beliefs in opposition to a "canonised" version of history?' Devenish clearly felt that, in the circumstances, 'a certain bias towards Clarkson [was] perhaps permissible'. Anticipating that the 1996 temporary exhibition at Wisbech might be criticised because 'the only abolitionists mentioned are the Clarkson brothers', Devenish admitted that 'this was intentional as I did not wish to become involved in the controversy and allegations that rocked the abolitionist movement in the period 1834–44, and which may well have distorted received history ever since'. Ironically, this unwillingness to problematise Clarkson is one of the biggest weaknesses of the current Clarkson display at Wisbech, but of far greater interest is the fact that, until recently, such arguments still had a purchase, and that people like Devenish still felt a responsibility to right what they perceived was an obvious injustice.[58]

Not surprisingly, what visitors can see at Wisbech today still reflects this pro-Clarkson 'bias'. The display begins with John Clarkson, who was the first governor of Sierra Leone, and ends with an enlarged cut-out of his brother, Thomas, together with his 'Africa box', opened to reveal its contents, many of which are remarkably still intact. Other exhibits illustrative of slavery and the slave trade include letters, newspapers, and maps; a purse with cowrie shells, African spears, 'aggrie' beads, manillas, foot locks, sugar snippers and sugar cones; commemorative medals, prints, and copies of paintings. Interestingly, there are no references to African or black perspectives, at least in the sense employed by many newer slave museums and galleries, and, as one might expect, little attempt is made to contextualise Clarkson or to explain how he fitted in. In contrast to Wilberforce House Museum, where there has been a conscious attempt to try and correct biased or distorted views of Wilberforce and his role in the abolitionist movement, Wisbech and Fenland Museum takes a largely uncritical view of Clarkson, throwing a veil over the 'Wilberforce controversy', and substituting in its place a cult of personality.[59]

Preoccupied with settling old scores, the Clarkson exhibit at Wisbech sits uncomfortably alongside many newer displays, especially those at Bristol and Liverpool. Therein lies the problem. By and large, British slave museums and galleries have reached a consensus over representations of transatlantic slavery; whether one visits Liverpool, Hull, or Bristol, the displays assume much the same shape and character and utilise many of the same technologies, slave ship reconstructions being an obvious case in point. Representations of British anti-slavery, on the other hand, are inconsistent and sometimes contradictory. At issue here is what to do about white voices. If, in the past, it seemed only natural to focus on figures like Wilberforce, newer museums and galleries have often been at pains to challenge such perspectives, and to adopt more critical positions that reflect unease with the European cultural meanings attached to the moral achievements of the 'Saints'. British antislavery has always been a contested space – this, after all, is the meaning of the 'Wilberforce controversy' – but today the debate is not so much whether Clarkson or Wilberforce deserves greater credit, but whether such orthodox 'histories' of British transatlantic slavery are any longer viable at all. Not surprisingly, a consensus has been slow to emerge. In the meantime, attention has shifted away from 'abolition' to 'slavery' as a site of national memory, a development that, if anything, has accentuated the conceptual distance between sites like Wisbech, on the one hand, and so-called 'maritime' displays, on the other.

Since the 1980s, we have witnessed an explosion in the number of slave museums and galleries. Moreover, as the bicentenary of the abolition of the slave trade approaches, interest in transatlantic slavery intensifies. By 2007 Liverpool will have a new £10m museum dedicated to slavery. In addition, the Heritage Lottery Fund has already funded several projects relating to transatlantic slavery, including a grant of £281,000 to the National Maritime Museum to purchase the Michael Graham-Stewart collection, thereby opening up for the first time the possibility of a major slavery exhibition in the nation's capital. More exciting still are the plans recently unveiled by Hull City Council as part of Wilberforce 2007, which involve investing £3.75m in Wilberforce House Museum 'to create a world leading state-of-the-art destination museum'.[60] What goes on in these museums has also undergone a radical change. New technologies and rising expectations have changed the nature of the museum experience and what visitors want (or demand) to take away from it. Responding to these challenges, slave museums have been quick to innovate, while at the same time forging important links with local action and community groups.

Perspectives have also changed, bringing with them a clearer sense of the need to address black or African approaches to transatlantic slavery.

While re-orientating our views of transatlantic slavery, however, these displays necessarily have their own internal logic and structure. Typically, more space is given to the slave trade than to slavery, for instance. Furthermore, as John Beech has argued, 'slavery' (really, the slave trade) is often defined and interpreted as a 'maritime activity'; that is, as a subset of transport history or the expansion of British trade. By contrast, slavery itself is frequently defined as a colonial activity, and therefore as something remote and distant. For this reason, it is still hard for many Britons to conceive of a history of British slavery, even though they might be willing to acknowledge, however grudgingly, British involvement in the transatlantic slave trade. In much the same way, attention has tended to focus on 'Abolition' – that is, the campaign to end the slave trade – rather than 'Emancipation' (the abolition of slavery). Wilberforce's legacy, of course, may have something to do with this bias, but, at the same time, it also reflects what Beech has described as the 'maritimization' of British transatlantic slavery, as evidenced by the fact that so many of these displays are located in former slave ports, principally Bristol and Liverpool.[61]

Interpreting British anti-slavery also poses problems of a different kind. This is not just a case of finding a way of reconciling 'white' and 'black' perspectives, although that is undoubtedly important. Slave museums also need to make more space for abolition. This means being more receptive to scholarly work on the dynamics of popular abolitionism – not least, as a way of making sense of abolitionist artefacts – as well as recent research on the role of women in the abolitionist movement: curiously, curators have been slow to take on board the implications of Clare Midgley's pioneering work on this subject, and, in particular, the link between women, popular protest, and issues like 'non-consumption' (that is, the boycotting of slave-grown produce).[62] Similarly, there is more to be said about black perspectives. In general, slave museums have tended to ignore nineteenth-century black abolitionists, scores of whom visited Britain between 1830 and 1860, and yet it is generally recognised that they played an important part in mobilising public opinion against slavery in the United States. Above all, there is a pressing need to reassess the significance of 'Abolition'– the 'first grassroots human rights campaign' – and to relate it to contemporary issues like the cancellation of Third World debt.[63]

Slave museums, like memorials and commemorations, play a vital role in shaping public memory and determining what should (or should not) be remembered. They also reflect contemporary political and ideological concerns, and, in this sense, there is little doubt that the current emphasis on the 'indignity' of transatlantic slavery informs, and is informed by, debates about reparations, as well as calls for a slavery remembrance day.[64] (Re)interpreting Britain's slave heritage, however, especially in the context of 2007, demands not only that we 'rescue people from enforced anonymity, [and] name the nameless', but also that we recognise how and why slavery came to an end, and what that tells us about Britain's slave past.[65] Here again, there is a need for good history and good education; indeed, over the coming decades, centres like the Wilberforce Institute in Hull and the new slavery museum in Liverpool will be critical in formulating responses to slavery and emancipation and, just as important, 'its modern human rights resonances'.[66]

Notes

1 For details, see www.slave-studies.net accessed 12 February 2005. Some of these sites, like *La site du musée de la traite et de l'escavage a Nantes*, are seemingly still at an embryonic stage. In the Netherlands, a National Institute for the Study of the Dutch Slave Trade and Slavery (NiNsee) was officially launched in June 2002. NiNsee sponsored the 'Break the Silence' exhibition in Amsterdam in 2003, and works closely with the Transaltantic Slavery Gallery in Liverpool. See www.ninsee.nl accessed 12 February 2005.

2 Eilean Hooper-Greenhill, *Museums and the Shaping of Knowledge* (London, 1992), p. 214.

3 Oldfield, *Popular Politics and British Anti-Slavery*, p. 75; Drescher, *The Mighty Experiment*, pp. 88–105.

4 Wood, *Blind Memory*, p. 223.

5 Oldfield, *Popular Politics and British Anti-Slavery*, pp. 155–63; Swann Auction Galleries, New York, sale 1926 (February 2002), lots 71, 261 and sale 1998 (February 2004), lot 43; Inga Bryden and Janet Floyd, *Domestic Space: Reading the Nineteenth-Century Interior* (Manchester, 1999), pp. 76–7.

6 Tim Schadla-Hall, *Tom Sheppard: Hull's Great Collector* (Beverley, 1989), p. 16; Deverell and Watkins, *Wilberforce and Hull*, pp. 75–6. See also minutes of Museums and Records Sub-Committee, *Hull Corporation Minutes*, 1906–41. An entry for 19 April 1906, for instance, records that 300 volumes from Wilberforce's library had been 'secured at an average of about a shilling a volume'.

7 Deverell and Williams, *Wilberforce and Hull*, pp. 76–7.

8 *Isle of Ely and Wisbech Advertiser*, 7 June 1933.

9 *Isle of Ely and Wisbech Advertiser*, 30 March 1960; *Wisbech Standard*, 25 March 1960; Wisbech and Fenland Museum, Museum Day Book, 1960.

10 J. B. Fry, *Wilberforce House, Hull: Its History and Collections* (Hull, 1946), pp. 11–14. All of these items were on display in 'Room A' of Wilberforce House, immediately east of the landing. Two other rooms contained Wilberforce memorabilia, one featuring his wax effigy, and the other (the birth room) containing 'an extensive collection of engraved portraits and photographs of paintings of Wilberforce'.

11 *Hull Daily Mail*, 21, 25 July 1933; *Hull and Lincolnshire Times*, 22 July 1933; Deverell and Watkins, *Wilberforce and Hull*, pp. 76–7.

12 *Hull and Lincolnshire Times*, 22 July 1933.

13 Ibid.

14 Celeste-Marie Bernier, exhibition review of 'Transatlantic Slavery: Against Human Dignity' and 'A Respectable Trade? Bristol and Transatlantic Slavery', *Journal of American History*, 88 (2001), pp. 1006–12; David C. Devenish, 'Exhibiting the Slave Trade', *Museum International*, 49 (1997), pp. 49–52; Anthony Tibbles, 'Against Human Dignity: The Development of the Transatlantic Slavery Gallery at Merseyside Maritime Museum, Liverpool', *Proceedings, IXth International Congress of Maritime Museums*, 1996,

pp. 95–6; Madge Dresser and Sue Giles, eds., *Bristol and Transatlantic Slavery* (Bristol, 2000), p. 9. For the British Empire and Commonwealth Museum, see www.empiremuseum.co.uk.

15 Eilean Hooper-Greenhill, *Museums and their Visitors* (London, 1994), p. 100. See also Vera L. Zolberg, '"An Elite Experience for Everyone": Art Museums, the Public, and Cultural Literacy', in Daniel J. Sherman and Irit Rogoff, eds., *Museum Culture: Histories, Discourses, Spectacles* (London 1994), pp. 49–65.

16 Hooper-Greenhill, *Museums and the Shaping of Knowledge*, p. 204.

17 Ibid, pp. 200–15. See also Hooper-Greenhill, *Museums and their Visitors*, esp. pp. 140–70; Peter Vergo, ed., *The New Museology* (London, 1989); Gaynor Kavanagh, ed., *Making Histories in Museums* (London, 1996).

18 Tibbles, 'Against Human Dignity', pp. 95–7.

19 Dresser and Giles, *Bristol and Transatlantic Slavery*, p. 9. For details on the National Maritime Museum I have relied on personal communications with Dr Robert Blyth, Curator, National Maritime Museum, London.

20 The literature on slavery is voluminous, but see, in particular, Ira Berlin, *Generations of Captivity: A History of American Slaves* (Cambridge, MA, 2003); Peter Kolchin, *American Slavery* (London, 1995); James Walvin, *Black Ivory: A History of British Slavery* (London, 1992); Eugene Genovese, *Roll, Jordan, Roll: The World the Slaves Made* (New York, 1974). For a recent challenge to 'revisionist' interpretations of slavery, see Wilma Dunaway, *The African-American Family in Slavery and Emancipation* (Cambridge, 2003).

21 Tibbles, 'Against Human Dignity', p. 98.

22 Dresser and Giles, *Bristol and Transatlantic Slavery*, pp. 25–32. The current display at the Industrial Museum in Bristol contains a much smaller range of African artefacts than is illustrated in the exhibition catalogue.

23 Wood, *Blind Memory*, pp. 300–301.

24 Dresser and Giles, *Bristol and Transatlantic Slavery*, pp. 13–17.

25 'Transatlantic Slavery Gallery: Summative Evaluation, 24 March 1995, prepared for National Museums and Galleries on Merseyside', pp. 11, 24, 34.

26 Tibbles, 'Against Human Dignity', p. 99. The 'Trench Experience' (1989) and the 'Blitz Experience' (1990), both at the Imperial War Museum in London, are part of the same broad phenomenon, as are the displays installed in many British and American folk museums. See, for instance, the recreation of an early slave village at Carter's Grove, Williamsburg, Virginia. Details can be found at www.history.org/history/museums/carters_grove.cfm accessed 21 January 2005.

27 Wood, *Blind Memory*, p. 295.

28 Tibbles, 'Against Human Dignity', pp. 99–100; Wood, *Blind Memory*, pp. 297–8.

29 Hooper-Greenhill, *Museums and the Shaping of Knowledge*, p. 211.

30 Ibid., p. 214; Merseyside Maritime Museum, Liverpool, typescript, 'Comments of the Transatlantic Slavery Gallery, based on notes left on the Transatlantic Slavery Gallery comments board from 25 October 1994 to 25 January 1995', p. 2; Tibbles, 'Against Human Dignity', p. 100.

31 Wood, *Blind Memory*, pp. 297–301; Ludmilla Jordanova, 'Objects of Knowledge: A Historical Perspective on Museums', in Vergo, ed., *The New Museology*, pp. 25–6.

32 Anthony Tibbles, ed., *Transatlantic Slavery: Against Human Dignity* (Liverpool, 1994), pp. 115, 150–4; Wood, *Blind Memory*, pp. 200–1; Celeste-Marie Bernier, exhibition review of 'Transatlantic Slavery: Against Human Dignity' and 'A Respectable Trade? Bristol and Transatlantic Slavery', pp. 1010–11.

33 Tibbles, 'Against Human Dignity', p. 100; Tibbles, *Transatlantic Slavery*, p. 152.

34 Here again, this mock-up has a timeless quality about it and is reminiscent of many enthnographical displays to be found in British museums. Interestingly, the interior

is bare except for a collection of pots and hoes, although it is not clear whether these are genuine, West Indian artefacts or simply props.

35   'Transatlantic Slavery Gallery: Summative Evaluation, 24 March 1995', pp. 18–22.
36   Tibbles, 'Against Human Dignity', p. 97.
37   Dresser and Giles, *Bristol and Transatlantic Slavery*, pp. 89–91.
38   'Transatlantic Slavery Gallery: Summative Evaluation', pp. 6, 36.
39   Jordanova, 'Objects of Knowledge', p. 26.
40   'Transatlantic Slavery Gallery: Summative Evaluation', pp. 9, 13–14; Wood, *Blind Memory*, p. 300.
41   Quite often, it would seem, consultations are carried out with each interested party, in turn, with the result that only the museum staff have a sense of the 'full picture'. Understandably, this way of doing things can lead to frustration, especially when community groups see the museum doing 'nothing'. How curators and research staff react to and interpret information received via this process is a subject that requires more careful academic study. What is evident, however, is that competing demands and expectations can, in some cases, result in paralysis.
42   All of these quotes are taken from the display panels at the British Empire and Commonwealth Museum.
43   For contemporary perspectives on labelling and texts in museums, see Hooper-Greenhill, *Museums and their Visitors*, pp. 115–39. Interestingly, most curators take a fairly minimalist approach to the labelling of abolitionist artefacts, describing them in terms of provenance, date, and form. Very few of the museums discussed here actually interpret these objects, or explain their production and use.
44   Tibbles, 'Against Human Dignity', p. 99.
45   For black abolitionists in Britain, see Fisch, *American Slaves in Victorian England*; R. J. M. Blackett, *Building an Antislavery Wall: Black Americans in the Atlantic Abolitionist Movement, 1830–1860* (Ithaca, NY, 1983).
46   Wood, *Blind Memory*, p. 131.
47   Tibbles, *Transatlantic Slavery*, pp. 87–95, 161–5.
48   Dresser and Giles, *Bristol and Transatlantic Slavery*, pp. 77–88.
49   Young, *The Texture of Memory*, p. 132; Charles Saumarez Smith, 'Museums, Artefacts, and Meanings', in Vergo, ed., *The New Museology*, p. 19.
50   As Jordanova puts it: '[Artefacts] have the same status as other historical documents: they are texts requiring interpretation, and they need to be set in their proper historical context.' See Jordanova, 'Objects of Knowledge', p. 29.
51   Brycchan Carey, 'The Equiano Portraits', www.brycchancarey.com/equiano/portrait.html accessed 24 February 2005; Reyahn King, 'Ignatius Sancho and Portraits of the Black Elite', in King, ed., *Ignatius Sancho: An African Man of Letters*, pp. 35–6; Lucy MacKeith, *Local Black History: A Beginning in Devon* (Exeter, 2003), pp. 23, 44–5; Wood, *Blind Memory*, p. 153.
52   Wood, *Blind Memory*, p. 131. See also Benjamin Zephaniah's brilliant deconstruction of the V&A's portrait of the eighteenth-century Jamaican scholar, Francis Williams, at www.vam.ac.uk/collections/british_galls/audio_talk_art/benzaph/8530_audio.html accessed 24 February 2005.
53   Deverell and Watkins, *Wilberforce and Hull*, p. 76.
54   For the Nelson gallery at Portsmouth Historic Dockyard, see www.flagship.org.uk/text/education_details.htm accessed 24 February 2005.
55   www.hullcc.gov.uk/wilberforce accessed 24 February 2005; John G. Beech, 'The Marketing of Slavery Heritage in the United Kingdom', *International Journal of Hospitality and Tourism and Administration*, 2 (2001), p. 100. At times, the website's handling of the early history of abolitionism comes close to endorsing Clarkson's version of events as

outlined in his controversial *History*. Clarkson's *Essay*, for instance, is described as 'one of the decisive influences in leading William Wilberforce to oppose slavery in Parliament'. Elsewhere, it is asserted clearly that Clarkson's 'single-minded determination turned slavery into the leading political issue of the day'; and that Wilberforce was 'invited' by the 'Committee for the Abolition of the Slave Trade' to 'press for Abolition in Parliament'.

56 Beech, 'The Marketing of Slavery Heritage in the United Kingdom', p. 100.
57 Devenish, 'Exhibiting the Slave Trade', pp. 49–52.
58 Wisbech and Fenland Museum, Clarkson Papers, TCC/157, David C. Devenish, 'The Slavery Exhibition at Wilberforce House, Hull', and TCC/158, David C. Devenish, 'Thomas Clarkson, Slavery and the Slave Trade: An Exhibition at Wisbech and Fenland Museum'; Devenish, 'Exhibiting the Slave Trade', p. 50.
59 In fairness, it is worth pointing out that Wisbech and Fenland Museum also labours under a number of disadvantages. One of these is that the museum's slavery collections are actually quite thin, at least in terms of three-dimensional objects. Many of the items in the current display, including prints, maps, and paintings, are copies of originals elsewhere, while others are on temporary loan. Just as important, Wisbech and Fenland Museum simply does not have the resources to compete with centres like Bristol, Liverpool, or Hull. Of necessity, funding for local museums and libraries is always on a tight rein, added to which there are always competing demands on the museum's space and time; in this connection, it is interesting to note that 90 per cent of the total expenditure on the temporary Clarkson exhibition put on in 1996 came from external sponsors. See Devenish, 'Exhibiting the Slave Trade', p. 49.
60 www.chn.ir/english/eshownnews.asp?no=3382 accessed 11 December 2004; www.hull.co.uk/newsDetail.aspx?NewsID=110 accessed 15 February 2005. At the time of writing, the National Maritime Museum's plans for 2007 have not been unveiled, but it seems likely that the history of transatlantic slavery will form part of a new gallery dedicated to 'The Atlantic World'. Personal communication from Dr Robert Blyth, Curator, National Maritime Museum, London.
61 Beech, 'The Marketing of Slavery Heritage in the United Kingdom', p. 103.
62 Clare Midgley, *Women Against Slavery: The British Campaigns, 1780–1870* (London and New York, 1992), and 'Slave Sugar Boycotts, Female Activism and the Domestic Base of British Antislavery Culture', *Slavery and Abolition*, 17 (1996), pp. 137–62. See also Charlotte Sussman, *Consuming Anxieties: Consumer Protest, Gender and British Slavery, 1713–1833* (Stanford, 2000).
63 Hochschild, *Bury the Chains*, pp. 3–5.
64 Celeste-Marie Bernier, exhibition review of 'Transatlantic Slavery: Against Human Dignity' and 'A Respectable Trade? Bristol and Transatlantic Slavery', p. 1012.
65 www.hull.co.uk/newsDetail.aspx?NewsID=110, 15 February 2005, quoting Professor David Richardson, Director of the Wilberforce Institute for the Study of Slavery and Emancipation.
66 www.hull.ac.uk/05/news/jan/oriel_chamber.html, 24 January 2005.

ᶜᴾ 6 ᶜᴾ

Transatlantic perspectives

Emancipation reverberated across the Atlantic world, signalling momentous changes that aroused complex emotions, ranging from excitement to hostility and contempt. In hard economic terms, it has to be said that the 'mighty experiment' was not a success. Put simply, it proved impossible for 'liberated' sugar colonies to compete with the slave-based economies of Brazil and Cuba, particularly when those economies benefited from the advantages of the international slave trade. The British government admitted as much when in the early 1840s it decided to permit the flow of indentured migration (that is, bonded labour) into the Caribbean.[1] But if, as Seymour Drescher suggests, Emancipation proved a fatal economic miscalculation, it continued to have a huge ideological and psychological impact, not least in the British Caribbean, where Emancipation Day remains an important reference point, signifying for many 'the liberation of an entire society, of masters and slaves, of rulers and ruled'.[2] As we shall see, Emancipation also had an impact on organised abolitionism. This was perhaps most obvious in the United States where what was often referred to as 'West India Emancipation' acted as a powerful catalyst for reformers like William Lloyd Garrison, and – no less important – helped to shape the rituals of the nineteenth-century American anti-slavery movement. In these different ways, Emancipation spilled out across the Atlantic world, and, in so doing, became a convenient 'symbol of the potential of freedom – a counter model to the example of Haiti – and [a] reminder of the possibility of moral progress'.[3]

As a slaveholding republic, the United States obviously took a close interest in events unfolding in the Caribbean. Responses varied. Slaveholders in the American South, for instance, drew undoubted comfort from the fact that Emancipation had proved such a costly failure, although, as Drescher points out, 'the actual results of the great experiment were very rarely invoked in discussions of the future of U.S. slavery'.[4] More significant, at least in retrospect, was the impact that Emancipation had on the development of American abolitionism. Links between British and American abolitionists dated back to the eighteenth century. One of the first acts of the Pennsylvania Abolition Society (PAS), for instance, following its reorganisation in 1787, was to open a correspondence with Thomas Clarkson. Eager to repay the compliment, in July 1787 the Society for Effecting the Abolition of the Slave Trade wrote to the societies at Philadelphia and New York 'to inform them of the measures they had taken for the abolition of the slave trade'.[5] Through these channels, which stretched from London to Philadelphia and New York, abolitionists exchanged ideas and information, in the process creating an 'imagined community' of reformers who offered each other support, advice, and encouragement.[6] Similarly, many British pamphlets, among them Clarkson's *Essay on the Impolicy of the African Slave Trade* (1788), were circulated on the other side of the Atlantic. As a result, Clarkson became one of the first international figures of the early abolitionist movement, as witness the decision of the New York Manumission Society in 1788 to make him one of its honorary members, along with Granville Sharp and Brissot de Warville.[7]

Cooperation between British and American abolitionists would continue into the nineteenth century; in fact, American reformers drew undoubted strength from the support they received from their British friends. Sympathetic bonds between abolitionists were further strengthened by personal contacts, made easier and cheaper by the advent of steamships. Many British abolitionists spent time in the United States, and most of the leading figures in the American movement visited Britain at one time or another, chief among them William Lloyd Garrison.[8] Garrison first visited Britain in 1833, during which time he called upon Clarkson at Playford Hall and stayed long enough to attend William Wilberforce's funeral in Westminster Abbey. He visited again in 1840 to attend the World Anti-Slavery Convention, when he led American protests over the refusal of the BFASS to seat women delegates, and accompanied Frederick Douglass during part of the latter's British tour in 1846.[9] Like many American visitors, Garrison viewed Britain in a sober light. This was not just a question of his republican sympathies, although these were undoubtedly important. Fervently Evangelical, Garrison also responded instinctively to the plight of British workers and the inequalities he thought he saw around him. As he noted in 1841: 'Until both man and woman be uncrowned in England, [and] the present government of that country be scattered to the four winds of heaven, the people will never be able to obtain or enjoy equal rights, nor to relieve themselves from the grievous burdens which are now crushing them to the earth.'[10] Nevertheless, in saying this, Garrison 'hailed the British abolition of the slave trade in 1807 as an epochal victory of "right over wrong, of liberty over oppression"'. Perhaps just as important, Garrison also sought to identify himself with British abolitionism, placing his own endeavours in a humanitarian tradition that stretched back to Granville Sharp and beyond.[11]

Garrison's visits to Britain over a period of twelve or more years coincided with the emergence of a new, reinvigorated American abolitionism that dates from 1831, when Garrison published his radical anti-slavery newspaper, *The Liberator*, calling for the immediate emancipation of Southern slaves.[12] The history of this movement, which fractured and split during the 1840s, lies beyond the scope of the present study. But what is interesting to note is how American abolitionists responded to 'West India Emancipation', and how they absorbed it into their rituals. For Garrisonians, in particular, this was a deliberate, pre-meditated choice. As a contributor to Garrison's *Liberator* put it in 1842, the anniversary of West India Emancipation 'is unattended by that chilling drawback upon the chastened festivities of the occasion which accompanied the celebration of the independence of a nation, who, to evince their gratitude for their own political freedom, enslave one sixth of their number'. In a similar vein, Edmund Quincy, one of Garrison's patrician allies, told a meeting in Abington, Massachusetts, in 1855 that 'it was not often that American abolitionists were called upon to rejoice. It was their mission, ordinarily, to weep with those who weep, rather than to rejoice with those who rejoice. On the great anniversaries which were held by the American people, they came together to recollect how unworthy the nation was to rejoice – how false their pretensions – how hollow the claims which they make to the exultation in which they indulge'.[13]

At the same time that they rejected American anniversaries, and, in particular, 4 July celebrations, Garrisonians elevated the anniversary of West India Emancipation to a central place in their calendar. '1 August deserves to be celebrated more than 4 July', Garrison declared in a typically uncompromising editorial. 'The instantaneous transformation of almost a million of chattels into rational and immortal beings is the greatest moral miracle of the age'.[14] Garrison, perhaps more than most, understood the importance of such rituals, not just in inventing what we might call an abolitionist tradition, but also in giving value and meaning to the lives of those who performed them. In Massachusetts, at least, most small towns held a 1 August festival. The *Liberator* for August 1842 carried news of ceremonials in Lynn, Fall River, South Scituate, Hingham, West Brookfield, and Dedham, the last attended by abolitionists from Boston, Dedham, Walpole, Medfield, Dorchester, Roxbury, and other towns in Norfolk county. In each case, the impetus usually came from the local anti-slavery society, either acting on its own initiative or in concert with other groups. As a result, some of these festivals were quite small. Others, however, enjoyed massive support. Particularly impressive were the annual meetings organised by the Massachusetts Anti-Slavery Society – in effect, the parent body – which for a period seem to have moved around the state before settling in Abington, south of Boston. Widely publicised, these meetings regularly attracted 'friends' from 'every quarter of the eastern part of Massachusetts', as well as from New Hampshire, New York, and Michigan, 'and even from Canada West and the province of New Brunswick'.[15]

Given the time of year, Emancipation Day festivals were normally held out of doors; in fact, most of them were advertised as 'picnics' and usually took place in shady 'groves' that provided relief from the afternoon sun. Travelling to and from these sites led to a further innovation, namely Emancipation Day parades. In 1844 delegates from Norfolk and Plymouth counties met in Hingham, Massachusetts, whereupon the 'Grand Line' was formed, led by 'the Chief Marshall and Aids on horseback', followed by 'a Legion of Honor, composed of fifty young ladies, dressed uniformly in white, with wreaths of oak leaves'. Behind them came the various delegates, organised into sections, each of them carrying a banner. Hanson's banner, for instance, depicted 'the Eagle of America trampling a prostrate slave, a bloodhound in the act of seizing the victim, and a file of soldiers pointing their muskets at his body, with the motto, "This is American Liberty", and below, "Truth shall set you free"'. Another represented 'a slave at sunrise on the 1st of Aug. 1834, with the chains falling from his limbs, from which they had just been broken, together with the motto, "This is the Lord's doing. Slavery abolished in the British West Indies, 1st August 1834"'. Describing the scene, the *Liberator* noted that 'the appearance of the Procession, as it passed through the principal streets, was beautiful in the extreme. Throughout its entire length, of nearly a mile and a half, splendid banners were displayed at short intervals, which, with the varied dresses and imposing numbers of its almost countless ranks, attracted universal attention and admiration'.[16]

As these few details suggest, abolitionists clearly managed Emancipation Day parades with military-like precision; the presence of marshals, 'aids on horseback', and, in many cases, bands, all gave these occasions a martial air, thereby reinforcing their orderliness and 'respectability', a key word in the abolitionists' vocabulary. Banners were also an important part of these spectacles, not only imparting colour to the proceedings, but also acting as visual cues that identified local groups and affiliations (and hence popular support for abolitionism) while at the same time advertising the abolitionists' cause in a series of uncompromising slogans and images. Among the twenty or more banners at Hingham in 1844 was one from Abington with the motto, 'No union with slaveholders, religiously or politically', and 'a beautiful device, representing the Genius of Freedom shrinking from the offered hand of the slave-driver'; another, this time from Milton, bore a 'Cap of Liberty', together with the motto, 'God never made a tyrant or a slave'. More difficult to read are the few references we have to styles of clothing, but the presence of children and young women in these processions, sometimes dressed 'uniformly in white', hints at a deliberate attempt on the part of organisers to emphasise the (Christian) purity of American anti-slavery, as well as the nobility of its leaders. It was not unusual, for instance, for Garrison's image to appear in Emancipation Day parades, often enclosed in an oak wreath, itself a symbol of strength and steadfastness.[17]

The focal point of these celebrations, however, was not so much the parades but the observances that followed them. Here – once the delegates had reached their various destinations – the proceedings usually took the form of religious services, involving hymns, prayers, bible readings, and orations.[18] Most leading white abolitionists made a point of speaking at these events, among them Garrison, Theodore Parker, Wendell Phillips, Samuel May, Parker Pillsbury, Charles Burleigh, and Edmund Quincy.[19] Significantly, some black abolitionists also attended white Emancipation Day celebrations. Henry 'Box' Brown, for instance, spoke at the 1 August meeting of the Massachusetts Anti-Slavery Society in 1849, as Charles L. Remond was to do in 1850 and again in 1858. Similarly, Frederick Douglass, the leading black spokesman of his generation, shared platforms with white abolitionists in upstate New York throughout the 1840s and 1850s.[20] Quite often, these exercises would last all afternoon, interspersed by short breaks for refreshments, which, in some cases, were clearly laid on by the organising committee. At Hingham in 1844 the assembly 'adjourned to the tables, which were erected on a rising ground in the rear of the platform, and partook of the abundant supply which covered them, which was distributed by the ladies of the "Legion of Honor", assisted by the Marshals'. Other events were advertised strictly as 'picnics', meaning that delegates were requested to 'bring their own provisions, drinking vessels, etc.' – although, in saying this, food was frequently on sale, certainly at many of the meetings held during the 1850s.[21]

Meticulously organised and orchestrated, Emancipation Day celebrations played an important part in shaping the political and cultural identity of the American abolitionist movement. They did so, crucially, by reminding abolitionists of the meaning of their campaign, while at the same time creating a continuous link between the (American) present and the (British) past. The performance of these rituals, in other words, in 'more or less invariant sequences of formal acts and utterances', helped to give radical abolitionism its own 'invented tradition'.[22] While American abolitionists clearly venerated Britain, however, they made a careful distinction between the British government, on the one hand, and the British people, on the other. Speaking to the Massachusetts Anti-Slavery Society's Emancipation Day celebration in Abington in 1855, Edmund Quincy declared that West India Emancipation 'was not brought about by the great men of England, by those who had their hand upon the tiller of State; but it was the triumph, emphatically, of the middling and labouring classes of England' who had 'extorted this act of justice from the hands of a reluctant ministry'. In a similar vein, Garrison believed that Emancipation was 'the triumph mainly of the middling classes', dismissing the £20m paid in compensation to colonial planters as one of the 'tricks of statesmanship which marred the beauty of this great act of national repentance and restitution', the other being 'the added boon of six years' unrequited toil' (that is, apprenticeship).[23]

For obvious reasons, American abolitionists drew inspiration from this idea of West India Emancipation as a triumph of the popular will. Reminding his listeners of the meaning of 1 August, Charles Burleigh told a meeting of the Massachusetts Anti-Slavery Society at Worcester in 1849 that 'every thing with which we, struggling in this anti-slavery enterprise of our day, have become so familiar, was the lot of the British philanthropist, when first he demanded that the slave trade shall be abolished, and afterwards claimed that the slave should be free'. Furthermore, British abolitionists had employed many of the same tactics, and the same peaceful means, to overcome their opponents – like many Garrisonians, Burleigh strongly rejected any notion that the two cases were actually quite different.[24] But this was not all. American abolitionists repeatedly used Britain as a stick to beat their fellow countrymen. 'We, that had exalted ourselves to Heaven, how have we cast ourselves down unto Hell', Garrison wrote in 1846, comparing the records of the two nations. 'We that had set ourselves up as models to the kingdoms of the world, and boasted ourselves of our nice sense of freedom, and scrupulous regard for civil rights, and superior enjoyment of civil liberty, how have we become a by-word and a hissing to the scoffing earth!' Echoing these sentiments, Wendell Phillips reflected bitterly in 1850 that 'it is England, now, not America, that is teaching the world lessons of liberty, and setting the examples which move and stir to noble deeds'.[25]

In much the same way, American abolitionists venerated figures like Wilberforce, Clarkson, and Sharp and delighted in their achievements. Clarkson, in particular, seems to have been held in high esteem, in part because of his longevity, in part because of his willingness to identify himself with the American cause. Significantly, Clarkson's *History* was republished in the United States in 1836 (an abridged version had been published earlier in 1816), and, as we have seen, American abolitionists made a special point of calling upon Clarkson when they visited Britain. Henry Wright assured Catherine Clarkson in 1843 that 'in the estimate of American Abolitionists, & of all our numerous *free* colored people', her husband was 'more intimately & *endearingly* associated with the holy cause of Anti-Slavery than any or all of those, who, in this kingdom [Britain] took part in it'.[26] Wilberforce, too, was commemorated in the United States, not least in the shape of Wilberforce College in Ohio, which was founded in 1856 by the Methodist Episcopal Church to provide educational instruction for blacks, and later (1863) reopened as Wilberforce University. Meanwhile, among free black communities in the North debating and temperance societies were frequently named for Wilberforce, as was the 'black utopia' settled on nearly 800 acres of land next to the town of Lucan, Upper Canada, during the 1830s. At least until the American Civil War both men enjoyed a special place within American abolitionism, as did Granville Sharp, who was frequently mentioned in the same breath as Clarkson and Wilberforce, and seems to have been better known in the United States than either Buxton or Brougham.[27]

Veneration for Britain undoubtedly helped to shape the political consciousness of American abolitionists. But it could also prove something of a distraction, just as it served to underline the status of American abolitionists as radicals and 'outsiders'.[28] Theodore Parker, for one, pointed out that had the 800,000 slaves in the British Caribbean 'been on the fast-anchored island of England, they would not have been freemen in '38. They would have been slaves to-day'. Parker's point was simple; that while American abolitionists eulogised England on the one hand, and 'while they spoke reproachfully of

America on the other, [they] a little over-rated the anti-slavery feeling in England, and a little under-rated the anti-slavery here'. 'There is nothing in the past history, there is nothing in the present condition of England,' he went on, 'which leads a man to believe, or to be certain, at least, that had the British people American slavery to deal with, they would have borne themselves more nobly than ourselves.'[29] Wendell Phillips, for his part, thought American abolitionists might find a more 'just' parallel in the position of 'missionaries Knibb and Smith in Jamaica'. If any man would learn 'aright the character of the American anti-slavery movement, and its spirit', he argued, 'if he would know the bitterness of its foes, the violence of their invective and their hate, let him go to the grave of the Smith, the martyr of Demarara'. Nevertheless, such doubts rarely led to an outright rejection of Britain; indeed, it was Parker who hailed Emancipation as 'one of the most remarkable acts of disinterested philanthropy ever performed by a nation'. Similarly, Wendell Phillips acknowledged that the British had taught the rest of the world an important lesson, namely that 'the Negro had a right to his freedom, as given to him by God, and no man, or nation, or human power, had a right to keep it from him'.[30]

In these and other ways, Britain (and Britain's moral example) was folded into American abolitionist discourse. Equally striking is the way blacks appropriated 1 August, sometimes joining forces with white abolitionists but, more often than not, organising their own ceremonials. The years immediately following the American Revolution witnessed the emergence, for the first time, of a large free black community in the United States. Estimates vary, but it seems likely that by 1840 there were approximately 170,000 free blacks in the North, and a larger number still in the South (approximately 215,000).[31] Though nominally free, most of these men and women faced considerable prejudice and discrimination, particularly those in the South. Nevertheless, during the second quarter of the nineteenth century they began to develop their own structures and institutions, as well as their own leaders; principally clergymen but also doctors, lawyers, large-scale farmers, undertakers, tradesmen, and entrepreneurs. Some of these communities were quite large. The free black population of New York, for instance, was 14,000 in 1830 (about one-third of the city's population), while that of Philadelphia was larger still.[32] As growing white proscription suggests, free blacks were to become an increasingly visible (and, to some, troublesome) feature of many American cities. Perhaps just as important, they were also able to find ways of making themselves heard, forging a political voice that tested the boundaries of their freedom, often with unforeseen results.[33]

One of the ways this deepening collective consciousness was expressed – at least, in the North – was through public festivities. As Patrick Rael has shown, the earliest of these celebrations, such as Election Day and Pinkster 'descended from the social practices of European America' and were essentially non-elite affairs that provided blacks with a 'cathartic release from pent-up frustration, as well as respite from daily toil'. Negro Election Day, for instance, 'served as African-Americans' take on white election day gatherings in New England';

Pinkster, meanwhile, had its origins in the Dutch celebration of Pentecost.[34] Over time, however, blacks' celebrations took on 'new forms and functions'. Following the abolition of the slave trade by Congress in 1808, free blacks in New York and Philadelphia adopted New Year's Day as the black 4 July, although just as quickly the parades and orations that marked these occasions appear to have been discontinued, largely in response to white entreaties. Similar concerns arose over the celebration of Emancipation Day in New York State (1827), which also happened to coincide with the annual 4 July festivities; in fact, white unease led blacks to abandon these festivals after 1831.[35] Far more enduring, however, were the celebrations connected with West India Emancipation. The speed of events – first the Emancipation Act of 1833 and then the end of apprenticeship in 1838 – rapidly established 1 August as an important date in the black calendar. Samuel Cornish, editor of the *Colored American*, declared in 1838 that henceforth 1 August should be 'remembered, observed and consecrated by every colored man'.[36] In a similar vein, William C. Nell told a meeting in Boston in 1842 that the observance of this day 'should not prove a spasmodic enthusiasm, a temporary excitement; but that a perpetual flame should burn vividly on the altar of their hearts, until the happy day should be ushered in, when the American bondman shall raise his hands with joyful shouting for his liberty'.[37]

This was not idle talk. Black elites everywhere in the North quickly grasped the meaning of 1 August and, just as quickly, made the day their own. Here again, the rituals associated with these occasions acquired a distinctive shape and character; in fact, black Emancipation Day celebrations seem to have evolved at the same pace, and along much the same lines, as their white counterparts. Prayers, music, bible readings, and addresses by prominent local figures, white and black, were all common features of these commemorative practices. Moreover, as time went on blacks took to the streets in increasing numbers, in a public display of strength and solidarity with the abolitionist cause. In 1844 in New Bedford, Massachusetts, a large procession under the direction of Paul C. Howard, the grand marshal, marched from the town hall to a 'beautiful grove, belonging to John Parker', led by 'a cavalcade of 40 young men, with a banner inscribed, "In commemoration of British West India Emancipation – 800,000 chattels restored to men"'.[38] A short distance away in Providence, Rhode Island, a procession 'embracing several benevolent societies and a large number of neatly-dressed and joyous children', marched from a local black church, through Main Street, to a 'pleasant grove', preceded by a 'full band of music'. Again, many of the societies carried banners: one inscribed on one side with a portrait of William Lloyd Garrison, and, on the other, 'a slave chained beneath the full spread stars and stripe; 'another the banner of the Female Assistant Society; and another, significantly, a banner of the Wilberforce Total Abstinence Society'. At the grove, those present listened to speeches, followed by dinner and yet more speeches. Then at 4 o'clock the procession re-formed and re-marched through 'the centre or square to Power street and then back to Rev. Atkin's Church'. In Boston in 1844 local blacks processed through Cambridge, Charles, Beacon, and Park streets to Tremont Chapel, where addresses were delivered 'by several gentlemen engaged for the occasion'.[39]

By this date most Emancipation Day celebrations were held out of doors, and invariably involved a dinner or picnic of some description. When the black abolitionist, Henry Bibb, attended a 'Liberty Festival' in Niles, Michigan, in 1848, he recalled that 'a regular and well formed procession moved from the grove appointed for the meeting to the table, where we found a sumptuous entertainment consisting of all the luxuries of the season awaiting us. A well-ordered or better repast is seldom got up'.[40] It also seems likely that many of these meetings included music (hence the presence of bands), 'promenading', and on occasion dancing. In other words, while Emancipation Day celebrations had a serious purpose, they were also social and family occasions and, as such, designed to attract as many people as possible. To judge from the available sources, it was not unusual for the largest of these events to attract 2,000 or 3,000 people. Even smaller towns like Niles, Michigan, could attract 'several hundred persons'. Organisers clearly worked hard to make these events a success. In New Bedford in 1844 arrangements were made with the New Bedford and Providence Railroad Company to discount '50 per cent, from their prices, for our Providence friends', while similar arrangements were made with the Nantucket steamboat company.[41] Featured speakers (Douglass, for instance) also proved popular attractions, as did processions, music, and martial displays. As a result, many of these events had a statewide appeal. At Dayton, Ohio, in 1854 local blacks were joined by 10 railway cars of supporters from Cincinnati, as well as contingents from Xenia, Hamilton, Troy, and Piqua. Similarly, 'of the 7,000 attending the celebration at New Bedford grove in 1855, some 500 came from Providence and 200 from Boston'.[42]

In part because Emancipation Day celebrations were elite-led affairs and therefore orderly and respectable, in part because they enjoyed the support and protection of prominent whites, these events seem to have passed off without serious incident. The *Liberator* noted in 1844 that 'great numbers' had turned out to see the Providence procession, adding significantly that 'not an insult or a sneer was bestowed upon it'. Similarly, when 500 blacks processed on horseback through Boston in 1847 a local (white) newspaper reported that there was 'not a word of ridicule or disrespect, but every thing passed off with apparent respect and quiet'. The irony of this situation was not lost on the newspaper's editor. Only 25 years before, he recalled, blacks celebrating 'the union of nations to abolish the slave trade' had been 'followed by the rabble; hissed, hooted and groaned at every turn, and one would have supposed that Bedlam had broken loose'.[43] Tolerated, for the most part, by local whites, black public celebrations helped to foster more radical forms of 'black community activism'. As Rael argues, such festivals also legitimised the status and authority of the men who organised them, which is presumably why black leaders in the North refused to abandon Emancipation Day celebrations, despite the pleas of figures like Garrison for them to do so.[44] But, in saying this, we should not lose sight of the significance of 1 August for free black communities in the United States, or the strength among them of black Anglophilia. Many of the banners on display at Emancipation Day festivities hint at this, as do many of the speeches and addresses; indeed, pro-British feeling played an important part in shaping an emerging political consciousness among free black communities during the 1840s and 1850s.[45]

At an elite level, identification with West India Emancipation was also reinforced by contacts with Britain and, just as important, with British abolitionists. Estimates vary, but something like 80 African Americans visited Britain between 1830 and 1865.[46] What drew them? In part, cash and a ready-made provincial circuit, made possible by the growth of provincial towns and by the speed and efficiency of the railways. But, at the same time, Britain offered black Americans sanctuary. Many of those who crossed the Atlantic in the 1840s and 1850s, among them Frederick Douglass, William Wells Brown, and Henry 'Box' Brown, were fugitive slaves or else had some other direct experience of slavery, and in Britain they found willing friends, as well as a home away from home. Alexander Crummell, who visited Britain in 1848, spoke for many when he told an audience in Liverpool: 'When I was in America I THOUGHT I was a man. In England I FEEL – I KNOW that I am'. Crummell's enthusiasm for his adopted home was boundless. 'The English have yet to learn Color-Phobia', he wrote to John Jay in 1851. 'My black complexion is a great privilege, and a real possession here, connected with other real qualities, which I am supposed to possess'.[47] Douglass also remarked upon the absence of colour prejudice in Britain. On his initial visit to Ireland in 1845 he told William Lloyd Garrison that 'one of the most pleasing features of my visit here thus far has been a total absence of all manifestations of prejudice against me, on account of my color'.[48]

Of course, it is impossible to judge how real these perceptions were. Because they were well mannered and well connected, most black visitors to Britain tended to move in fairly select circles. During his first six months in Britain, for instance, Crummell breakfasted with Sir Harry Inglis, Judge Lewin of the East Indies, and the masters and fellows of several Cambridge colleges.[49] Similarly, Douglass was guided and protected by his Garrisonian friends, many of whom welcomed him into their own homes. Nevertheless, the sense of relief was palpable. As Douglass put it: 'I find no difficulty here in obtaining admission into any place of worship, instruction or amusement, on equal terms with people as white as any I ever saw in the United States. I meet nothing to remind me of my complexion'. Douglass would return to this theme time and time again. 'Eleven days and a half gone, and I have crossed three thousand miles of perilous deep', he wrote to Garrison from Ireland in January 1846. 'Instead of a democratic government, I am under a monarchical government. Instead of the bright, blue sky of America, I am covered with the soft, gray fog of the Emerald Isle. I breathe, and lo! The chattel becomes a man! I gaze around in vain for one who will question my equal humanity, claim me as a slave, or offer me an insult.'[50]

What gave these visits added poignancy, certainly during the 1830s and 1840s, was the opportunity for black Americans to pay their respects to British abolitionists and, in doing so, to establish their own credentials. Nathaniel Paul, who had been sent to Britain to raise funds for the Wilberforce community in Upper Canada, wrote excitedly to Garrison in April 1833 that he had had 'the pleasure of breakfasting twice with the venerable Wilberforce', adding: 'I now have a letter in my pocket that I received from him, a few weeks since, which I would not take pounds for. Once I have been in the company of the patriotic Clarkson. I must say I viewed them both as Angels of Liberty. God bless and reward them.'[51] Some fifteen years later, Douglass visited Clarkson – 'the last of the noble line of Englishmen who inaugurated the anti-slavery movement for England and the civilized world' – at Playford Hall, near Ipswich, in the company of Garrison and George Thompson. Describing the visit in his *Life and Times* (1893), Douglass recalled that 'the scene was impressive. It was the meeting of two centuries'. He went on: 'After shaking hands with my two distinguished friends, and giving them welcome, he [Clarkson] took one of my hands in both of his, and, in a tremulous voice, said, "God bless you, Frederick Douglass! I have given sixty years of my life to the emancipation of your people, and if I had sixty years more they should all be given to the same cause."'[52]

In Douglass's case, these memories and associations left an indelible mark; in fact, few black leaders, certainly in the post-Civil War era, attached quite so much significance to West India Emancipation, or, for that matter, to the moral example set by the British. In a series of Emancipation Day addresses delivered in the 1840s and 1850s, Douglass sketched out in detail what for him was the meaning of 1834/1838, both as an idea and a fact. Interestingly, he began with first principles. West India Emancipation, he told a meeting in Canandaigua, New York, in 1857, was 'the most interesting and sublime event of the nineteenth century', and as such, had a universal significance that transcended national or geographical boundaries. As he pointed out: 'In the great Drama of Emancipation, England was the theatre, but universal and everywhere [the] applying principles of Righteousness, Liberty, and Justice were the actors.' For this reason, Douglass argued, black Americans could reasonably claim Emancipation as their own, 'at least until we shall have an American celebration to take its place'.[53] 'The annals of the world show no brighter page than that on which West India Emancipation is written', he reminded a meeting in Poughkeepsie, New York, in 1858. 'It is an exhibition of conscience – a manifestation of Christian virtue – an acknowledgment of duty – a confession and a renunciation of profitable sin at great expense, on a grand and commanding scale, by a great nation.'[54]

In saying this, Douglass was also keenly aware that Britain's actions had shifted the terms of debate, setting an example for others to follow. Emancipation, he claimed, had 'made the name of England known and loved in every Slave Cabin, from the Potomac to the Rio Grande, and has spread alarm, hatred, and dread in all the accursed slave markets of our boasted Republic from

Baltimore to New Orleans'.[55] Throughout the 1840s and 1850s, Douglass would use these images, and Britain's example, to exert moral pressure on the American republic, at the same time rejecting the notion that West India Emancipation could be dismissed out of hand as an unsuccessful 'experiment'. Like many others, Douglass was not blind to the failings of Emancipation. But, to his mind, Americans had 'approached it as though it were a railroad, a canal, a steamship, or a newly invented mowing machine', demanding to know 'WILL IT PAY? Will it increase the growth of sugar?' In other words, all their tests of the 'grand measure' had proceeded from the 'slaveholders' side, and never from the side of the emancipated slave'. As Douglass put it in 1858: 'Liberty is not a device or an experiment, but a law of nature dating back to man's creation, and if this fundamental law is a failure, the responsibility is not with the British Parliament, not with the British people, but with the great Author of this law.'[56]

Perhaps more than any other black leader, Douglass also stressed the obvious links and continuities between British and American abolitionists. Imbued with a deep sense of history, Douglass saw all too clearly that the American movement, like many other American institutions, was 'largely derived from England'. What he meant by this was the application of ideas and strategies. To take an obvious example, Douglass traced the doctrine of 'immediatism' (that is, the immediate emancipation of slaves) back to Elizabeth Heyrick, whose *Immediate, Not Gradual Abolition* had been published in 1824. Similarly, Douglass noted that Garrison had 'applied British abolitionism to American slavery. He did that and nothing more. He found its principles here plainly stated and defined; its truths glowingly enunciated, and the whole subject illustrated, and elaborated in a masterly manner. The sin – the crime – the curse of slavery, were all demonstrated in the light of reason, religion, and morality, and by a startling array of facts'.[57] Equally striking is Douglass's habit of drawing analogies between American and British abolitionists, thereby setting the movement in its appropriate historical context. Charles Sumner, the outspoken senator from Massachusetts, is heralded at different times as the American Wilberforce, William Lloyd Garrison as its Thomas Clarkson, and Wendell Phillips as its Granville Sharp.[58] Douglass was not alone in doing this – many white abolitionists also looked to Britain as a way of historicising American abolitionism – but in his case the reverential tones in which he refers to Britain speak to a more pronounced Anglophilia, that, in turn, derived from Douglass's sense that in Britain he had been allowed to become his own man, freed from all constraints and expectations.[59]

Significantly, Douglass never lost his enthusiasm for Britain or for the meaning of West India Emancipation, even when challenged by figures like James McCune Smith, who believed that blacks would do better to celebrate the actions of Denmark Vesey or Nat Turner; that is, figures who were prepared to fight for their freedom, rather than wait for it to be 'given' to them.[60] Douglass understood only too well the appeal of such arguments. Yet he still insisted on recognising the anniversary of West India Emancipation. In a remarkable speech delivered in Elmira, New York, on 1 August 1880, long after slavery had been abolished in the United States, Douglass returned to this theme, reminding his listeners that 'the downfall of slavery under British power meant the downfall of slavery, ultimately, under American power, and the downfall of negro slavery everywhere'. Here, in other words, was an anniversary of universal significance that, at the same time, proclaimed an important truth, namely that 'men have in their own hands the peaceful means of putting all their moral and political enemies under their feet and of making this world a healthy and happy dwelling-place, if they will but faithfully and courageously use these means'. More controversially, he also pointed out that 'English emancipation' had 'one advantage over American emancipation. Hers has a definite anniversary. Ours has none. Like our slaves, the freedom of the Negro has no birthday'. Reminding his readers of the claims of the (British) past, Douglass hailed West India Emancipation as 'the first bright star in a stormy sky; the first smile after a long providential frown; the first ray of hope; the first tangible fact demonstrating the possibility of a peaceable transition from slavery to freedom, of the Negro race'. [61]

Despite Douglass's pointed reminders, 1 August would eventually lose much of its relevance for African Americans, although, as Douglass feared, no obvious (single) alternative emerged to take its place. Instead, blacks seem to have celebrated a number of different anniversaries connected with 'American emancipation', among them passage of the Emancipation Proclamation (1 February 1863), Lincoln's birthday (12 February 1809), and ratification of the Fifteenth Amendment (30 March 1870).[62] Few whites paid 1 August much attention either, particularly after the American Civil War (1861–65) had brought slavery to an end. Yet, as we have seen, for a good part of the nineteenth century – and particularly the years between 1838 and 1861 – West India Emancipation held a special place in the rituals of American abolitionists. For obvious reasons, black and white activists looked to Britain for support and encouragement, mindful of the special bonds that tied the two countries together. But this identification went beyond the exchange of ideas and personnel. American abolitionists folded Britain's moral example into the rituals of the American anti-slavery movement, creating not only a continuous link with the past but also holding out the promise of a future that was radically different. Emancipation Day celebrations cemented these emotional ties and sympathies, at the same time habitually reminding American abolitionists of the wider significance of their struggle and their special role within it. The importance of these rituals should not be under-estimated. Highly elaborate performances, they helped to define the meaning of American abolitionism and, just as important, how it should be remembered.

At least up until 1861, Emancipation in the United States remained a distant hope. In the Caribbean, however, it was a stark reality – a social and economic revolution that for most whites, at least, represented the end of their world as they knew it. Fiercely protective of their economic interests, the planter elite had for years resisted any attempt to end or even ameliorate slavery, predicting that such 'interference' would lead to black insurrection, the 'extermination of whites', and the utter ruin of the colonies.[63] The Emancipation Act of 1833, which not only granted planters £20m in compensation but also rejected the notion of immediate emancipation in favour of a period of apprenticeship, did little to allay these fears. As 1 August 1834 approached, rumours of insurrection spread throughout the Caribbean. In Barbados, for instance, troops were dispatched to Bridgetown as a show of imperial strength, and there were similar alarms in Trinidad, Montserrat, and St Kitts.[64] Clearly, in some cases such precautions proved timely but on the whole Emancipation passed off peaceably, as did the ending of apprenticeship four years later (1 August 1838). Sir Lionel Smith, Governor of Barbados and the Windward Islands, reported to the Colonial Secretary in 1838 that in Jamaica Emancipation Day 'was observed, by proclamation, as one of thanksgiving and prayer'. 'It is quite impossible for me to do justice to the good order, decorum and gratitude which the whole of the labouring population manifested on the happy occasion', he went on. 'Tho' joy beamed on every countenance, it was throughout the island tempered with solemn thankfulness to God; and the churches and chapels were everywhere filled with these happy people, in humble offerings of praise for the great blessing he has conferred upon them.'[65]

For obvious reasons, abolitionists on both sides of the Atlantic seized eagerly upon this image of Emancipation as a peaceful passage or transformation. James Thome and J. Horace Kimball, who visited the Caribbean in 1837, reported that in St John's, Antigua, 1 August 1834 had been spent 'by the great mass of negroes in the churches and chapels', adding that the day had been 'like a sabbath'. Equally striking, so the two men thought, was the lack of any 'frivolity'. 'There were no riotous assemblies, no drunken carousals. It was not in such channels that the excitement of the emancipation flowed. They were as far from dissipation or debauchery, as they were from violence and carnage.'[66] It was the same thing in 1838, when apprenticeship came to an end. Charles Stuart, a flamboyant former army officer and a loyal Garrisonian, reported to Theodore Weld in December 1838 that 'while the military were watching for insurrection [in Barbados], the emancipated bondsmen were thronging in multitudes to the houses of God, to render thanks for the great benefit, which they had received at His hands'.[67] Whether exaggerated or not, such accounts helped to reinforce nationalistic and imperialistic discourses that interpreted Emancipation as a 'gift' that had been bestowed upon a pious, grateful people. A popular image of the period portrays an emancipated slave standing with his arms outstretched above his head, shackles at his feet, together with the inscription, 'England I Revere. God I Adore. Now I Am Free'. Similar images can be found in school textbooks of the 1860s and 1870s, where again crowds of grateful blacks gather together respectfully to receive news of their impending emancipation.[68]

Abolitionists were inclined to attribute black 'passivity' to the legacy of slavery, or, alternatively, to the civilising work of white missionaries.[69] As

Catherine Hall has shown, evangelical Christians struggled long and hard to impose their values on post-emancipation societies in the Caribbean, starting with Emancipation Day itself.[70] A case in point is the Revd. James Phillippo, a prominent Baptist missionary, who served in Jamaica for over fifty years. Like many other whites, Phillippo saw Emancipation (or, rather, the ending of apprenticeship) as a test of black loyalty. In *Jamaica: Its Past and Present* (1843) he describes in detail how on 1 August 1838 he arranged for his congregation to march from the Baptist chapel in Spanish Town to the square opposite Government House, where they were addressed by the Governor, Sir Lionel Smith. In a manner that anticipated many celebrations in the United States, the members of the congregation carried flags and banners, some of them dedicated to 'Sturge', 'Brougham', 'Victoria', and the 'Marquis of Sligo', others hailing 'England' as 'the land of liberty, of light, of life', or else anticipating an end to 'strife and conflict' in the Caribbean. One banner, for instance, bore the inscription, 'Emancipation in peace, in harmony, in safety and acquiescence, on all sides'; another, 'Education, social order, and religion'. Phillippo also arranged for three triumphal arches to be erected at the principal entrances to his chapel, each of them 'decorated with leaves and flowers, and crowned with flags bearing the several inscriptions of "Freedom's come", "Slavery is no more", "Thy chains are broken, Africa is free", while in addition to these and the flags and banners borne by the procession, one was seen waving from the cupola of the metropolitan school-room, bearing "the 1st of August, 1838", ornamented by a painted wreath of laurel'.[71]

As these few details suggest, Phillippo conceived of the Spanish Town celebration as a respectable, orderly affair that spoke in different ways to the freedmen's sense of obligation, as well as their duties and responsibilities. (The naming of free villages in Jamaica after prominent British abolitionists – Sligoville, Clarkson Town, Wilberforce, Buxton – reflected many of the same values and preoccupations.)[72] Also revealing are the 'rural fetes' that Phillippo and others organised to celebrate Emancipation. In one of these at Dawkins Caymanas, near Spanish Town, Governor Smith and his suite sat down to dinner with 300 'apprentices' in a 'spacious Arcade in the Gothic style' woven out of cocoa-nut branches.[73] The scene is visualised in a contemporary print, published by R. Cartwright of London in 1838. In the foreground, the Governor sits at a separate table with his back to the apprentices, who are arranged behind him in two long rows, the men on the left, and the women on the right. Above them are arranged coloured silk banners bearing the names of 'Victoria', 'Sligo', 'Sturge', 'Brougham', 'Mulgrave', and Smith himself.[74] Clearly designed for a British audience, the scene was again one of order and respectability, and, as such, a far cry from the scenes of bloodshed that many in the Caribbean (and in Britain) had predicted. Emancipation, according to this sentimental discourse, denoted 'peace' and 'harmony', even if it also meant maintaining a safe distance between the governor and the black apprentices.

White missionaries would continue to play an important role in shaping Emancipation Day celebrations, even if they were unable to recapture the

19   *Celebration of the 1st of August 1838 at Dawkins Caymanas, near Spanish Town, Jamaica* (1838)

excitement that had characterised the ceremonials in 1838.[75] By mid-century, large public demonstrations, like those held in Spanish Town, seem to have given way to more private rituals that, instead of applauding the achievements of the 'Saints', made explicit the connection between Emancipation and baptism, 'the crossing over from one identity to another'.[76] In 1854 Phillippo and his congregation observed 1 August with an open-air baptismal service at Clair Park Penn. The crowds, it seems, gathered the night before, 'encamping under the trees'. At daylight a thanksgiving meeting was held, after which the candidates (42 in all) were taken to the riverside and baptised.[77] To judge from the few surviving records, these rituals appear to have been repeated each year, assuming an 'explicitly backward-looking and calendrical character'.[78] They also became more elaborate. Phillippo's journal for 1869 records that on 1 August he baptised ten persons in the river near Turnbull's Penn, Spanish Town. Two days later, he conducted the 'usual annual thanksgiving meeting', and in the evening 'delivered a lecture on the progress of anti-slavery principles throughout the world'. Finally, on 4 August large crowds gathered for the 'annual festival of children' at the Metropolitan School.[79] While it would be misleading to describe these rituals as specifically 'black' ceremonials, it is clear that they established a (black) tradition that survived well into the twentieth century and beyond; indeed, we can find traces of them in the anniversary celebrations held in 1933 and again in 1983. In this sense, at least, Emancipation Day celebrations helped to nurture (and, in turn, were nurtured by) a sense of black identity that had its roots deep in the black church.

Church-oriented activities were only part of a much broader picture, however. Some blacks, particularly those in rural districts, obviously preferred their own 'African' celebrations, turning for inspiration to the 'crop-over' festivals that survived from the days of slavery.[80] In Jamaica in 1847 it was reported that labourers in Trelawny celebrated 1 August by going about 'from one estate to another, drumming, fifing, dancing, and john-canooing, in the demi-savage spirit of the olden time'. Though vigorously suppressed by the white elite, who associated such rituals with idolatry, sorcery, and vulgarity, elements of these popular folk activities survived into the twentieth century in the shape of the all-night 'tea meetings' and 'bruckins parties' described by Claude McKay and others.[81] Then there were the celebrations organised by 'race-conscious, educated blacks and coloureds'. As Bridget Brereton has shown, around 1850 coloured Trinidadians were openly using 1 August dinners to criticise government policy in the Caribbean, while at the same time painting lurid pictures of the horrors of colonial slavery (this in an attempt to stress their solidarity with ex-slaves rather than whites). Yet what is also revealing about the Trinidad experience is the difficulty in forming some kind of consensus. Despite the blandishments of educated coloureds, many ex-slaves clearly showed little interest in Emancipation Day celebrations; others (white as well as black) took the view that slavery was best forgotten or 'regarded merely as a matter of History'. Emancipation, in other words, quickly became a contested realm of memory, involving not only different interpretations of the past, but also *lieu d'amnesie* (realms of forgetting).[82]

By mid-century there were signs that Emancipation Day celebrations were in decline.[83] However, the 50th anniversary of the ending of apprenticeship in the Caribbean (1 August 1888) afforded West Indians an opportunity to reassess the meaning and legacy of Emancipation. Throughout the region, the anniversary was marked by special thanksgiving services, accompanied in many cases by processions and illuminations. In some islands – Grenada, for instance – 1 August was celebrated as a public holiday. At 8 o'clock in the morning the Union Jack was displayed at Fort George, which 'was the signal for the appearance of coloured bunting in all parts of the town'. Then, at midday, a procession of over 800 schoolchildren was led from York House to the Queen's Park, 'where athletic sports were got up', and later in the afternoon a large crowd gathered in Market Square to raise 'three cheers for Queen Victoria and three for the Administrator who had kindly granted them the holiday'. Similar celebrations were held in British Guiana, where the committee of management organised a special commemorative concert, as well as an industrial exhibition 'demonstrating the progress achieved during 50 years of Freedom'.[84] The increasing 'secularisation' of these festivities, a trend that can be dated back to the 1860s and 1870s, marked yet another subtle shift in commemorative practices in the Caribbean. Equally striking is the determination to celebrate Emancipation in terms of social and economic progress. 'It is not that a bond has been made by an individual here and there, but the people have advanced', editorialised the *Barbados Globe*, surveying the progress that had been made since 1834. 'Religion, education, and freedom have done their work, and in trade, in commerce, in agriculture, [and] in professions the on-ward march is to be seen'.[85]

Nevertheless, the 1888 ceremonials were conceived, by and large, as 'white' rituals, and when local organisers chose to ignore this reality they could quickly run into difficulties. Take the case of Trinidad. In June 1888 a delegation of 'blacks' led by Edgar Maresse-Smith, a coloured lawyer, called upon the governor, Sir William Robinson, and asked him to declare 1 August a public holiday. Robinson refused, citing among other things Trinidad's mixed population (it seems to have been assumed that Emancipation would have no meaning for Indians, Chinese, French, Spaniards, or Portuguese) and the likely disruption to local shops and businesses. At the same time, the governor offered the delegation some advice. To his mind, thanksgiving services were the 'most appropriate manner in doing honour to the occasion'. 'I rejoice that progress has been made,' he went on, 'but I hardly think that the advance has been rapid enough and sufficiently widespread'. What was called for, then, was some plan of celebrating 1 August 'which will have for its object the improvement of the moral and condition of those who are in a humbler state of life that yourselves'. Significantly, Robinson also took this opportunity to remind the members of the delegation that 'the freedom of the African Race was won not by your efforts – not by your orators, not by your warriors'. Rather, 'it was fought for by white men and gained after fierce struggles against authority and power, and after unwearied sacrifices'. It followed, therefore, that these men, and William Wilberforce, in particular, needed to be thanked and praised.[86]

The whole matter might have ended there. But so far from accepting the governor's decision, and the reasoning behind it, the delegation dismissed Robinson's views as 'a calumny on the coloured race' and, as such, racially motivated. For Maresse-Smith and other educated blacks and coloureds, celebrating the Jubilee of Emancipation was inextricably linked to notions of black consciousness. As one of them explained at a public meeting following the delegation's interview with the governor, 1 August was not only an opportunity to prove that 'we are able to appreciate the boon which was conferred upon us', but also to 'show that we are not at all ashamed of acknowledging our [African] origin'. Another member of the delegation went so far as to describe 1888 as 'the jubilee of a nation'.[87] Predictably, Robinson was unnerved by this turn of events, as were sections of the local white press. The Trinidad *New Era*, for instance, dismissed the members of the eight-man delegation as 'shallow pated seekers after notoriety', and poured contempt on what it described as their 'Voltarian [sic] tenets'. A pointed contrast was also drawn between events in Trinidad and the preparations already under way in Demerara, where, it was claimed, it had been 'positively determined that there will be an absence of all party feelings'. The implication was clear. The members of the delegation were trying to turn the Jubilee of Emancipation to their own political advantage, not least by introducing into the debate the troublesome concepts of 'race' and 'class'.[88]

By this stage, it seemed possible that the 1888 anniversary might pass unnoticed. But then late in July another delegation, backed this time by the mayor of Port of Spain, approached the governor with a view to putting on a banquet in the Prince's Building. Robinson supported the project, and even offered to preside, but not before he had received assurances (freely given, as it turns out) that the celebration would not be made 'a question of class, colour, or party', and that 'order and decorum' would be observed throughout. It is probably not accidental, either, that the delegation mentioned the possibility of raising a statue to Wilberforce in the eastern end of the town, should finances permit.[89] Efforts to reach some sort of understanding with Maresse-Smith proved much less successful, however, with the result that when 1 August arrived there were, in fact, two banquets, one at the Prince's Building and the other at St Rose's School. Inevitably, this confusion cast a shadow over the celebrations in Port of Spain; indeed, the local white press noted with some satisfaction that 'on the whole the Jubilee [had] excited less interest than the promoters seemed to have anticipated'.[90] Yet what is also striking is the perseverance of Robinson's 'black' opponents, as well as their political vision. This is perhaps best illustrated by comparing the toasts delivered at the two banquets. While the guests at the Prince's Building were invited to drink to the health of the Queen, the Governor, and to the 'memory of Wilberforce', thereby reaffirming the essential 'Britishness' of these occasions, those assembled at St Rose's School drank to the health of the Queen and her representatives in the colonies, to 'the Pioneers and Champions of Negro Emancipation', and to 'the Rising Generation of African Descent'.[91]

Similar tensions were evident again in 1933–34 (significantly, the 1907 anniversary of the abolition of the slave trade seems to have passed largely unnoticed in the Caribbean). Inasmuch as there was a tradition in the British West Indies, 1838 and not 1834 was recognised as the key anniversary date.[92] But, taking their cue from the 'mother country', most British colonies celebrated 1933–34, adding their voices to an imperial chorus that was designed to pay tribute to, and, to some extent, recover Britain's tradition of humanitarian interventionism. As was the case 'at home', many islands set up special Wilberforce Centenary Committees, usually composed of clergymen and local (black) civic dignitaries. In Barbados, for instance, the centenary of Wilberforce's death was marked by thanksgiving services at St Michael's Cathedral and the Methodist and Moravian churches, as well as a 'monster meeting' at Queen's Park, presided over by the Acting Governor.[93] More elaborate still were the celebrations held in Port of Spain (Trinidad), which began on 29 July with a 'demonstration' of 200 schoolchildren at the Prince's Building. This was followed by a dinner for 800 'poor people', another aspect of 'cropover', and a fireworks display at Queen's Park Savannah (31 July), which brought the 'Wilberforce Celebrations' to an end.[94] Similar events were also held in St Lucia, where the day's ceremonials climaxed with fireworks and the lighting of a bonfire at Vigie Point.[95] Only Jamaica, it seems, held aloof from the Wilberforce centenary, although even here there were 'special' thanksgiving services in some of the island's churches.[96]

Many of the same rituals – thanksgiving services, parades, fireworks, and 'special' dinners for the poor – were repeated in August 1934. Across the Caribbean, thousands of West Indians took to the streets to celebrate Emancipation Day. Nowhere was this more apparent than in Trinidad, where local authorities organised an ambitious programme of events, including a mass meeting of Friendly Societies and black working men's groups at the Queen's Park Savannah, a night concert of 'Negro music' at the Royal Victoria Institute, a 'masked pageant', complete with carnival bands and calypso singers, and a 'Grand Emancipation Dance' at the Prince's Building. In what was presumably a conscious attempt to mimic celebrations in Britain, the organisers also devised and put on a historical pageant, which ran over four different nights between 29 July and 3 August.[97] Meanwhile, in St Kitts Emancipation Day was observed by 'a church parade of civic dignitaries', as well as a children's parade, which was followed by 'athletic sports' at Warner Park. Elsewhere in the Caribbean organisers put on industrial, arts, and crafts exhibitions, thereby introducing into the celebrations an element of economic nationalism.[98] In other words, the ceremonials in 1933–34 took on a wider function than hitherto, in part social, in part patriotic, and in part a celebration of local folklore and culture.

In these and other ways, West Indian societies claimed a distinctive voice in what was essentially a white imperialistic discourse. Inevitably, Emancipation Day celebrations took place under the watchful eye of colonial authorities that were only too quick to remind West Indians of the significance of Emancipation and the respect due to figures like Wilberforce.[99] Colonists responded in kind, dutifully passing resolutions pledging allegiance to the Crown, but at the same time attaching to these gestures a meaning that was frequently at odds with imperial priorities in the region.[100] By the 1930s a new generation of leaders had emerged in the Caribbean, shaped by the experiences of the First World War and severe economic recession. A case in point is Arthur Andrew Cipriani, a white of Corsican descent who had served overseas with the British West Indian Regiment, and who on his return to Trinidad took over the leadership of the largely black Trinidad Working Men's Association and later became Mayor of Port of Spain and a member of the Legislative Council. As Eric Williams points out, Cipriani 'considered it his duty to attack or censure the government wherever the opportunity presented itself', leading a vigorous campaign against what he considered to be the worst effects of colonialism: low wages, poor housing, disease, a failing educational system, and rising unemployment.[101]

Interestingly, Cipriani played a leading role in the 1933–34 celebrations in Trinidad. Not only was he chairman of the local Wilberforce Centenary Committee, but he also presided over many of the events held in Port of Spain in 1934, including the 'carnival' at Queen's Park Oval. Cipriani obviously wanted the festivities in 1933–34 to be a spectacle and to provide an opportunity for

West Indians to express themselves and their own local culture.[102] More seriously, however, he also wanted the ceremonials to make a point. For instance, Cipriani took a close interest in the historical pageant, which, unlike its British counterpart, adopted a more Afrocentric view of British transatlantic slavery, as evidenced by the inclusion of scenes depicting the 'capture of the Ashanti tribe', a 'slave auction in the West Indies', and 'a protest from Barbados against the liberation of slaves'.[103] In much the same way, he was careful to link the Emancipation Day celebrations to the delicate question of Trinidad's political future. Like many 'radicals', Cipriani was highly critical of Trinidad's continued status as a Crown Colony, believing that the Caribbean islands should be placed on the same footing as Britain's white settler colonies, that is, made 'autonomous communities' within the British Empire. As he told a mass meeting at Queen's Park Savannah: 'We are British, yes, but subjects, no'. Returning to this theme in his Emancipation Day message, Mayor Cipriani urged Trinidadians to 'strive earnestly to achieve the goal of Self-Determination. Refuse to have yourselves dubbed as British subjects, a modified term for British slaves! Consider yourself British Colonial Citizens – Members of the great Commonwealth of Nations!'[104]

Cipriani was not alone in seeing the 1933–34 celebrations as a vehicle for black self-advancement. In Jamaica, Marcus Garvey's Universal Negro Improvement Association (UNIA) staged an ambitious programme of events to coincide with Emancipation Day (1934) that included an open-air 'service' in Edelweiss Park, a grand parade through the streets of Kingston, and a grand ball. Seizing his opportunity, Garvey also organised the 7th International Convention of the Negroes of the World around these celebrations, thereby giving the UNIA and its radical, 'separatist' programme maximum publicity (a fact not lost on colonial authorities that monitored Garvey's movements with growing concern).[105] Also revealing is the Jamaica *Daily Gleaner's* report of a meeting of the 'Quill and Ink Club' at Port Maria, whose members, mainly black and coloured professionals, celebrated the centenary of Wilberforce's death in July 1933 with a series of exercises charting 'the wonderful progress' the 'race' had made since 1834 and identifying the challenges that still lay ahead. A recurring theme here was the need to go on working for 'full emancipation'. As one of the speakers, Amy Bailey, put it: 'No country had ever progressed as it should and reached its full national vigour until it had had emancipation within itself'. What Bailey had in mind, clearly, was a programme of cultural rejuvenation. 'The young had no definite outlook', she went on, insisting that, 'right or wrong', they should put their country first and take pride in its 'local produce, scenery, proverbs and "anancy" stories and digging match songs'. Perhaps just as important, Bailey and her friends placed these concerns within a wider international context. As the *Daily Gleaner's* report makes clear, the members of the 'Quill and Ink Club' were in close contact with Dr Harold Moody's League of Coloured Peoples, based in London, and like Garvey's followers, therefore, were part of complex transatlantic networks that, in different ways, stressed the idea of black self-determination.[106]

For the most part, the celebrations in 1933–34 passed off peacefully. Four years later, however, the mood and the expectations were very different. Between 1935 and 1938 the Caribbean region was engulfed by a series of riots, fires, and strikes that reflected growing frustration among black workers, many of whom were landless and facing increasing social and economic dislocation brought on by worldwide recession and falling sugar prices.[107] The trouble seems have started in 1935 when coal workers went on strike in St Lucia. There were similar disturbances in 1937, not only in St Lucia but also in Antigua (a dock strike) and British Guiana (a strike of seamen and postal workers). That same year trouble erupted in the Trinidad oilfields and Barbados was convulsed by riots following the deportation of the black labour leader, Clement Payne.[108] Jamaica seems to have been in an almost continuous state of unrest. In May 1938 there were serious labour disturbances at Tate and Lyle's Frome Estate in Westmoreland, during which 3,000 workers demolished the company's office and attacked staff and police with 'stones, sticks and iron bars'. This was followed by disturbances in Kingston, which soon escalated into a general strike involving wharf workers and conservancy men in the Corporation area. Perhaps more worrying still, the unrest quickly spread into the outlying parishes, where roads were barricaded, telegraph lines cut, and mobile police patrols had to be deployed to deal with 'disorderly crowds'. By early June the governor, Sir Edward Denham, was seriously considering the use of tear gas to disperse 'unlawful assemblies', and in several incidents police opened fire on rioters. Owen Wright, the Inspector General, reported to the Colonial Secretary on 23 June that eight civilians had been killed in disturbances in Jamaica, a further 25 wounded, and 139 injured.[109]

For obvious reasons, this chain of events cast a shadow over the 1938 centenary celebrations – an anniversary that many whites now looked forward to with mounting apprehension. Here again, Jamaica proved a flashpoint. As Emancipation Day approached, rumours surfaced that blacks intended to rise up again on 1 August, seemingly under the impression that in 1838 the British had entered into an agreement whereby 'all lands were granted to the Proprietors by the Crown for 100 years, as a kind of compensation'; and that after that they were to 'fall to the Slaves, or their descendants, or in fact, the People, who can select what they like'.[110] Of course, the government denied any such claims, and yet the rumours still persisted. Fearful of another uprising (it was said that owners who did not hand over their land on 1 August would be 'massacred'), the colonial authorities mobilised over 2,000 special constables, many of them armed, in addition to the regular police force. The Acting Governor even took the precaution of requesting the presence of a cruiser in Jamaica on or around Emancipation Day. So serious was the situation (or so it was thought) that questions were raised in the House of Lords, and at one point Chamberlain's government considered issuing a Royal Message to coincide with the anniversary, by way of thanking the colonies for their loyalty and 'averting anything likely to mar what ought to be such a joyful occasion'. The proposal was eventually rejected, but it speaks volumes about imperial priorities, as well as the nervousness of the planter elite, many of whom seem to have anticipated the 1938 anniversary in much the same way that their ancestors had anticipated Emancipation one hundred years before.[111]

If an insurrection was imminent in 1938, then the threat quickly evaporated. As far as one can judge, Emancipation Day in Jamaica was celebrated in the usual manner, although there is little doubt that white alarmist fears and a heavy police presence curbed the enthusiasm of many Jamaicans. At James Philippo's former church in Spanish Town, 1 August was marked by a special thanksgiving service, followed (on 2 August) by a 'young people's demonstration', a tradition that, as we have seen, went back to the mid-nineteenth century. 'In the realm of sports the day was no different to any popular holiday', observed the *Daily Gleaner*. 'Race meetings – horse and cycle – were well patronised; garden parties and fairs, principally in country districts, attracted fair attendances and cricket was played'. Meanwhile, in Kingston the Native Industries Protection Committee organised a 'monster Emancipation Centenary Celebration', which, significantly, began at 6 a.m. with the laying of wreaths on Queen Victoria's statute in the capital's South Parade, and was followed later in the morning by a 'patriotic meeting' which adopted a 'resolution of loyalty and allegiance to the throne'. Such gestures seem to have had the desired effect. According to the *Daily Gleaner* – hardly an unbiased source – 'no excess enthusiasm, no great show of either thanksgiving or pride or achievement, and none of the rumoured disorder [had] marked the day'.[112]

Similar reports came from other parts of the Caribbean. Some islands (Trinidad is a case in point) clearly decided not to recognise the anniversary at all, particularly if they had staged ceremonials in 1933 and 1934. On the other hand, blacks in Barbados observed the centenary of Emancipation by holding a mass meeting at the 'Lemon Grove' in Bridgetown, which was addressed by J. A. Martineau and Grantley Adams, both of whom were active in the local labour movement. Here, at least, blacks continued to invest Emancipation Day with its own special meaning. Seemingly undaunted by the rioting of the previous year, the meeting called upon the governor to release some of those imprisoned in November 1937 for sedition, while another of the speakers chose as his theme 'Negro leaders in Barbados during the last 100 years'.[113] Nevertheless, there is no disputing the fact that the celebrations in 1938 were generally muted, certainly when compared to those in 1933 and 1934, and for this the government must share some of the responsibility. Shaken by the events of 1935–38, colonial authorities used Emancipation Day celebrations to reassert British authority, demanding of blacks not only their loyalty but also their respect and gratitude. As the local white Administrator told a meeting of blacks in St Lucia, 'they were now enjoying the same measure of freedom as anyone else in the Empire to do and say what they pleased, within the provisions of the law'. In return, what was expected of them – and these words might have been spoken in 1888 or, indeed, 1838 – was to be 'thrifty' and to 'work harder'.[114]

Celebrating freedom in the Caribbean was never straightforward. As we have seen, white clergymen and colonial officials tended to view these celebrations as essentially didactic, imperialistic rituals that were designed to celebrate Britain's tradition of humanitarian interventionism. Blacks, in turn, were invited to share in these rituals – to engage, if you will, in a 'cult of gratitude'.[115] Up to a point they did. Indeed, what is noteworthy about celebrations in the Caribbean is that very few blacks openly rejected white insistence on privileging figures like Wilberforce over what might be described as black 'loss'. Instead, they folded into these (white) rituals their own priorities, focusing on black achievements since Emancipation, or the need for greater unity and cooperation. In each case, the result was something different, the forging of a black tradition that over time played an important role in shaping an emerging black consciousness – even if white scrutiny and white imperial control imposed obvious constraints on black assertiveness, at least in the period up to 1938. Insofar as there was an alternative to all this, then it was to ignore or 'forget' Emancipation; and throughout this period (1838–1938) there were voices on both sides of the racial divide who chose to do just that, either because they were originally opposed to Emancipation (as in the case of the planter elite), or because they felt that celebrating 1 August was divisive in some way.[116] In this sense, Emancipation was always a contested space, not least because it pressed heavily on questions of remembering and forgetting, just as it pressed heavily on notions of guilt and shame.

In the years following independence, it was these same considerations that led some territories to abandon Emancipation Day celebrations, hoping thereby to break their ties with the slave past. In Jamaica, for instance, the festival was abandoned in 1962, 'when it was replaced by Independence Day, which was observed on the first Monday of August'.[117] Yet, as hopes of a 'bold new era' receded, many began to call for the restoration of Emancipation Day, on the grounds that 1 August marked not only an important turning-point in the history of the region but was also an important source of pride and self-esteem.[118] Interest in Emancipation Day was also revived by the 150th anniversary of Emancipation in 1984. Despite fears in some quarters that 'overemphasising abolition' at this time might produce only 'negative results', celebrations were planned throughout the Caribbean.[119] In Trinidad, a special committee organised a twelve-day programme of events that started on 26 July in Point Fortin, before moving on to Port of Spain, where 1 August was marked by a civil ceremony at City Hall, followed by a thanksgiving service at Trinity Cathedral and a 'flambeau procession' from Woodward Square to the bottom of Charlotte Street.[120] Meanwhile, in Jamaica there were thanksgiving services in Spanish Town and at James Phillippo's church in Sligoville; and in Barbados Emancipation Day was commemorated by an ecumenical midnight service at the Moravian Church in Roebuck Street. Not to be outdone, on 30 July the citizens of St Kitts and Nevis launched a weeklong programme of activities, which took as its theme 'Proud, dignified and black, none can take my freedom back'.[121]

If the shape of these celebrations was familiar, however, their content often revealed a tougher, independent stance. For one thing, there was a much greater readiness to challenge 'white' interpretations of the past, stimulated, in part, by the revisionist works of Eric Williams and C. L. R. James. So, for instance, Forbes Burnham, Prime Minister of modern day Guyana, told his 1 August audience that Britain did not abolish slavery in 1834 for humanitarian reasons but because the system had become 'unprofitable, risky and expensive'.[122] Similarly, there was a much greater determination to stress black perspectives on slavery and emancipation. Particularly striking in this regard are some of the postage stamps issued to coincide with the 1984 anniversary. Anguilla, for instance, marked 1 August by issuing a set of eight stamps commemorating the 'heroes' of abolition, among them Olaudah Equiano and Henri Christophe. Trinidad and Tobago took the more radical step of commemorating black loss through two stamps depicting the Middle Passage (in this case, represented

20   Stamps commemorating the 150th anniversary of emancipation
in Trinidad and Tobago, 1984.

by a slave ship and broken slave manacles) and the 'triangular trade'. Perhaps just as significant, the other two stamps in the series commemorated Eric Williams' *Capitalism and Slavery*, originally published in 1944, and the black 'liberator', Toussaint L'Ouverture. St Vincent, meanwhile, juxtaposed a portrait of William Wilberforce with three plantation scenes, the last of which shows a white planter idly watching two slaves cutting sugar canes.[123] In other words, while the celebrations in 1984 reinforced 'an emphasis on abolition that harked back to an earlier [nineteenth-century] historiography', they also commemorated 'a revised pantheon of heroes' and, just as important, 'a revised interpretation of motives'.[124]

If anything, the enthusiasm for Emancipation Day celebrations increased during the 1990s, most notably in Jamaica where the anniversary was finally restored in 1997 following a six-year campaign led by, among others, Rex Nettleford, Professor of Continuing Studies at the University of the West Indies.[125] But, more recently, the viability of Emancipation Day has been challenged by the United Nations Educational, Scientific and Cultural Organisation (UNESCO), which in 1998 inaugurated an International Day for the Remembrance of the Slave Trade and its Abolition. Significantly, the date chosen, 23 August, commemorates the slave uprising that took place in Saint Domingue in 1791, an event that in the words of Koichiro Matsuura, Director-General of UNESCO, 'shook the foundations of slavery to the core and marked the start of the process that led to the abolition of the slave trade'.[126] That is to say, 23 August celebrates black 'agency' and black self-determination, rather than what might be described as a culture of (white) abolitionism. As we have seen, the internationalisation of 23 August is still far from complete (it has yet to be recognised in Britain, for instance), but in the Caribbean there are already signs that it has replaced Emancipation Day, or, rather, that the two anniversaries have been merged into each other, in order to create a 'Season of Emancipation'. In 2005, for instance, the government of Barbados organised a series of events to mark its 'Season of Emancipation', including a multi-media musical and dramatic presentation, 'Memories of the Forgotten Children', and the unveiling of the Monument of Freedom at Rock Hall, St Thomas, the island's 'first free village'.[127]

For obvious reasons, it is still too early to predict what the fate of Emancipation Day in the Caribbean will be. But, as we approach the bicentenary of the abolition of the slave trade, there are indications on both sides of the Atlantic that the old orthodoxies are being replaced by new perspectives that in a Caribbean context, at least, are inextricably linked to questions of black identity and psychological well being. The relatively recent elevation of figures like Olaudah Equiano and Toussaint L'Ouverture in many ways hints at what is at stake here, namely black empowerment (it is significant, for instance, that the celebrations in 1984 made little or no reference to Wilberforce or to his 'coadjutors').[128] To this extent, what we are witnessing in the Caribbean echoes events in contemporary Britain. In each case, the challenge, as many see it, is to create a narrative (a specific 'history') that not only makes sense of transatlantic slavery, and its attendant sense of loss, but also gives appropriate space and attention to black 'agency' and to black self-determination. The 'truth' or validity of such 'histories' is not at issue here. Rather, they should be understood as part of an ongoing process of re-writing and revising the past in order to meet the demands of the present.

Notes

1 See Drescher, *The Mighty Experiment*, esp. chapters 12 and 13.
2 Rex Nettleford, quoted in B. W. Higman, 'Remembering Slavery: The Rise, Decline and Revival of Emancipation Day in the English-speaking Caribbean', *Slavery and Abolition*, 19 (1998), p. 97.
3 Ibid., p. 90.
4 Drescher, *The Mighty Experiment*, p. 199.
5 Oldfield, *Popular Politics and British Anti-Slavery*, pp. 51–4.
6 See, for instance, Historical Society of Pennsylvania, Philadelphia, Pennsylvania Abolition Society Papers, microfilm edition, Reel 11, James Pemberton to Granville Sharp, 6 May 1794.
7 New-York Historical Society, New York, New York Manumission Society Papers, General/Quarterly Committee Minutes, 1785–97, entries for 9 November 1786, 28 August, 24 September, 20 November 1788.
8 For transatlantic cooperation between British and American abolitionists, see Betty Fladeland, *Men and Brothers: Anglo-American Antislavery Cooperation* (Chicago and London, 1972); Clare Taylor, ed., *British and American Abolitionists: An Episode in Transatlantic Understanding* (Edinburgh, 1974).
9 Mayer, *All on Fire*, pp. 151–65.
10 Ibid, pp. 285–95, 372; *Liberator*, 20 August 1841.
11 Mayer, *All on Fire*, pp. 151–2.
12 For Garrison and Garrisonians, see Mayer, *All on Fire*; Newman, *The Transformation of American Abolition: Fighting Slavery in the Early Republic*; James Brewer Stewart, *Holy Warriors: The Abolitionists and American Slavery* (revised edn, New York, 1996); Ronald G. Walters, *The Antislavery Appeal: American Abolitionism after 1830* (Baltimore, 1976).
13 *Liberator*, 5 August 1841, 10 August 1855.
14 *Liberator*, 20 August 1841.
15 *Liberator*, 5, 12, 19 August 1841, 4 August 1854, 1 August 1856.
16 *Liberator*, 9 August 1844.
17 *Liberator*, 9 August 1844, 8 August 1845. For styles of clothing, see Connerton, *How Societies Remember*, pp. 10–11.
18 As Mitch Kachun notes, parades and orations were the 'two central public components of July Fourth celebrations' in the United States. See Mitch Kachun, *Festivals of Freedom: Memory and Meaning in African American Emancipation Celebrations, 1808–1915* (Amherst and Boston, 2003), pp. 22–3.
19 *Liberator*, 8 August 1845, 13 August 1847, 17 August 1849, 10 August 1855.
20 *Liberator*, 10 August 1849, 9 August 1850, 6 August 1858; John W. Blassingame, ed., *The Frederick Douglass Papers, series 1: Speeches, debates, and interviews, vol. 2: 1847–54* (New Haven, c. 1982), p. 69; John W. Blassingame, ed., *The Frederick Douglass Papers, series 1: Speeches, Debates, and Interviews, vol. 3: 1855–63* (New Haven, c. 1985), pp. 214–15.
21 *Liberator*, 9 August 1844, 1 August 1845, 1 August 1856.

22 Connerton, *How Societies Remember*, pp. 12–13, 44–5, 70–1; Hobsbawn and Ranger, eds., *The Invention of Tradition*, pp. 1–2.
23 *Liberator*, 31 July 1846, 10 August 1855.
24 *Liberator*, 17 August 1849.
25 *Liberator*, 31 July 1846, 9 August 1850.
26 Howard University, Washington, DC, Clarkson Papers, Henry C. Wright to Catherine Clarkson, 25 October 1845.
27 Ripley, ed., *The Black Abolitionist Papers*, *vol. I*, p. 57 n. 2; William Pease and Jane Pease, *Black Utopia: Negro Communal Experiments in America* (Madison, WI, 1963), pp. 46–62. For Wilberforce College, see www.petersons.com/blackcolleges/profiles/wilberforce.asp?sponsor=2904 accessed 8 June 2005.
28 Stewart, *Holy Warriors*, pp. 45–9, 64–73.
29 *Liberator*, 17 August 1849.
30 *Liberator*, 9 August 1850.
31 Kolchin, *American Slavery*, pp. 80–5, 241. For free black communities in the North, see Gary B. Nash, 'Forging Freedom: The Emancipation Experience in Northern Seaport cities, 1775–1820', in Ira Berlin and Ronald Hoffman, eds., *Slavery and Freedom in the Age of the American Revolution* (Charlottesville, VA, 1983), pp. 3–48; Litwack, *North of Slavery*. For free blacks in the South, see Ira Berlin, *Slaves Without Masters: The Free Negro in the Antebellum South* (New York, 1974); Marina Wikramanayake, *A World in Shadows: The Free Black in Antebellum South Carolina* (Columbia, SC, 1973).
32 Thomas Hershberg, 'Free Blacks in Antebellum Philadelphia: A Study of Ex-Slaves, Freeborn, and Socioeconomic Decline', *Journal of Social History*, 5 (1971), p. 183. By contrast, the free black population of Charleston, South Carolina, in 1860 was just over 3,000, and that of Richmond, Virginia, around 2000. See Michael Johnson and James L. Roark, *Black Masters: A Free Family of Color in the Old South* (New York and London, 1984), pp. 206–7; Midori Takagi, *'Rearing Wolves to Our Own Destruction': Slavery in Richmond, Virginia, 1782–1865* (Charlottesville, VA, 1999), pp. 17.
33 See Shane White, *Stories of Freedom in Black New York* (Cambridge, MA, 2002), esp. pp. 7–67; Patrick Rael, *Black Identity and Black Protest in the Antebellum North* (Chapel Hill, NC, 2002).
34 Rael, *Black Identity and Black Protest*, p. 57. See also Kachun, *Festivals of Freedom*, pp. 17–19.
35 Kachun, *Festivals of Freedom*, pp. 25–8, 42–53; Gary Nash, *Forging Freedom: The Formation of Philadelphia's Black Community, 1720–1840* (Cambridge, MA, 1988), pp. 189–90; Benjamin Quarles, *Black Abolitionists* (New York, 1969), pp. 118–21.
36 Quoted in Quarles, *Black Abolitionists*, p. 124.
37 *Liberator*, 19 August 1842.
38 *Liberator*, 9 August 1844.
39 *Liberator*, 26 July (Boston), 16 August (Providence) 1844. For a detailed overview, see Kachun, *Festivals of Freedom*, pp. 54–96.
40 Quoted in Rael, *Black Identity and Black Protest*, p. 64.
41 *Liberator*, 9 August 1844.
42 Quarles, *Black Abolitionists*, p. 125.
43 *Liberator*, 16 August 1844, 13 August 1847; Kachun, *Festivals of Freedom*, pp. 73–5.
44 Rael, *Black Identity and Black Protest*, pp. 56, 81; *Liberator*, 9 August 1844.
45 For 'black Anglophilia', see Elisa Tamarkin, 'Black Anglophilia: or, The Sociability of Antislavery', *American Literary History*, 14 (2002), pp. 444–78.
46 Ripley ed., *The Black Abolitionist Papers*, pp. 571–3.
47 Quoted in J. R. Oldfield, *Alexander Crummell (1819–1898) and the Creation of an African-American Church in Liberia* (Lewiston, NY, 1990), pp. 28, 37.

48 Quoted in Waldo Martin, *The Mind of Frederick Douglass* (Chapel Hill, NC, 1984), p. 114.

49 Oldfield, *Alexander Crummell*, p. 25.

50 Frederick Douglass, *Autobiographies: Narrative of the Life of Frederick Douglass, an American Slave, My Bondage and My Freedom, Life and Times of Frederick Douglass* (Library of America edition, New York, 1994), pp. 688–9.

51 Ripley ed., *The Black Abolitionist Papers*, p. 39.

52 Douglass, *Autobiographies*, p. 686.

53 Blassingame, ed., *The Frederick Douglass Papers, series 1: Speeches, debates, and interviews, vol. 3: 1855–63*, pp. 194, 199.

54 Ibid., p. 216.

55 Ibid., p. 189.

56 Ibid., pp. 196–7, 219.

57 Ibid., pp. 190–1.

58 Ibid., p. 371 (1 August 1860); Douglass, *Autobiographies*, p. 929.

59 Douglass, *Autobiographies*, pp. 129–30 (James McCune Smith's introduction to *My Bondage and My Freedom*).

60 Blassingame, ed., *The Frederick Douglass Papers*, vol. 3, p. 201n.

61 Douglass, *Autobiographies*, pp. 926, 930.

62 Bernard Powers notes that in Charleston, South Carolina, during the 1870s and 1880s local blacks celebrated Crispus Attuck's death (5 March 1770), Liberian Independence Day (26 July 1847), 4 July, the passage of the Emancipation Proclamation, and the anniversary of the Fifteenth Amendment. See Bernard Powers, *Black Charlestonians: A Social History, 1822–1885* (Fayetteville, AR, 1994), p. 165. For whatever reason, the anniversary of the ratification of the Thirteenth Amendment (18 December 1865), which formally abolished slavery in the United States, does not seem to have been observed by African Americans. For the 'expansion and fragmentation' of African-American celebrations after 1862, see Kachun, *Festivals of Freedom*, pp. 97–146.

63 Studholme Hodgson, *Truths from the West Indies* (London, 1838), pp. 30–4, 250–6. See also National Archives, London, CO318/116 and CO324/88; James A. Thome and J. Horace Kimball, *Emancipation in the West Indies: A Six Months' Tour in Antigua, Barbados and Jamaica in the Year 1837* (New York, 1838), p. 36.

64 Hilary McD. Beckles, *Great House Rules: Landless Freedom and Black Protest in Barbados, 1834–1937* (London, 2003), pp. 33–4, 38–9; Bridget Brereton, 'A Social History of Emancipation Day in the British Caribbean: The First Fifty Years', in Patrick Bryan, ed., *August 1st: A Celebration of Emancipation* (Mona, Jamaica, 1995), p. 29; Hodgson, *Truths from the West Indies*, pp. 266–311.

65 *Parliamentary Papers*, vol. 35 (1839), p. 212.

66 Thome and Kimball, *Emancipation in the West Indies*, pp. 36–7.

67 Gilbert H. Barnes and Dwight L. Dumond, eds., *Letters of Theodore Dwight Weld, Angelina Grimke Weld and Sarah Grimke, 1822–1844* (New York, 1970), p. 70 (Charles Stuart to Theodore Weld, 11 December 1838). In the same letter Stuart recorded the gratitude of the freedmen, viz: 'Massa freedom too much sweet', 'Bless de ladies in England', 'Bless Queen Victoria, who gave me free'.

68 See, for instance, 'Slaves Receiving News of Emancipation, British West Indies, ca. 1834', http://hitchcock.itc.virginia.edu/Slavery/details.php?filename=cass2 accessed 8 June 2005 (taken from *Cassells' Illustrated History of England*, London, 1863).

69 See Hodgson, *Truths from the West Indies*, pp. 129–32.

70 Catherine Hall, *Civilising Subjects: Metropole and Colony in the English Imagination, 1830–1867* (London, 2000), esp. pp. 84–208. All of the missionary churches in the Caribbean gained numbers up to 1845, but thereafter suffered a serious decline. One observer

noted in 1850 that the missionaries 'no longer [had] the same hold on the Negro population'. See David King, *The State and Prospects of Jamaica* (London, 1850), p. 100 and Hall, *Civilising Subjects*, pp. 229–43, 264.

71 James Phillippo, *Jamaica: Its Past and Present State* (London, 1843), pp. 175–85. For similar celebrations at Falmouth and Montego Bay, see Hall, *Civilising Subjects*, pp. 117–18; William Fitz-er Burchell, *Memoir of Thomas Burchell, 22 Years a Missionary in Jamaica* (London, 1849), pp. 342–3.

72 Hall, *Civilising Subjects*, pp.120–39.

73 Phillippo, *Jamaica: Its Past and Present*, pp. 179–83.

74 National Maritime Museum, London, Michael Graham-Stewart Collection, ZBA2501, *Celebration of the 1st August 1838 at Dawkins Caymanas, near Spanish Town, Jamaica* (1838).

75 In retrospect, it is clear that the 1840s were the peak of missionary activity in the Caribbean, but in the case of Jamaica it also worth noting that Sir Lionel Smith left the Caribbean in October 1839. His successor, Sir Charles Metcalfe, appears to have been much more hostile towards the freedmen and their missionary friends, which may explain why the public parades in Spanish Town came to an abrupt end after 1839. See Hall, *Civilising Subjects*, pp. 201–2.

76 Hall, *Civilising Subjects*, pp. 124–5.

77 Edward Bean Underhill, *Life of James Mursell Phillippo, Missionary in Jamaica* (London, 1881), p. 270.

78 Connerton, *How Societies Remember*, p. 45.

79 Underhill, *Life of James Mursell Phillippo*, p. 375. Brereton, on the other hand, argues that 'by the end of the 1840s, certainly in Jamaica and in Trinidad, special services ceased to be held on August 1, and the churches lost interest in using the anniversary for didactic purposes'. See Brereton, 'A Social History of Emancipation Day in the British Caribbean', p. 34

80 B. W. Higman, 'Slavery Remembered: The Celebration of Emancipation in Jamaica', *Journal of Caribbean History*, 12 (1979), esp. pp. 56–62; Edwina Ashie-Nikoi, 'Cohobblopot: Africanisms in Barbadian Culture through the Lens of Crop-Over', *Journal of Caribbean History*, 32 (1998), pp. 82–120.

81 Higman, 'Slavery Remembered', pp. 70–2; Claude McKay, *Banana Bottom* [1933] (London, 1986), pp. 48–86; Maureen Rowe, 'Bruckins Party: A Celebration of "Full Free"', in Bryan, ed., *August 1st: A Celebration of Emancipation*, pp. 67–72. For 'John Canoe' or 'John Connu', see Martha Warren Beckwith, *Black Roadways: A Study of Jamaican Folk Life* (Chapel Hill, 1929), pp. 150–51.

82 Bridget Brereton, 'The Birthday of Our Race: A Social History of Emancipation Day in Trinidad, 1838–1888', in B. W. Higman, ed., *Trade, Government and Society in Caribbean History, 1700–1920* (Kingston, Jamaica, 1983), pp. 70–73; Higman, 'Remembering Slavery', pp. 91–2; Stipriaan, 'July 1, Emancipation Day in Suriname: A Contested *Lieu de Memoire*, 1863–2003', p. 269.

83 Higman, 'Slavery Remembered', pp. 60–61; Brereton, 'The Birthday of Our Race', pp. 74–5.

84 *Barbados Globe*, 6 August 1888. Experiences did vary, however. To judge from local newspapers, there were no public celebrations in Barbados, for instance, and while the jubilee was declared a public holiday in British Guiana, Grenada, and Tobago, it was not recognised as such in Barbados, Trinidad, Dominica or St Vincent. See Higman, 'Remembering Slavery', p. 92.

85 Brereton, 'The Birthday of Our Race', p. 74; *Barbados Globe*, 30 July 1888.

86 *Port-of-Spain Gazette*, 27 June 1888.

87 Ibid. See also Brereton, 'The Birthday of Our Race', pp. 77–80.

88 (Trinidad) *New Era*, 29 June and 20 July 1888; *Port-of-Spain Gazette*, 27, 30 June 1888.

89 *Port of Spain Gazette*, 18, 21 July 1888; *Barbados Herald*, 2 August 1888; (Trinidad) *New Era*, 27 July 1888.

90 *Port of Spain Gazette*, 1, 4 August 1888; (Trinidad) *New Era*, 3 August 1888.

91 *Port of Spain Gazette*, 1 August 1888.

92 For comments on the respective merits of 1833–34 and 1838, see (Jamaica) *Daily Gleaner*, 30, 31 July, 2 August 1934.

93 *Barbados Advocate*, 31 July, 1 August 1933.

94 *Trinidad Guardian*, 29, 30 July, 6 August 1933. The celebrations in Trinidad clearly had a wider regional appeal. Local newspapers reported that many 'Barbados people' were expected to visit Port of Spain during the Wilberforce Centenary, and that a special excursion had been arranged, leaving Bridgetown on 23 July and travelling by way of St Vincent and Grenada, 'thus giving an opportunity to people of these two other islands of witnessing the celebrations'. See *Trinidad Guardian*, 11 July 1933.

95 Ibid., 9 August 1933; *Barbados Advocate*, 9 August 1933.

96 (Jamaica) *Daily Gleaner*, 29 July 1933.

97 *Trinidad Guardian*, 31 July, 1, 3, 4, 5 August 1934.

98 Ibid., 4, 5 August 1934; (Jamaica) *Daily Gleaner*, 4 August 1934.

99 Speaking during the 1934 celebrations, the Acting Governor of Trinidad urged a large group of schoolchildren to 'realise your responsibilities when you grow up and play your part as men and women worthy of your citizenship in this glorious British Empire'. See *Trinidad Guardian*, 31 July 1934. For Wilberforce, see *Barbados Advocate*, 1 August 1933, *Trinidad Guardian*, 29 July 1933.

100 For loyalty addresses, see *Trinidad Guardian*, 31 July, 5 August 1934; (Jamaica) *Daily Gleaner*, 4 August 1934.

101 Eric Williams, *History of the People of Trinidad and Tobago* (London, 1964), pp. 216–24. See also Beckles, *Great House Rules*, esp. pp. 1–30;

102 *Trinidad Guardian*, 31 July, 1, 3, 5 August 1934.

103 Ibid. Cipriani went so far as to describe the historical pageant as the 'most important feature of the Centenary'.

104 *Trinidad Guardian*, 31 July, 1 August 1934.

105 (Jamaica) *Daily Gleaner*, 28 July 1934. Characteristically, Garvey composed or 'arranged' a number of poems, hymns, and anthems especially for the occasion.

106 (Jamaica) *Daily Gleaner*, 31 July 1933. See also Patricia Stafford, 'Refining "Bajan" Identity, 1930–1980', *Journal of Caribbean History*, 39 (2005), pp. 102–22.

107 Williams, *History of the People of Trinidad and Tobago*, pp. 226–36; W. M. Macmillan, *Warning from the West Indies* (London, 1938), pp. 5–15; Cary Fraser, 'The Twilight of Colonial Rule in the British West Indies: Nationalist Assertion vs. Imperial Hubris in the 1930s', *Journal of Caribbean History*, 30 (1996), pp. 1–27.

108 Macmillan, *Warning from the West Indies*, pp. 8–10; National Archives, London, CO321/362/8 and CO321/367/8 (St Lucia); National Archives, London, CO295/599/13 (Trinidad).

109 National Archives, London, CO137/826/9, Denham to W. Ormsby Gore, 2/3, 23, 28 May, 2, 4 June 1938; Owen F. Wright to Colonial Secretary, 23 June 1938.

110 Ibid., C. C. Woolley to Colonial Secretary, 23 July 1938; National Archives, London, CO137/827/1, extract of a letter from Messrs. Cargill, Cargill, and Dunn, solicitors, 13 June 1938; CO137/827/2, Arthur Davis to Sir John Simon, 15 July 1938; (Jamaica) *Daily Gleaner*, 27, 28, 30 July 1938.

111 National Archives, London, CO137/827/2, extract of a letter from J. H. Emmens, 23 June 1938; CO137/826/9, extract from a private and personal letter from C. C. Woolley to Sir Henry Moore, 3 August 1938; CO137/826/9, telegram, Officer administering

the Government of Jamaica to the Secretary of State for the Colonies, 14 June 1938 (cruiser); CO318/435/1, Secretary of State for the Colonies to William Macmillan, 21 July 1938 and telegram, Secretary of State for the Colonies to all West Indies Colonies, 23 July 1938; (Jamaica) *Daily Gleaner*, 30 July 1938.

112 (Jamaica) *Daily Gleaner*, 28 July, 2 August 1938.

113 *Barbados Advocate*, 6, 8 August 1938.

114 *West Indian Crusader*, 3 August 1938; *Voice of S. Lucia*, 3 August 1938.

115 Stipriaan, 'July 1, Emancipation Day in Suriname', p. 275.

116 See, for example, *Barbados Globe*, 30 July 1888; *Port of Spain Gazette*, 23 June 1888; (Jamaica) *Daily Gleaner*, 21 July 1934.

117 Higman, 'Remembering Slavery', p. 95.

118 Ibid., p. 97.

119 For opposition to Emancipation Day celebrations see (Jamaica) *Daily Gleaner*, 31 July 1984; *Trinidad Guardian*, 6 August 1984.

120 *Trinidad Guardian*, 31 July, 2, 3 August 1984. Building on these initiatives, in 1984 Trinidad also decided to make Emancipation Day a public holiday (that is, from 1985 onwards), thereby replacing 'Discovery Day'.

121 (Jamaica) *Daily Gleaner*, 21, 30, 31 July, 1, 2, 3 August 1984; *Barbados Advocate*, 29, 30 July 1984. In Jamaica, 'Emancipation Day' was made the theme of the island's Independence Day celebrations, and the *Daily Gleaner* marked the occasion with a special pull-out section entitled, 'Thanksgiving: 150th Anniversary of the Birth of Free Jamaica'. There were also special exhibitions in many of Jamaica's libraries.

122 *The Times*, 3 August 1984.

123 Author's own collection. Also highly significant is the fact that in Jamaica a local company produced sets of 'Abolition bookmarkers' to coincide with the 150th anniversary, featuring 'photographs and messages from the lives of our National Heroes'. 'Not by Wishbone but by Backbone people build themselves' was the slogan featured on the Marcus Garvey bookmark. See *Daily Gleaner*, 6 August 1984.

124 Higman, 'Remembering Slavery', p. 103.

125 Ibid., p. 97.

126 http://portal.unesco.org/culture/en/ev.php-URL_ID=5420 (22 August 2005); www.lifebridge. org/undays/august23.htm (22 August 2005).

127 www.barbados.gov.bb/ViewNews.asp?ID=2851&Dat=8/16/2005 (22 August 2005).

128 Speaking to this theme, Lancelot Layne, who was a key figure in the 150th anniversary celebrations in Trinidad, emphasised in a press release that 'though parliamentary lobbying in Britain helped to rouse the conscience in British citizenry, the catalyst to the said freedom was the will of our bondaged people to change their condition in these our native lands'. See *Trinidad Guardian*, 1 August 1984. In a similar vein, Mike Henry, Chairman of the Abolition 150 Committee in Jamaica, told readers of the *Daily Gleaner* that 'slavery was destroyed throughout the British Empire in 1834 as the direct result of the collective action of the Jamaican slaves led by Samuel Sharpe'. See (Jamaica) *Daily Gleaner*, 21 July 1984.

Conclusion

As Iwona Irwin-Zarecka has argued, 'if the terrain of collective memory is vast and varied, it is also structured'. That is to say, it involves a process of selection – of remembering and forgetting.[1] Agency is also important here. In the case of transatlantic slavery, it is hardly insignificant that the memory-work was led, for the most part, by those who had most at stake in preserving Britain's humanitarian tradition, namely abolitionists themselves. Of course, there were aberrations, the failure to commemorate the 1907 anniversary of the abolition of the slave trade being an obvious case in point. But the controversy surrounding Haydon's *The Anti-Slavery Convention, 1840*, and its removal from Ipswich to London, points to a more deliberate attempt to preserve an abolitionist view of the past, as do many of the sites of memory discussed in Chapter 3. As we have seen, abolitionists also took an important lead in 1933–34, in this case evoking a common tradition of humanity in order to rouse the British to fresh endeavours, this time against the international slave trade. Organised on a nationwide scale, and involving thousands of people, the 1933–34 celebrations did as much as anything to shape what I have described here as a 'culture of abolitionism' and to ensure that transatlantic slavery was seen – by the majority of whites, at least – through the moral victory of Emancipation.

Yet, in saying this, it is also clear that the chief reason this particular version of the past proved so strong and so pervasive was that it served the state's interests, at least until the Second World War. Consistent with their imperialistic interests and ambitions, Britons attached special significance to their 'altruistic presence' in Africa, India, and the English-speaking Caribbean. In practice, this meant absolving themselves of responsibility for transatlantic slavery and, instead, highlighting the role the British had played in bringing slavery to an end. Perhaps just as important, it also meant placing those who *were* held responsible, Africans and Europeans, beyond the pale of 'civilisation'.[2] As has been well documented, such assumptions were at the heart of the 'New Imperialism' that emerged in the late nineteenth century, and they continued to influence the actions of the British state down to the 1930s and beyond. For this reason, abolitionists found a willing audience, particularly during periods of crisis and self-doubt, when Emancipation was eagerly seized upon by the British public as evidence of the nation's true mission in a rapidly changing world.

For those at the margins of empire, Britain's tradition of humanity was also an important organising principle. As we have seen, British colonial officials attached great importance to Britain's humanitarian record and the example set by figures like Wilberforce. And, for the most part, blacks in the British West Indies were willing to share in this 'cult of gratitude'. Even radicals like Cipriani embraced many imperialistic perspectives, combining a genuine regard for Wilberforce and the values he represented with their own nationalist ambitions for the Caribbean region (later generations, of course, were to take a rather different view of the matter, but even for them Britain represented an ambiguous legacy, embracing realms of remembering as well as forgetting). The United States presents a very different case study. But here again, Britain's moral example proved an inspiration and a guiding principle for black and white abolitionists alike. African-Americans, in particular, employed 1834/1838 as a platform for community activism and new, more radical forms of black protest. Just as important, for many blacks, notably Frederick Douglass, West India Emancipation was to prove an enduring source of pride and self-esteem.

Put another way, Britain's humanitarian record was one of the 'common denominators' that bound the nation and the empire together.[3] Following the Second World War and the onset of decolonisation, however, this imperial narrative became much more difficult to sustain, although Britain's tradition of humanity remained (and remains) an important part of the dominant white discourse. The real challenge, however, has come in the last twenty years. Since the 1980s there has been a concerted effort to re-think the parameters of transatlantic slavery and, as a result, to re-shape our frames of remembrance. Slave museums have been at the forefront of this shift or transformation, but, as we have seen, there is now broad agreement, both inside and outside Parliament, that the nation must face up to its responsibilities and 'do justice' to transatlantic slavery, even if many are still unsure what an appropriate response might be. As I have argued, this ongoing debate was stimulated in large part by questions about diversity and multiculturalism, and about who and what constitutes the British nation. It was also influenced by the increasing self-confidence and independence of black communities in the Caribbean and the United States, and by the process of globalization, meaning, in this instance, the initiatives taken by organisations like UNESCO, which continue to play an important part in shaping current debates about remembering transatlantic slavery.

Negotiating these different narratives (an imperial discourse, on the one hand, and multiculturalism, on the other) is not always easy. Indeed, in

multicultural societies in Britain and the United States it has become legitimate
to ask the question what, if any, are the 'common denominators' that bind
these nations together.[4] Thanks to the pioneering work of scholars and curators, most of us now recognise the need to acknowledge the true horror and
enormity of transatlantic slavery, and its role in building Britain's national
wealth – and, for the most part, the result has been a much more nuanced
view of the history and legacy of this 'foul iniquity'. Nevertheless, in highlighting the 'indignity' of transatlantic slavery it is important that we do not
lose sight of the specific, British roots of abolitionism and Britain's tradition
of humanitarian interventionism. This is not a simple matter of choice. Rather,
it is a matter to be pondered, as twenty-first century Britons struggle to come
to terms with their pasts and out of them create new memory projects that are
based on shared assumptions, even if they cannot always be based on shared
experiences.[5]

Notes

1   Irwin-Zarecka, *Frames of Remembrance*, p. 87.
2   See Castle, *Britannia's Children*, pp. 64–8.
3   Confino, 'Collective Memory and Cultural History', p. 1400.
4   Levinson, *Written in Stone*, pp. 37–8.
5   Ibid., pp. 130–9.

Bibliography

MANUSCRIPTS

Bodleian Library, Oxford
Wilberforce Papers

Boston Public Library
William Lloyd Garrison Papers

British Library
Clarkson Papers

Chapin Library, Williams College, Massachusetts
Amelia Opie Papers

Corporation of London Record Office
Court of Common Council Minutes

Historical Society of Pennsylvania, Philadelphia
Pennsylvania Abolition Society Papers (microfilm edition)

Howard University, Washington, DC
Clarkson Papers

Ipswich Museum
Museum Committee Minutes

Ipswich Record Office
George Ransome Scrapbooks
Town Council of Ipswich, Reports of Committees

Lionel Robbins Library, London School of Economics
League of Nations Union Papers (microfilm edition)

London Guildhall Library
Granger Scrapbooks

Merseyside Maritime Museum, Liverpool
Transatlantic Slavery Gallery: Summative Evaluation, 24 March 1995
Typescript, 'Comments on the Transatlantic Slavery Gallery, based on notes left on the Transatlantic Slavery Gallery comments board from 25 October 1994 to 25 January 1995'

National Archives, London
Colonial Office Records

National Maritime Museum, London
Michael Graham-Stewart Collection

National Portrait Gallery, London
Archives Correspondence
Minutes of Trustee Meetings
Secretary's Journals
The Anti-Slavery Convention, 1840, hanging history
The Anti-Slavery Convention, 1840, keys, lists, photos, studies

New-York Historical Society
New York Manumission Society Papers

Rhodes House Library, Oxford
British and Foreign Anti-Slavery Society Papers
Anti-Slavery and Aborigines' Protection Society Papers

Royal Institute of British Architects Library, London
John Oldrid Scott Papers

University College, London
Brougham Papers

Westminster Abbey Library and Muniments
Correspondence of the Sub-Deans of Westminster Abbey

Wilberforce House Museum, Hull
Wilberforce and Anti-Slavery Collection

Wisbech and Fenland Museum
Clarkson Papers
Day Book of Wisbech Museum and Literary Institution
Minute Book of Wisbech Museum and Literary Institution
Papers of the Thomas Clarkson 150th Anniversary Committee
Wisbech General Cemetery, Minutes of the Board of Management

Wordsworth Library, Grasmere
Wordsworth Papers

NEWSPAPERS AND PERIODICALS

Britain

Anti-Slavery Reporter
Anti-Slavery Reporter and Aborigines' Friend
Athenaeum
Bournemouth Daily Echo
British Magazine
Bury Post
Cambridge Weekly News
Carlisle Journal
Christian Observer

Daily Express
Daily Telegraph
East Anglian Daily Times
Eastern Morning News and Hull Advertiser
Eclectic Review
Edinburgh Review
Evening Star
Flashback
Gentleman's Magazine
Guardian
Harrogate Advertiser
Headway
Hertfordshire Mercury
Hull Advertiser
Hull and Lincolnshire Times
Hull Daily Mail
Hull Packet
Hull Rockingham
Hull Times
Illustrated London News
Isle of Ely & Wisbech Advertiser
Lancaster Guardian
League of Nations Union News
Manchester Guardian
Methodist Recorder
Morning Post
NMM Community News
Notes & Queries
Quarterly Review
Reading Mercury
Salisbury Times
Sheffield Daily Telegraph
Suffolk Chronicle
The Art Union
The Builder
The Friend
The Spectator
The Times
Wisbech Advertiser
Wisbech Standard
Wisbech Telegraph
York Herald
Yorkshire Gazette

Overseas

Barbados Advocate
Barbados Globe
Barbados Herald

Colonial Standard and Jamaica Despatch
(Jamaica) Daily Gleaner
Liberator
Port of Spain Gazette
The New Yorker
Trinidad Guardian
(Trinidad) New Era
Voice of St Lucia
West Indian Crusader

OFFICIAL PUBLICATIONS

Alumni Cantabrigiensis
Hansard
Hull Corporation Minutes
Parliamentary Papers
Proceedings of the General Anti-Slavery Convention called by the Committee of the British and Foreign Anti-Slavery Society and held in London, from Friday, June 12 to Tuesday, June 23, 1840 (London, 1841)
Victoria County History: City of York (London, 1961)

BOOKS AND PUBLICATIONS

Ahier, John, *Industry, Children and the Nation: An Analysis of National Identity in School Textbooks* (London, New York, and Philadelphia, 1988)
Allerston, Jack, *Statues, Busts and Ornamentation of Hull* (Hull, 1984)
Altick, Robert, *The Shows of London* (Cambridge, MA, 1978)
Anderson, Benedict, *Imagined Communities: Reflections on the Origin and Spread of Nationalism* (London, 1983)
Anon, *A Guide to Ipswich Museum* (Ipswich, 1871)
Anon, *A Sketch of the Life of Thomas Clarkson* (London and Wisbech, 1876)
Anon, *The Manor House, York: The Yorkshire School for the Blind* (Hull, 1883)
Ashie-Nikoi, Edwina, 'Cohobblopot: Africanisms in Barbadian Culture through the Lens of Crop-Over', *Journal of Caribbean History*, 32 (1998), pp. 82–120
Bailyn, Bernard, *To Begin the World Anew: The Genius and Ambiguities of the American Founders* (New York, 2003)
Barnes, Gilbert H. and Dumond, Dwight L., eds., *Letters of Theodore Dwight Weld, Angelina Grimke Weld and Sarah Grimke, 1822–1844* (New York, 1970)
Beckles, Hilary McD, *Great House Rules: Landless Freedom and Black Protest in Barbados, 1834–1937* (London, 2003)
Beckwith, Martha Warren, *Black Roadways: A Study of Jamaican Folk Life* (Chapel Hill, NC, 1929)
Beech, John, 'The Marketing of Slavery Heritage in the United Kingdom', *International Journal of Hospitality and Tourism Administration*, 2 (2001), pp. 85–105
Ben-Amos, Avner, *Funerals, Politics and Memory in Modern France, 1789–1996* (Oxford, 2000)

Berlin, Ira, *Generations of Captivity: A History of American Slaves* (Cambridge, MA, 2003)

Berlin, Ira, *Slaves Without Masters: The Free Negro in the Antebellum South* (New York, 1974)

Bernier, Celeste-Marie, exhibition review of 'Transatlantic Slavery: Against Human Dignity' and 'A Respectable Trade? Bristol and Transatlantic Slavery', *Journal of American History*, 88 (2001), pp. 1006–12

Best, G. F. A., 'The Evangelicals and the Established Church in the Early Nineteenth Century', *Journal of Theological Studies*, new series, 10 (1959), pp. 68–78

Bindman, David, *From Ape to Apollo: Aesthetics and the Idea of Race in the Eighteenth Century* (London, 2002)

Blackett, R. J. M., *Building an Anti-Slavery Wall: Black Americans in the Atlantic Abolitionist Movement, 1830–1860* (Ithaca, NY, 1983)

Blassingame, John W., *The Frederick Douglass Papers, series 1: Speeches, debates and interviews, vol. 2: 1847–54* (New Haven, CT, c. 1982)

Blassingame, John W., ed., *The Frederick Douglass Papers, series 1: Speeches, Debates and Interviews, vol. 3: 1855–63* (New Haven, CT, c. 1985)

Blight, David, *Beyond the Battlefield: Race, Memory and the American Civil War* (Boston, 2002)

Boime, Albert, *The Art of Exclusion: Representing Blacks in the Nineteenth Century* (London and Washington, DC, 1980)

Bradley, Simon and Pevsner, Nikolaus, *The Buildings of England: London 6: Westminster* (London, 2003)

Brereton, Bridget, 'A Social History of Emancipation Day in the British Caribbean: The First Fifty Years', in Patrick Bryan, ed., *August 1ˢᵗ; A Celebration of Emancipation* (Mona, Jamaica, 1995), pp. 27–44

Brereton, Bridget, 'The Birthday of Our Race: A Social History of Emancipation in Trinidad, 1838–1888', in B. W. Higman, ed., *Trade, Government and Society in Caribbean History, 1700–1920* (Kingston, Jamaica, 1983), pp. 69–83

Brown, David Blayney, '"Fire and Clay": Benjamin Robert Haydon – Historical Painter', in David Blayney Brown, Robert Woof and Stephen Hebron, *Benjamin Robert Haydon, 1786–1846: Painter and Writer, Friend of Wordsworth and Keats* (Grasmere, 1996), pp. 1–24.

Brown, Ford K., *Fathers of the Victorians: The Age of Wilberforce* (Cambridge, 1961)

Brown, John, *Wilberforce House, High Street, Hull: A Memoir and a Memorial* [1896] (Hull, 1985)

Bryant, G. E. and Baker, G. P., eds., *A Quaker Journal: Being the Diary and Reminiscences of William Lucas of Hitchin (1804–1861)*, 2 vols (London, 1934)

Bryden, Inga and Floyd, Janet, *Domestic Space: Reading the Nineteenth-Century Interior* (Manchester, 1999)

Burchell, William Fitz-er, *Memoir of Thomas Burchell, 22 Years a Missionary in Jamaica* (London, 1849)

Buxton, Charles, *Memoirs of Sir Thomas Fowell Buxton, Bart., with Selections from his Correspondence* (London, 1848)

Buxton, Travers, *Wilberforce: The Story of a Great Crusade* (London, 1907)

Cannadine, David, 'Introduction: Divine Rites of Kings', in David Cannadine and Simon Price, eds., *Rituals of Royalty: Power and Ceremonial in Traditional Societies* (Cambridge, 1987)

Castle, Kathryn, *Britannia's Children: Reading Colonialism through Children's Books and*

Magazines (Manchester, 1996)

Chadwick, Owen, *The Victorian Church*, 2 vols (London, 1966)

Clarkson, Thomas, *Strictures on a Life of W. Wilberforce by the Rev. R. I. Wilberforce and the Rev. S. Wilberforce. With a Correspondence between Lord Brougham and Mr Clarkson; also a Supplement containing Remarks on the Edinburgh Review of Mr Wilberforce's Life* (London, 1838)

Clarkson, Thomas, *The History of the Rise, Progress and Accomplishment of the Abolition of the Slave Trade by the British Parliament*, 2 vols (London, 1808)

Clarkson, Thomas, *The History of the Rise, Progress and Accomplishment of the Abolition of the Slave Trade by the British Parliament*, new edn (London, 1839)

Cole, David, *The Works of Sir Gilbert Scott* (London, 1980)

Colquhoun, John Campbell, *William Wilberforce: His Friends and His Times* (London, 1866)

Confino, Alon, 'Collective Memory and Cultural History: Problems of Method',*American Historical Review*, 102 (1997), pp. 1386–1403

Connerton, Paul, *How Societies Remember* (Cambridge, 1989)

Cormack, Patrick, *Wilberforce: The Nation's Conscience* (Pickering, 1983)

Coupland, Reginald, *The Empire in these Days: An Interpretation* (London, 1935)

Coupland, Reginald, *William Wilberforce* [1923] (London, 1945)

Cowie, Leonard W. ed., *William Wilberforce, 1759–1833: A Bibliography* (Westport, CT, 1992)

Credland, Arthur G., *Harry Cartlidge, 1893–1987: Hull Photographer* (Hull, 1998)

Dabydeen, David, *Hogarth's Blacks: Images of Blacks in Eighteenth-Century English Art* (Manchester, 1987)

Devenish, David C., 'Exhibiting the Slave Trade', *Museum International*, 49 (1997), pp. 49–52

Deverell, Liz and Watkins, Gareth, *Wilberforce and Hull* (Hull, 2000)

Douglass, Frederick, *Autobiographies: Narrative of the Life of Frederick Douglass, an American Slave, My Bondage and My Freedom, Life and Times of Frederick Douglass* (New York, 1994)

Drescher, Seymour, *The Mighty Experiment: Free Labor versus Slavery in British Emancipation* (New York, 2002)

Dresser, Madge and Giles, Sue, eds., *Bristol and Transatlantic Slavery* (Bristol, 2000)

Dunaway, Wilma, *The African-American Family in Slavery and Emancipation* (Cambridge, 2003)

Eley, Geoff and Suny, Ron, eds., *Becoming National: A Reader* (Oxford, 2000)

Elmes, James, *Thomas Clarkson: A Monograph. Being a Contribution towards the History of the Abolition of the Slave Trade and Slavery* (London, 1854)

Elwin, David, ed., *The Autobiography and Memoirs of Benjamin Robert Haydon* (London, 1950)

Fay, J. B., *Wilberforce House, Hull: Its History and Collections* (Hull, 1946)

Fisch, Audrey,*American Slaves in Victorian England: Abolitionist Politics in Popular Literature and Culture* (Cambridge, 2000)

Fitzgerald, Frances, 'Peculiar Institutions: Brown University looks at the Slave Trade in its Past', *The New Yorker*, 12 September 2005, pp. 68–77

Fladeland, Betty, *Men and Brothers: Anglo-American Antislavery Cooperation* (Chicago and London, 1972)

Forster, E. M., *Marianne Thornton, 1797–1887: A Domestic Biography* (London, 1956)

Fraser, Cary, 'The Twilight of Colonial Rule in the British West Indies: Nationalist

Assertion vs. Imperial Hubris in the 1930s', *Journal of Caribbean History*, 30 (1996), pp. 1–27

Furneaux, Robin, *William Wilberforce* (London, 1974)

Gardiner, Frederick John, *History of Wisbech and Neighbourhood during the last Fifty Years* (Wisbech, 1898)

Gedi, Noa and Elam, Yigal, 'Collective Memory: What is it?', *History and Memory*, 8 (1996), pp. 30–50

Genovese, Eugene, *Roll, Jordan, Roll: The World the Slaves Made* (New York, 1974)

George, Eric, *The Life and Death of Benjamin Robert Haydon, 1786–1846* (Oxford, 1948)

Gibson, Ellen Wilson, *Thomas Clarkson: A Biography* (London, 1990)

Gillett, Edward and MacMahon, Kenneth A., *A History of Hull* (Oxford, 1980)

Gittings, Robert and Manton, Jo, *Dorothy Wordsworth* (Oxford, 1985)

Glassberg, David, *American Historical Pageantry: The Uses of Tradition in the Early Twentieth Century* (Chapel Hill, 1990)

Grayling, A. C., *The Quarrel of the Age: The Life and Times of William Hazlitt* (London, 2000)

Griggs, Earl Leslie, *Thomas Clarkson: The Friend of Slaves* (London, 1936)

Gurney, Joseph John, *Familiar Sketch of the late William Wilberforce* (Norwich, 1838)

Halbwachs, Maurice, *On Collective Memory*, edited, translated and with an Introduction by Lewis A. Coser (Chicago, 1992)

Hall, Catherine, *Civilising Subjects: Metropole and Colony in the English Imagination, 1830–1867* (London, 2002)

Harford, John Scandrett, *Recollections of William Wilberforce, Esq. MP for the County of York during nearly Thirty Years; with brief Notices of some of his personal Friends and Contemporaries* (London, 1865)

Haydon, Benjamin Robert, *Description of Haydon's Picture of the Great Meeting of Delegates at Freemason's Tavern, June 1840, for the Abolition of Slavery and the Slave Trade* (London, 1844)

Haynes, Samuel, *The Auden Generation: Literature and Politics in England in the 1930s* (London, 1976)

Hayter, Alethea, *A Sultry Month: Scenes of London Literary Life in 1846* (London, 1965)

Hazlitt, William, *The Spirit of the Age* [1825] (Plymouth, 1991)

Hershberg, Thomas, 'Free Blacks in Antebellum Philadelphia: A Study of Ex-Slaves, Freeborn, and Socioeconomic Decline', *Journal of Social History*, 5 (1971), pp. 183–204.

Higman, B. W., 'Remembering Slavery: The Rise, Decline and Revival of Emancipation Day in the English-Speaking Caribbean', *Slavery and Abolition*, 19 (1996), pp. 90–105

Higman, B. W., 'Slavery Remembered: The Celebration of Emancipation in Jamaica', *Journal of Caribbean History*, 12 (1979), pp. 55–74

Hind, R. J., 'Wilberforce and the Perceptions of the British People', *Historical Research*, 60 (1987), pp. 321–35.

Hoare, Prince, *Memoirs of Granville Sharp* (London, 1820)

Hobsbawn, Eric and Ranger, Terence, eds., *The Invention of Tradition* (Cambridge, 1983)

Hochschild, Adam, *Bury the Chains: Prophets and Rebels in the Fight to Free an Empire's Slaves* (New York, 2005)

Hochschild, Adam, *King Leopold's Ghost: A Story of Greed, Terror, and Heroism in Colonial Africa* (Boston, 1998)

Hodgson, Studholme, *Truths from the West Indies* (London, 1838)

Honour, Hugh, *The Image of the Black in Western Art, vol. 4, From the American Revolution to World War I*, 2 parts (Cambridge, MA, 1989)

Hooper-Greenhill, Eilean, *Museums and their Visitors* (London, 1994)

Hooper-Greenhill, Eilean, *Museums and the Shaping of Knowledge* (London, 1992)

Hughes-Hallet, Penelope, *The Immortal Dinner: A Famous Evening of Genius and Laughter in Literary London, 1817* (London, 2001)

Hynes, Samuel, *The Auden Generation: Literature and Politics in England in the 1930s* (London, 1976)

Irwin-Zarecka, Iwona, *Frames of Remembrance: The Dynamics of Collective Memory* (New Brunswick, 1994)

Johnson, Michael and Roark, James L., *Black Masters: A Free Family of Color in the Old South* (New York and London, 1984)

Jordanova, Ludmilla, 'Objects of Knowledge: A Historical Perspective on Museums', in Peter Vergo, ed., *The New Museology* (London, 1989), pp. 22–40

Kachun, Mitch, *Festivals of Freedom: Memory and Meaning in African American Emancipation Celebrations, 1808–1915* (Amherst and Boston, 2003)

Kammen, Michael G., *Mystic Chords of Memory: The Transformation of Tradition in American Culture* (New York, 1993)

Kapferer, Bruce, *Legends of Peoples, Myths of State* (Washington, D.C., 1988)

Kavanagh, Gaynor, ed., *Making Histories in Museums* (London, 1996)

King, David, *The State and Prospects of Jamaica* (London, 1850)

King, Reyahn, 'Ignatius Sancho and Portraits of the Black Elite', in Reyahn King, ed., *Ignatius Sancho: An African Man of Letters* (London, 1997), pp. 15–43

Kolchin, Peter, *American Slavery* (London, 1995)

Lean, Garth, *God's Politician: William Wilberforce's Struggle* (London, 1980)

Levinson, Sanford, *Written in Stone: Public Monuments in Changing Societies* (Durham, NC, and London, 1998)

Lewis, C. T. Courtenay, *George Baxter (Colour Printer): His Life and Work* (London, 1908)

Litwack, Leon, *North of Slavery: The Negro in the Free States, 1790–1860* (Chicago, 1961)

Lowenthal, David, *The Past is a Foreign Country* (Cambridge, 1985)

McFeely, William S., *Frederick Douglass* (New York, 1991)

McKay, Claude, *Banana Bottom* [1933] (London, 1986)

MacKeith, Lucy, *Local Black History: A Beginning in Devon* (Exeter, 2003)

Macmillan, W. M., *Warning from the West Indies* (London, 1938)

Marsh, Jan, ed., *Black Victorians: Black People in British Art, 1800–1900* (Aldershot, 2005)

Martin, Waldo, *The Mind of Frederick Douglass* (Chapel Hill, NC, 1984)

Mayer, Henry, *All On Fire: William Lloyd Garrison and the Abolition of Slavery* (New York, 1998)

Merriman-Labor, A. B. C., *Britons through Negro Spectacles or a Negro on Britons* (London, 1909)

Midgley, Clare, 'Slave Sugar Boycotts, Female Activism and the Domestic Base of British Antislavery Culture', *Slavery and Abolition*, 17 (1996), pp. 137–62

Midgley, Clare, *Women Against Slavery: The British Campaigns, 1780–1870* (London and New York, 1992)

Morel, E. D., *Red Rubber: The Story of the Rubber Slave Trade flourishing on the Congo in the Year of Grace 1906* (London, 1906)

Morley, Edith, *Henry Crabb Robinson on Books and their Writers*, 2 vols (London, 1938)

Nash, Gary, *Forging Freedom: The Formation of Philadelphia's Black Community, 1720–1840* (Cambridge, MA, 1988)

Nash, Gary, 'Forging Freedom: The Emancipation Experience in Northern Seaport Cities, 1775–1820', in Ira Berlin and Ronald Hoffman, eds., *Slavery and Freedom in the Age of the American Revolution* (Charlottesville, VA, 1983), pp. 3–48

Newman, Richard S., *The Transformation of American Abolitionism: Fighting Slavery in the Early Republic* (Chapel Hill, 2002)

Newsome, David, 'Fathers and Sons', *The Historical Journal*, 6 (1963), pp. 292–310

Nora, Pierre, dir., *Realms of Memory: Rethinking the French Past*, edited and with a foreword by Lawrence D. Kritzman, translated by Arthur Goldlammer, 3 vols (New York, c. 1996–98)

Oldfield, J. R., 'Transatlanticism, Slavery and Race', *American Literary History*, 14 (2002), pp. 131–40.

Oldfield, J. R., *Popular Politics and British Anti-Slavery: The Mobilisation of Public Opinion against the Slave Trade, 1787–1807* (Manchester, 1995)

Oldfield, J. R., *Alexander Crummell (1819–1898) and the Creation of an African-American Church in Liberia* (Lewiston, NY, 1990)

Olney, Clarke, *Benjamin Robert Haydon: Historical Painter* (Atlanta, GA, 1952)

Ormand, Richard and Rogers, Malcolm, eds., *Dictionary of British Portraiture: Late Georgians and Early Victorians*, 2 vols (New York, 1979)

Ousby, Ian, *Blue Guide England* (London, 1995)

Passerini, Luisa, 'Memories between Silences and Oblivion', in Katherine Hodgkin and Susannah Radstone, eds., *Contested Pasts: The Politics of Memory* (London and New York, 2003), pp. 238–54

Paston, George, *B. R. Haydon and His Friends* (London, 1905)

Paulin, Tom, *The Day-Star of Liberty: William Hazlitt's Radical Style* (London, 1998)

Pease, William and Pease, Jane, *Black Utopia: Negro Communal Experiments in America* (Madison, WI, 1963)

Pevsner, Nikolaus, *London* 2 vols (third revised edition, London, 1973)

Phillippo, James, *Jamaica: Its Past and Present State* (London, 1843)

Pollock, John, *Wilberforce* (London, 1977)

Pool, Bernard, ed., *The Croker Papers, 1808–1857* (London, 1967)

Pope, Willard Bisell, ed., *The Diary of Benjamin Robert Haydon*, 5 vols (Cambridge, MA, 1960–63)

Powell, Richard J., 'Cinque: Antislavery Portraiture and Patronage in Jacksonian America', *American Art*, 11 (1997), pp. 48–73

Powers, Bernard, *Black Charlestonians: A Social History, 1822–1885* (Fayetteville, AR, 1994)

Quarles, Benjamin, *Black Abolitionists* (New York, 1969)

Rael, Patrick, *Black Identity and Black Protest in the Antebellum North* (Chapel Hill, 2001)

Reynolds, Madeline G. H., *The Peckovers of Wisbech* (Wisbech, 1994)

Rice, Alan, *Radical Narratives of the Black Atlantic* (London, 2003)

Ripley, C. Peter, *The Black Abolitionist Papers, vol. 1, The British Isles, 1830–1865* (Chapel Hill, 1985)

Robinson, Henry Crabb, *Exposure of Misrepresentations contained in the Preface to the Correspondence of William Wilberforce* (London, 1840)

Rowe, Maureen, 'Bruckins Party: A Celebration of "Full Free"', in Patrick Bryan, ed.,

August 1ˢᵗ: A Celebration of Emancipation (Mona, Jamaica), pp. 67–72

Rowlands, Michael, 'Memory, Sacrifice and the Nation', *New Formations*, 30 (1996–97), pp. 8–17

Sadler, Thomas, ed., *Reminiscences and Correspondence of Henry Crabb Robinson*, 3 vols (London, 1859)

Samuel, Raphael, *Island Stories: Unravelling Britain, Theatres of Memory, Volume II*, edited by Alison Light (London, 1998)

Samuel, Raphael, *Theatres of Memory* (London, 1994)

Savage, Kirk, *Standing Soldiers, Kneeling Slaves: Race, War, and Monument in Nineteenth-Century America* (Princeton, NJ, 1999)

Schadla-Hall, Tim, *Tom Sheppard: Hull's Great Collector* (Beverley, 1989)

Sheahan, J. J., *History of the Town and Port of Kingston upon Hull* (Beverley, 1866)

Sheppard, Thomas, *William Wilberforce: Emancipator of Slaves, 1759–1833* (Exeter, 1937)

Sheppard, Thomas, *Medals, Tokens, etc. Issued in connection with Wilberforce and the Abolition of Slavery* (Hull, 1916)

Sikes, Herschel Moreland, ed., *The Letters of William Hazlitt* (London, 1979)

Smith, Charles Saumarez, 'Museums, Artefacts, and Meanings', in Peter Vergo, ed., *The New Museology* (London, 1989), pp. 6–21

Smith, Nicola C., 'George Gilbert Scott and the Martyrs' Memorial', *Journal of the Warburg and Courtauld Institute*, 42 (1979), pp. 195–206

Stafford, Patricia, 'Refining "Bajan" Identity, 1930–1980', *Journal of Caribbean History*, 39 (2005), pp. 102–22

Stanley, Arthur Penrhyn, *Historical Memorials of Westminster Abbey* (London, 1868)

Stephen, George, *Anti-Slavery Recollections: In a Series of Letters addressed to Mrs. Harriet Beecher Stowe* (London, 1854)

Stephen, James, *Essays in Ecclesiastical Biography* (London, 1872)

Stewart, James Brewer, *Holy Warriors: The Abolitionists and American Slavery* (revised edition, New York, 1996)

Stott, Ann, *Hannah More: The First Victorian* (Oxford, 2003)

Stoughton, John, *William Wilberforce* (London, 1880)

Stowe, Harriet Beecher, *Sunny Memories of Foreign Lands*, 2 vols (London, 1854)

Sturge, Joseph, *A Visit to the United States in 1841* (London, 1842)

Sussman, Charlotte, *Consuming Anxieties: Consumer Protest, Gender and British Slavery, 1713–1833* (Stanford, CA, 2000)

Takagi, Midori, *'Rearing Wolves to Our Own Destruction': Slavery in Richmond, Virginia, 1782–1865* (Charlottesville, VA, 1999)

Talfourd, Thomas Noon, *The Letters of Charles Lamb, with a Sketch of his Life*, 2 vols (London, 1837)

Tamarkin, Elisa, 'Black Anglophilia: or, The Sociability of Antislavery', *American Literary History*, 14 (2002), pp. 444–78

Tattersfield, Nigel, *The Forgotten Trade: Comprising the Log of the* Daniel *and* Mary *of 1700 and Accounts of the Slave Trade from the Minor Ports of England, 1698–1725* (London, 1991)

Taylor, Clare, *British and American Abolitionists: An Episode in Transatlantic Understanding* (Edinburgh, 1974)

Temperley, Howard, *British Anti-Slavery, 1833–1870* (London, 1972)

Thome, James A. and Kimball, J. Horace, *Emancipation in the West Indies: A Six Months' Tour in Antigua, Barbados and Jamaica in the Year 1837* (New York, 1838)

Thompson, J. A., 'The League of Nations Union and Promotion of the League Idea in

Great Britain', *Australian Journal of Politics and History*, 18 (1972), pp. 52–61

Thornhill, Alan, *Mr Wilberforce, MP* (London, 1965)

Thorpe, Andrew, *Britain in the 1930s* (Oxford, 1992)

Tibbles, Anthony, 'Against human Dignity: The Development of the Transatlantic Slavery Gallery at Merseyside Maritime Museum, Liverpool', *Proceedings, IXth International Congress of Maritime Museums*, 1996, pp. 95–102

Tibbles, Anthony, ed., *Transatlantic Slavery: Against Human Dignity* (Liverpool, 1994)

Trouillot, Michel-Rolph, *Silencing the Past: Power and the Production of History* (Boston, MA, 1995)

Underhill, Edward Bean, *Life of James Mursell Phillippo, Missionary in Jamaica* (London, 1881)

Van Stipriaan, Alex, 'July 1, Emancipation Day in Suriname: A Contested *Lieue de Memoire*, 1863–2003', *New West Indian Guide*, 78 (2004), pp. 269–304

Vergo, Peter, ed., *The New Museology* (London, 1989)

Walker, Richard, *Regency Portraits*, 2 vols (London, 1985)

Walters, Ronald G., *The Antislavery Appeal: American Abolitionism after 1830* (Baltimore, PA, 1976)

Walvin, James, *Black Ivory: A History of British Slavery* (London, 1992)

Warner, Oliver, *William Wilberforce* (London, 1962)

Webster, Mary, *Francis Wheatley* (London, 1970)

Wheeler, Henry M., *The Slaves' Champion: a Sketch of the Life, Deeds and Historical Days of William Wilberforce* (London, 1860)

White, Shane, *Stories of Freedom in Black New York* (Cambridge, MA, 2002)

Wikramanayake, Marina, *A World in Shadows: The Free Black in Antebellum South Carolina* (Columbia, SC, 1973)

Wilberforce, Robert Isaac, and Samuel Wilberforce, *The Life of William Wilberforce. By his Sons, Robert Isaac Wilberforce [and] Samuel Wilberforce*, 5 vols (London, 1838)

Wilberforce, William, *The Correspondence of William Wilberforce. Edited by his Sons, Robert Isaac Wilberforce and Samuel Wilberforce*, 2 vols (London, 1840)

Wildridge, T. Tindall, *The Wilberforce Souvenir* (Hull, 1884)

Williams, Eric, *History of the People of Trinidad and Tobago* (London, 1964)

Winter, Jay, *Sites of Memory, Sites of Mourning: The Great War in European Cultural History* (Cambridge, 1995)

Wood, Marcus, *Blind Memory: Visual Representations of Slavery in England and America, 1780–1865* (Manchester, 2000)

Woof, Pamela, ed., *Dorothy Wordsworth: The Grasmere Journals* (Oxford, 1991)

Woof, Robert, 'Haydon, Writer and the Friend of Writers', in David Blayney Brown, Robert Woof, and Stephen Hebron, *Benjamin Robert Haydon, 1786–1846: Painter and Writer, Friend of Wordsworth and Keats* (Grasmere, 1996), pp. 25–64

Woolnough, Frank, *A History of Ipswich Museum* (Ipswich, 1908)

Wordsworth, William, *Sonnets* (London, 1838)

Wordsworth, William, *Poems, in Two Volumes by William Wordsworth* (London, 1807)

Yarrington, Alison, *The Commemoration of the Hero, 1800–1864: Monuments to the British Victors of the Napoleonic Wars* (New York and London, 1988)

Young, James, *The Texture of Memory: Holocaust Memorials and Meaning* (New Haven, CT, 1993)

Zolberg, Vera L., '"An Elite Experience for Everyone": Art Museums, the Public, and Cultural Literacy', in Daniel J. Sherman and Irit Rogoff, eds., *Museum Culture: Histories, Discourses, Spectacles* (London, 1994), pp. 49–65

WEBSITES AND ELECTRONIC RESOURCES

www.antislaveryarch.com
www.barbados.gov.bb
www.blink.org.uk
www.brycchancarey.com
www.ccfwebsite.com
www.chn.ir
www.digitalstroud.com
www.empiremuseum.co.uk
www.flagship.org.uk
www.guardian.co.uk
www.history.org
www.hitchcock.its.virigina/edu/Slavery
www.hull.ac.uk
www.hull.co.uk
www.hullcc.gov.uk
www.lancaster.gov.uk
www.lifebridge.org
www.ninsee.nl
www.petersons.com/blackcolleges
www.portal.unesco.org
www.stpaulschurchmillhill.co.uk
www.slave.studies.net
www.thisisstroud.com
www.vam.ac.uk

Eltis, David, *The Trans-Atlantic Slave Trade: A Database on CD-ROM* (Cambridge, 1999)

Index